Economic and Social Perspectives on European Migration

D1740012

This book addresses a wide range of migration-related issues in the European context and examines the socioeconomic consequences of migratory flows throughout Europe, focusing on a number of emblematic European countries. The book is divided into three parts. The first part deals with the tension between migrants and their integration processes in the receiving country, which is deeply influenced by the attitude of the local population and the different approach to highly and less skilled immigrants. The second part analyses the impact of migration on the economic structure of the receiving country, while the third part explores the varying degree of immigrants' socio-economic integration in the country of destination.

The book offers an essential interdisciplinary contribution to the issue of migration and provides readers with a better understanding of the effects that different forms of migration have had and will continue to exert on economic and social change in host countries. It also examines migration policy issues and builds on historical and empirical case studies with policy recommendations on labour market, integration and welfare policy issues. The book is addressed to a wide audience, including researchers, academics and students of economics, sociology, politics and history, as well as government/EU officials working on migration topics.

Francesca Fauri is associate professor of Economic History at the Department of Economics of the University of Bologna, Italy.

Debora Mantovani is associate professor of Sociology at the Department of Political and Social Science of the University of Bologna, Italy.

Donatella Strangio is full professor of Economic History at the Department of Memotef of Sapienza University of Rome, Italy.

Routledge Studies in Labour Economics

The Economics of Trade Unions
A Study of a Research Field and Its Findings
Hristos Doucouliagos, Richard B. Freeman and Patrice Laroche

Young People and the Labour Market
A Comparative Perspective
Floro Caroleo, Olga Demidova, Enrico Marelli and Marcello Signorelli

Women's Economic Empowerment in Turkey
Edited by Onur Burak Çelik and Meltem İnce Yenilmez

A Comparative Perspective of Women's Economic Empowerment
Edited by Meltem İnce Yenilmez and Onur Burak Çelik

Mediterranean Migration and the Labour Markets
Policies for Growth and Social Development in the Mediterranean Area
Edited by Salvatore Capasso and Eugenia Ferragina

The Digital Transformation of Labor
Automation, the Gig Economy and Welfare
Edited by Anthony Larsson and Robin Teigland

Labour Market Institutions and Productivity
Labour Utilisation in Central and Eastern Europe
Edited by Beata Woźniak-Jęchorek and Michał Pilc

Economic and Social Perspectives on European Migration
Edited by Francesca Fauri, Debora Mantovani, and Donatella Strangio

For a full list of titles in this series, please visit: www.routledge.com/Routledge-Studies-in-Labour-Economics/book-series/RSLE

Economic and Social Perspectives on European Migration

Edited by
Francesca Fauri, Debora Mantovani, and Donatella Strangio

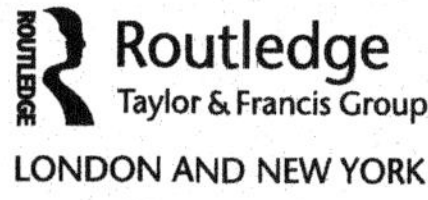

LONDON AND NEW YORK

First published 2021
by Routledge
2 Park Square, Milton Park, Abingdon, Oxon OX14 4RN

and by Routledge
52 Vanderbilt Avenue, New York, NY 10017

Routledge is an imprint of the Taylor & Francis Group, an informa business

© 2021 selection and editorial matter, Francesca Fauri, Debora Mantovani, and Donatella Strangio; individual chapters, the contributors

The right of Francesca Fauri, Debora Mantovani, and Donatella Strangio to be identified as the authors of the editorial material, and of the authors for their individual chapters, has been asserted in accordance with sections 77 and 78 of the Copyright, Designs and Patents Act 1988.

All rights reserved. No part of this book may be reprinted or reproduced or utilised in any form or by any electronic, mechanical, or other means, now known or hereafter invented, including photocopying and recording, or in any information storage or retrieval system, without permission in writing from the publishers.

Trademark notice: Product or corporate names may be trademarks or registered trademarks, and are used only for identification and explanation without intent to infringe.

British Library Cataloguing-in-Publication Data
A catalogue record for this book is available from the British Library

Library of Congress Cataloging-in-Publication Data
A catalog record has been requested for this book

ISBN: 978-0-367-49362-2 (hbk)
ISBN: 978-1-003-04591-5 (ebk)

Typeset in Sabon
by Newgen Publishing UK

Contents

Contributors

Anna Attias is Associate Professor of Applied Mathematics at Sapienza University of Rome and Invited Professor at the Pontificia Universitas Gregoriana (Vatican City). Her research activity mainly focuses on actuarial subjects related to the healthcare field (econometric models to rationalize health expenditure in a qualitative and quantitative view) and the social security field (to measure sustainability and adequacy of pensions systems particularly concerning pay-as-you-go systems).

Patrizia Battilani is Associate Professor of Economic History at the Alma Mater Studiorum-University of Bologna's Department of Economics. She is the Director of the Centre for Advanced Studies in Tourism of the University of Bologna. Her more recent research interests include cultural tourism, social enterprises and welfare systems in a historical perspective. She has also worked on Chinese migration to Italy.

Anikó Bernát is a researcher at the TARKI Social Research Institute (Budapest, Hungary). She specialises in areas related to migration, poverty and social inclusion of vulnerable groups, especially ethnic minorities. She is involved in several European and national research projects. She also runs projects that are exploring the volunteer movement of migrant solidarity groups and the social aspects of the recent migration flow in Hungary and Europe.

Francesca Fauri is Associate Professor of Economic History at the Alma Mater Studiorum-University of Bologna's Department of Economics. She has published extensively on issues concerning the history of European economic integration, local business history, Italy's postwar economic and business history, and Italian and European migration movements. She is Vice-President of Europe Direct in Forlì and holds a Jean Monnet Chair in European Economic and Migration History.

Giancarlo Gasperoni is Professor of Sociology at the Alma Mater Studiorum-University of Bologna's Department of Political and Social Science, where he teaches Education Systems and Policies and Method and Data Analysis Techniques. His research interests include the sociology of education, social inequality, immigrants' life experiences, voting behaviour and social research methodology.

Pedro Góis is Professor of Sociology and Methodology at the University of Coimbra's Faculty of Economics, and a researcher at the Centre for Social Studies (CES). Recently he was a consultant and country expert for the International Organization for Migration (OIM), Caritas, ICMPD, European Commission and European Migration Network (EMN). His main research interests include refugees in Europe, transnational ethnic identity, Portuguese and Brazilian migration flows.

Debora Mantovani is Associate Professor of Sociology at the Alma Mater Studiorum-University of Bologna's Department of Political and Social Science, where she teaches Sociology of Inequality and Quantitative Methods for the Social Sciences. Her main research interests include the sociology education, social inequality, educational achievement and integration of immigrant-origin students and social research methodology.

José Carlos Marques is Professor at the Polytechnic Institute of Leiria and a researcher at CICS.NOVA (unit Leiria)-Interdisciplinary Centre of Social Sciences of the Universidade Nova Lisbon. His areas of interest are Portuguese migration flows, migrants' integration and transnational practices and highly skilled migration. Recently he participated in several research projects on post-2000 Portuguese migration flows.

Donatella Strangio is Professor of Economic History at the Sapienza University of Rome's Department of Methods and Models for Economics, Land and Finance. She is Director of the Master's programme in Business Management in Sapienza University of Rome. Her more quoted works are on famine in the pre-industrial age, migration, public finance, colonization and decolonization, institutions and long run economic growth and the history of tourism.

Paolo Tedeschi is Associate Professor in Economic History at the University of Milan-Bicocca, where he also teaches History of the European Integration, History of the Financial Markets and Food History. His research focuses on the history of European integration, the economic history of rural and Alpine Lombardy and the history of Lombard business interest associations, trade unions and friendly societies. He is also a member of the Robert Schuman Institute of European Affairs (University of Luxembourg) and of the Best4Food (Bicocca).

Francesca Tosi is Assistant Professor of Social Statistics at the Alma Mater Studiorum-University of Bologna's Department of Statistical Sciences "Paolo Fortunati", where she teaches Social Statistics and International Demography. Her current research focuses on international migrations and the transnational family, student mobility in Italy, theories and metrics for the construction of social indicators, and the transition to adulthood.

Eleonora Vlach is currently a post-doctoral researcher in Social Stratification and Social Policy at the Institute of Sociology, Goethe University Frankfurt am Main. She teaches Comparative Social Structure Analysis, Sociology of Migration and Sociology of Education. Her research interests lie in the field of social stratification and social mobility, with a specific focus on the educational and occupational inequalities on the basis of individuals' migration background and social origins.

Helena Winiarska is a policy officer at the European Commission. Her career evolves around the European social policies, notably in the fields of employment and social dialogue, legal and irregular migration management, work with third countries on return and readmission. In her current role at the Directorate-General for Home Affairs, Migration and Integration, she holds an operational position in Italy, where she follows the disembarkation events and coordinates the work of EU agencies in Italy as part of the European Regional Migration Taskforce, based in Catania.

Introduction

1 European Agenda on Migration between progress and challenges

Situational overview

Helena Winiarska

"Migration is here to stay"; the President of the European Commission Ursula Von der Leyen said at the beginning of her new mandate in 2019. This is why the European Union (EU) proposes to implement a common, sustainable and effective approach to migration. Migration management is among the Union's top political priorities and the European Commission has developed a number of concrete initiatives to address the challenges of this large and complex phenomenon. At the same time, migration remains among the most sensitive areas of all EU policies. Migration management requires continuous striking of careful balances between humanitarian principles and respect for human rights, which constitute core European principles, the economic and demographic interests of European societies, and respect for the rule of law and the protection of external borders.

Before addressing these elements, it is important to clarify the legal context, namely the EU competence in the area of migration based on articles 79 and 80 of the Treaty on the Functioning of the European Union (TFEU).

On regular migration, the EU is competent to lay down the conditions governing entry into and legal residence in a Member State, including for the purposes of family reunification, for third-country nationals. Member States retain the right to determine volumes of admission for people coming from third countries to seek work.

On integration, the EU may provide incentives and support for measures taken by Member States to promote the integration of legally resident third-country nationals; EU law makes no provision for the harmonization of national laws and regulations, however.

When it comes to combating irregular immigration, the European Union is required to prevent and reduce irregular immigration, in particular by means of an effective return policy, in a manner consistent with fundamental rights.

And, finally, on readmission agreements, the European Union is competent to conclude agreements with third countries for the readmission to their country of origin or provenance of third-country nationals who do not fulfil or no longer fulfil the conditions for entry into, or presence or residence in, a Member State.

This contribution aims to address the main challenges and the key milestones achieved by the 2015 *European Agenda on Migration* and to detail the main axes of support the European Union and its Member States provided to Italy in the face of the 2015–2016 migration crisis. Furthermore, it will touch upon the challenges that the outbreak of the COVID-19 posed to EU Member States and migrants, and, finally, try to outline the main policy areas of the upcoming Migration *Pact*.

European Agenda of Migration: a four pillar based approach to migration

In 2015, the European Union faced an exceptional challenge when around two million people arrived on its shores in the space of two years, in search of refuge or a new life, often risking their lives to escape war, political oppression or poverty. Faced with the human tragedy unfolding in the Mediterranean, the EU took swift and determined action to avert the loss of life at sea. However, at the time, the EU Member States also lacked a collective take on migration management and border security. It quickly became clear that Member States could not address the challenge of migration alone and only a common European approach could address the issues collectively. In response, in May 2015, the Juncker Commission presented a *European Agenda on Migration* (European Commission 2015) intended to address immediate challenges and equip the EU with the tools to manage migration in the medium to long term in the areas of irregular migration, borders, asylum and legal migration.

The *Agenda* was built on four comprehensive policy pillars: *i*) reducing incentives for irregular immigration; *ii*) border management – saving lives and securing external borders; *iii*) developing a stronger common asylum policy; *iv*) establishing a new policy on regular migration, modernizing and revising the "Blue Card" system, setting fresh priorities for integration policies, and optimizing the benefits of migration policy for the individuals concerned and for countries of origin.

The *Agenda* also launched the idea of setting up EU-wide relocation and resettlement schemes, announced the "Hotspot" approach where relevant EU agencies work on the ground with frontline Member States to swiftly identify, register and fingerprint incoming migrants, and a possible common security and defence policy (CSDP) operation in the Mediterranean to dismantle smuggling networks and combat trafficking in persons. The latter was launched soon afterwards as EUNAVFOR MED "Operation Sophia".

On 6 April 2016, the European Commission published its guidelines on regular migration, as well as on asylum, in a communication. There are four main strands to the guidelines on legal migration policies: revising the *Blue Card Directive*; attracting innovative entrepreneurs to the EU; developing a more coherent and effective model for regular immigration to the EU by assessing the existing framework; and strengthening cooperation with the key countries of origin, with a view to ensuring legal pathways to the EU, while improving returns of those who have no right to stay.

In particular, solutions leading to a proper social and economic integration of migrants and refugees in European societies are an integral part of a successful migration management policy. This is why the European Commission adopted in 2016 an ambitious *Action Plan on Integration* with measures to support Member States in further developing and implementing effective actions across all relevant policy areas. Labour market integration and support in terms of education and training were key dimensions of this Action Plan.

All policy developments are closely monitored by the European Migration Network, established in 2008 as an EU network of migration and asylum experts from all Member States, who work together to provide objective, comparable and policy-relevant information.

What has the *Agenda* achieved?

Since 2016, the *European Agenda on Migration* has guided the work of the Commission, EU agencies and Member States. This led to the development of a new EU migration infrastructure, with new laws, new systems for coordination and cooperation, and direct operational and financial support from the EU. Although there is still ground to cover, the progress made over the past few years should not be underestimated.
Among others:

- irregular border crossings into the EU fell to 150,000 in 2018 – the lowest figure in five years. Key to this have been innovative approaches to partnership with third countries, such as the *EU-Turkey Statement* of March 2016 (European Council 2016);
- EU action has helped to save lives: almost 760,000 rescues at sea and the rescue of over 23,000 migrants in the Nigerian desert since 2015;
- the EU has shown tangible and rapid support to the Member States under most pressure: hotspots now serve as an operational model to quickly and efficiently bring support to key locations. Five hotspots are operational in Greece, and four in Italy; EU internal funding for migration and borders has more than doubled since the start of the crisis to over €10 billion; Member States relocated 34,700 people from Italy and Greece under the dedicated EU schemes. 1,103 people have also benefitted from relocation since summer 2018 under voluntary relocations, an exercise that the Commission continues to coordinate since January 2019;
- the new European Border and Coast Guard Agency (Frontex) has supported Member States to protect the EU external borders, with a second phase of reform under way to boost its capacity by a standing corps of 10,000 operational staff;

- the EU has stepped up the legal pathway of resettlement of persons in need of international protection to Member States, with almost 63,000 people resettled since 2015;
- the EU has provided protection and support for millions of refugees in third countries – the Facility for Refugees in Turkey is delivering on the ground with 90 projects currently up and running in Turkey, supporting almost 1.7 million refugees on a daily basis and building new schools and hospitals; the EU Regional Trust Fund in Response to the Syrian Crisis is delivering with more than 75 projects providing health, education, livelihoods and socio-economic support to Syrian refugees, internally displaced persons and hosting communities across the region; work to help those facing appalling conditions in Libya has included evacuating over 4,000 people, as well as the voluntary return of over 49,000 since 2017 – with the African Union–European Union–United Nations Taskforce as an innovative partnership model; 210 projects in 26 countries under the EU Trust Fund for Africa delivering concrete results, including basic support to over 5 million vulnerable people.
- action to disrupt smuggling networks on all routes, including work in the Niger leading to a major decrease in migrants entering Libya from the South.
- formal readmission agreements or practical arrangements on return and readmission are in place with 23 countries of origin and transit, with extra support from the EU to push for effective return.

The EU has stronger systems to control its borders and can now quickly bring the necessary financial and operational support to Member States under pressure. It has new channels to support the vulnerable and provide alternative, safe and legal pathways to Europe for those in need of protection. It is cooperating more closely on migration management than ever before with partner countries outside Europe.

It is on these building blocks that work now must continue to complete a sustainable system to ensure an efficient and humane migration management equal to the likely challenges of the future, not least in establishing the right framework for a Common European Asylum System that is managed responsibly and fairly. This will need further efforts across the board, and migration will remain high on the political agenda in the years to come.

European Agenda for Migration: what did it mean for Italy?

Since 2014, the EU has supported Italy with nearly €1 billion of funding for asylum, migration, security and border management. The EU allocated €0.7 million emergency assistance to the Italian Ministry of Interior and UN High Commissioner for Refugees (UNHCR) in July 2019 to support the humanitarian evacuation of approximately 450 persons from Libya and Niger to Italy. Another recent example is a €30 million project in five Italian regions to address the exploitation of migrant labour in agriculture and to help the integration of migrants into the regular labour market. Support has also come through expertise from EU agencies and Member States with a total of 144 experts deployed by Frontex in 2019 and 180 by the European Asylum Support Office (EASO). This expertise remains an essential part of the EU contribution to migration management and preparedness in the Central Mediterranean and Member States need to maintain the required level of deployments.

Despite significant progress in the past four years, the situation remains volatile and geopolitical developments have created new challenges for the EU. We should continue to work to address immediate key challenges and to make progress on on-going work. Despite solidarity efforts in the context of disembarkations in the Central Mediterranean, lives continue to be lost at sea and the *ad hoc* relocation solutions coordinated by the Commission are clearly not long-term solutions.

The Commission is fully supporting the process initiated with the signature of the *Joint Declaration of Intent* on 23 September 2019 by Malta, Italy, Germany and France setting out the contours of a predictable and structural set of arrangements. However, long-term solutions can only come from the reform of the Common European Asylum System to which we remain committed, in the framework of a comprehensive approach to migration.

COVID-19: the pandemic impact on the migrants' lives and integration in the EU

The coronavirus pandemic has affected all spheres of our lives. It has severely reduced our mobility as citizens and workers, has brought European economies to a standstill and is still threatening to trigger one of the most severe global economic crises in recent decades. Over the last weeks and months, the Commission has nevertheless worked to respond to this new pandemic and acted much faster and more effectively than many thought possible.

At the same time, for the European Commission it remained imperative that the crisis should not undermine the rule of law or the fundamental values of the European Union. From the very first moment, President Von der Leyen, Vice-President Schinas and Commissioner Johansson highlighted the need for immediate operational action but also for solidarity.

In the area of migration management, similarly to many others, the Commission has taken on a coordination role in this crisis at the request of Member States. The recently adopted *Guidelines on Asylum and Return Procedures and on Resettlement* (European Commission 2020a) are a product of this role given to the Commission. Protection needs do not disappear because of the pandemic; therefore, the guidelines illustrate how to ensure continuity of procedures as much as possible while fully guaranteeing the protection of people's health and rights.

Among the key challenges that needed addressing, the migrants' camps in countries of first reception are severely ill equipped to support a large number of persons who already live in precarious conditions. In this respect and in the context of the health emergency, we are helping Greece to implement a dedicated emergency plan.

As regards the situation at the Greek-Turkish borders, the Commission immediately put in place an Action Plan in early March, including additional financial support of €700 million combined with operational and humanitarian support.

The Commission has also put great emphasis on the overriding interests of migrant children as one of the most vulnerable categories. We are now working on the relocation of unaccompanied minors from Greece and other frontline Member States such as Cyprus and Malta. Member States have already pledged for the relocation of 1,600 unaccompanied minors and particularly vulnerable children accompanied by their families. Despite the pandemic, the first relocations have already taken place and more will follow soon.

Beyond the frontline measures, several observations are worth noting in the context of the 2020 health and economic crisis driven by the coronavirus pandemic across the EU countries and the situation of migrant workers in the European labour market:

1. Migrant workers are more likely to have temporary contracts than average workers, both EU-wide and more specifically in Poland, Cyprus, Slovenia and Spain and to some extent in Germany and the Netherlands. This means migrants are more likely to lose their job and income, especially in specific sectors and occupations such as construction, tourism, and hospitality and food service activities.[1] Migrant households are already at a higher risk of in-work poverty (especially in Luxembourg, Spain, Italy, Cyprus and Bulgaria) and severe material deprivation (especially in Greece as well as in Belgium, Denmark, Italy and Spain) (European Commission 2018a).
2. Another aspect is the adaptation of education services during the lockdown period, in line with the European Commission horizontal line.[2] Programme for International Student Assessment (PISA) data confirm the significant impact of both socio-economic and migrant background on educational outcomes (OECD 2019a; 2019b). After controlling for socio-economic background, educational inequalities related to migrant background were most pronounced in Finland, Slovenia, Austria and Estonia. During the coronavirus lockdown, access to support by schools and teachers, availability of IT equipment and the possibility for parents to provide education support at home are likely to vary widely across households depending on their socio-economic and migrant background, thereby exacerbating educational and language disparities. This may be even more severe for pupils seeking asylum and refugees whose access to education is often difficult.

3. The third dimension is access to health services for migrants across EU countries. While migrants may be less likely to be severely affected by coronavirus due to their age composition, *EU Statistics on Income and Living Conditions* data confirm that when adjusting for age composition, unmet medical needs were more likely among foreign-born populations (compared to native-born) especially in Estonia and Greece and to a lesser extent in Sweden, Italy, Denmark and Latvia (OECD/EU 2018).[3] This situation draws back to various factors such as lack of legal access due to residence status or limited health insurance in some countries. Moreover, there is a lack of knowledge on how to access services, lack of financial resources, concentration of migrants in some disadvantaged areas with lower access to health services) and lack of adaptation of national systems to the specific needs of migrants.[4] Proper information in the relevant languages is therefore essential in order to ensure that migrants can effectively take protective measures against the COVID-19 virus and that they have effective access to the healthcare system care including translation of essential information into other languages, interpretation and use of local community and diaspora media. Again, among migrants residing in the EU, refugees and asylum seekers may be particularly at risk (The Guardian 2020). Beyond access to healthcare, refugees and migrants may be more exposed to the virus because of their greater reliance on public transport, precarious housing conditions, with no individual separate spaces, or the low-paid jobs where little or no protective measures are available.
4. The fourth horizontal point to monitor is the impact of the pandemic on mobility and migration. There is already evidence of severe limitations on visas and residence permits issued to third-country nationals. This will affect all categories of migrants, including seasonal workers and other labour migrants, students, researchers, family migrants and resettled refugees. Some sectors (typically agriculture[5]) and some Member States (Spain, Italy, France, Germany, Poland and the Czech Republic) are more likely to be affected by the potential lack of (seasonal) labour force. More specifically with regard to shortages in the health workforce, some Member States may need to facilitate the recognition of foreign qualifications in the healthcare sector in response to the coronavirus pandemic.[6]

The way ahead and the *New Pact on Migration and Asylum*

In migration management, which lies at the sensitive crossroads between social, security and economic policies, *ad hoc* solutions are not satisfactory. At the time of this publication going to print, the Von Der Leyen Commission continues to work on the *New Pact on Migration and Asylum*. This will be a fresh start for the EU asylum and migration framework that is not only fair, humane and effective, based on the principle of solidarity and fair responsibility, but also that contributes to the proper functioning of the Schengen area. The *Pact* will notably aim to identify consensual solutions to the difficult asylum reform, as part of the wider comprehensive approach we will take on migration. We need a reformed, solid, and comprehensive *Common European Asylum System* that can operate effectively both in normal times and at times of crisis.

The need for a geopolitical solution remains as strong as ever. It continues to be important to engage with Turkey in the framework of the *EU-Turkey Statement* and to keep the channels of communication with Turkey open.

Despite these difficult times, the European Union upholds its commitments vis-à-vis third countries hosting large numbers of refugees. Though resettlement procedures have been temporarily suspended due to the COVID-19 outbreak, we are working closely with the Member States to ensure a smooth resumption as soon as this is again possible under safe conditions for all.

Migration should be at the heart of strong, mutually beneficial partnerships with third countries of origin and transit. We need to work with third partners to protect those in need, prevent irregular migration, fight against smuggling, foster the implementation of returns and develop new pathways to Europe. The coronavirus outbreak has significantly affected all these issues and it remains difficult or sometimes impossible for non-EU nationals to reach the EU. Workers, for instance those working seasonally in agriculture, have not been able to reach the places where they were needed. Families struggle to be reunited. National administrations have also slowed down, which poses difficulties for those who need to renew residence permits, for example.

While it is too early to assess the full and long-term effects of coronavirus on legal migration, the European Commission will continue to monitor compliance by Member States with EU law. For example, the European Migration Network is gathering evidence on how Member States are adapting the rules on residence permits for those third-country nationals who have lost their job due to the pandemic.

At the same time, it is clear that we need to scale up the legal migration pilot projects. The Commission has been supporting such projects to encourage Member States to test new ways to better organize legal migration for work and training purposes with key partner countries. Projects are based on labour and skills needs in the EU as well as origin countries, so we will closely monitor how these needs develop in the future.

How do we explain, however, the fact that the issue of migration and in particular incoming legal migration – unlike many other policy areas such as trade and competition policies – is considered such a controversial and sensitive issue?

Migration policy resonates closely with a citizens' *perception* of control over a national or European territory and national culture, as well as with an issue of *perception* of access not only to the labour market, but also to social services. It is also one of the areas where public perceptions have been most influenced by media images. For instance, in the 2018 special Eurobarometer survey on *Integration of Immigrants in the European Union* (European Commission 2018b), nearly half of respondents said that there are at least as many foreigners irregularly present on the territory of the European Union as legally staying ones. This is far from being the case. The reality is that most (non-EU) migrants come to stay legally, temporarily or permanently in Europe. It does not mean that their integration is an easy endeavour and they still face a difficult labour market situation in a number of EU countries.

An important fact is that only a minority of migrants from third countries come to the EU for work reasons. Among the 3 million new residence permits issued in 2018, around 27 per cent came for labour reasons while a majority came without a job offer, for family reasons (28%), to study (20%), to receive "international protection" (10%) or for other reasons (14%). Nevertheless, these other groups also bring relevant skills and experience that can and need to be valued.

Public opinion surveys in Europe have shown that citizens tend to overestimate the size of the immigrant population. For instance, a Eurobarometer survey published in 2018 shows that in 19 out of the 28 Member States, the estimated proportion of immigrants in the population is at least twice the actual proportion. In reality, persons born outside the EU represented in 2018 around 7.5 per cent of its population, much below the share found in a number of non-EU OECD countries. These figures are far from a perception of *invasion* created by some media and picked up by extreme-right politicians in recent years.

Beyond attracting talents that the EU needs, decision makers in Europe should therefore also devote attention to better using the skills of immigrants, whether new arrivals or long-term residents, and upgrading those skills as needed. This can be done through active integration policies that engage all relevant levels of government and civil society. Moreover, closing the current employment gap between third-country nationals and EU nationals – and making sure that people are in jobs in line with their qualifications – could help maintain the labour force and improve fiscal balances in a number of EU countries.

However, integration is not only an economic issue. It is crucial to ensure social cohesion and the promotion and respect of the EU's fundamental values. In January 2020, the European Commission adopted a communication about *Social Europe* (European Commission 2020b), which elaborates on how to put the *European Pillar of Social Rights* into practice. We see it as a social strategy to make sure that the climate, digital and demographic transitions are socially fair and just. One of these pillars is "equal opportunities and jobs for all" including the promotion of gender equality and supporting the integration of migrants in Europe.

While integration of migrants is primarily a competence of each EU Member State, the EU nevertheless can play an important supporting role through different means: fostering exchange of good practices and mutual learning between EU Member States, supporting actors on the ground, and through financial support via EU funds.

Despite the impact of the coronavirus pandemic on the adoption of the *New Pact on Migration and Asylum*, it is clear that we need to move ahead as soon as possible. The *New Pact* will present a comprehensive approach covering all aspects of migration, also addressing border management and ensuring more coherence between our internal and external policies.

Notes

1 The ILO report *COVID-19 and World of Work: Impacts and Responses* stresses the risk of vulnerabilities among migrant workers (ILO 2020).
2 "The suspension of classes at all education levels points to the need to ensure that education institutions and educators are well prepared to provide distance learning. This requires adequate digital infrastructure, teaching materials and that teachers are equipped with the necessary skills and support to deliver online learning effectively. It is also crucial to ensure that all learners can access distance learning, in particular those from disadvantaged backgrounds and in remote/rural areas".
3 See Figure 4.11: "Unmet medical needs" OECD/EU (2018).
4 MPG analysis for European Web Site on Integration (EWSI) on availability of services for long-term integration concludes that while intercultural competence in healthcare systems is increasingly recognized as an essential element of adequate healthcare provision, only a handful of EU MS make interpretation or cultural mediation services widely available and standards or guidelines on providing culturally competent or diversity sensitive services exist in fewer than half of countries' public health services.
5 There are already reports that a foreign labour force will be lacking in the agricultural sector from the next month in several countries (e.g. France, Germany).
6 OECD Migration Division is currently surveying OECD delegates regarding adaptations to mobility and migration rules due to the COVID-19 pandemic. The survey includes a question about this dimension (measures for Recognition of Foreign Qualifications in the healthcare sector).

References

European Commission (2015). *Communication from the Commission to the European Parliament, the Council, the European Economic and Social Committee and the Committee of the Regions: A European Agenda on Migration*, https://ec.europa.eu/home-affairs/sites/homeaffairs/files/what-we-do/policies/european-agenda-migration/background-information/docs/communication_on_the_european_agenda_on_migration_en.pdf.

European Commission (2018a). *Toolkit on the Use of EU Funds for the Integration of people with a Migrant Background*, https://ec.europa.eu/regional_policy/sources/policy/themes/social-inclusion/integration-of-migrants/toolkit-integration-of-migrants.pdf.

European Commission (2018b). *Results of special Eurobarometer on integration of immigrants in the European Union*, https://ec.europa.eu/home-affairs/news/results-special-eurobarometer-integration-immigrants-european-union_en.

European Commission (2020a). *Coronavirus: Commission presents guidance on Implementing EU Rules on Asylum and Return Procedures and on Resettlement*, https://ec.europa.eu/commission/presscorner/detail/en/IP_20_666.

European Commission (2020b). *A Strong Social Europe for Just Transitions*, https://ec.europa.eu/commission/presscorner/detail/en/qanda_20_20.

European Council (2016). *EU-Turkey statement, 18 March 2016*, www.consilium.europa.eu/en/press/press-releases/2016/03/18/eu-turkey-statement/.

ILO (2020). *COVID-19 and World of Work: Impacts and Responses*, www.ilo.org/wcmsp5/ groups/public/---dgreports/---dcomm/documents/briefingnote/wcms_738753.pdf.

OECD (2019a). *Pisa 2018 Results (Volume I): What Students Know and Can Do*. Paris: OECD Publishing.

OECD (2019b). *Pisa 2018 Results (Volume II): Where All Students Can Succeed*. Paris: OECD Publishing.

OECD/EU (2018). *Settling in 2018: Indicators of Immigrant Integration*. Paris/European Union, Brussels: OECD Publishing.

The Guardian (2020). *NGOs Raise Alarm as Coronavirus Strips Support from EU refugees*, www.theguardian.com/global-development/2020/mar/18/ngos-raise-alarm-as-coronavirus-strips-support-from-eu-refugees.

2 Migrants in Europe

From a production factor to social actors

Francesca Fauri, Debora Mantovani and Donatella Strangio

Migration is a constant feature of the human species and has been an intrinsic characteristic of the world population to the present day (Lucassen and Lucassen 2009; 2014). People have always moved across Europe to work at crops and to escape hunger, famine and war. But these were not the only reasons. It was the high human mobility of pre-industrial Europe that led to the spread of new techniques across the continent. Artisans of various skills migrated because they were offered better paid jobs and living conditions in neighbouring states. In the words of Cipolla (1997: 190): "The attachment of the pre-industrial worker to the place of residence was directly proportional to his standard of living, that is to say it was minimal". This has not changed over the centuries, and even nowadays moving across borders creates a conduit for the global transmission of ideas.

With the onset of the second industrial revolution, new technologies allowed modern means of transportation to connect the world and create a global labour market. The number of people moving across the world soared and was supported by the fact that restrictions on migrants were virtually non-existent. "The surprise is less that they were willing to migrate than they were allowed to do so" (Foreman-Peck 1995: 140). Despite the undeniable difficulties in facing integration in a new destination country, millions of Europeans went to look for a better future abroad; this free circulation of workers seemed for a while to allocate its positive economic effects on both receiving and sending countries (migration accounted for very large shares of the international convergence in GDP per worker and real wages, though a much smaller share in GDP per capita: Taylor and Williamson 1994).

However, in the interwar period both the United States (after the First World War) and most Latin America and European receiving countries (after the 1929 crisis) introduced stricter immigration laws and quotas on the number of incomers. This new approach inaugurated by the US (the greatest recipient country at the time) both discouraged the arrival of workers from traditional departure countries and changed the flows' origins (Italians, who were the largest immigrant group to the US before 1914, were cut off from its shores after the 1924 Quota Act, whereas Mexicans were not affected: Fauri 2015).

Since then migration movements have become increasingly dependent on the laws and regulations of each single destination nation. The only exception to this worldwide reality is the European Union's internal market: people are allowed, since the end of the 1960s, to move freely across its borders and look for a job in any of the 27 EU states, a tangible benefit of being European citizens.

Immigration laws and work permits regulate human mobility in the rest of the hemisphere. Today, from a strictly economic point of view, this production factor, labour, is the most penalized as far as free circulation is concerned. There exists "a cognitive dissonance in economics about globalization: trade and capital flows are unambiguously, good, labour flows are unambiguously complicated" (Hanson 2010). Often rich countries implement barriers against immigration that contrast with their pro-liberalization stance on trade and investment. Certainly, of all production factors, people are the most difficult to handle, regulate and integrate in a new market.

This is because labour is not only an economic factor and immigration success is not only about job and housing access (even though these are important): it is a sensitive social issue and touches upon a wide array of matters such as equal opportunity, gender equality, youth education and integration. Migration is not only an income-maximizing choice; it can be driven by other factors (non-economic reasons such as ethnic chains or welfare benefits) and is often the result of a decision taken within the family context. The family still remains the unit of analysis that best describes the complexity of migratory projects and cross-border mobility patterns.

Finally, migration also raises questions about what kind of values European countries share with their multiethnic immigrant communities and what kind of society they want to be: open or closed, welcoming or anti-melting-pot/assimilation possibilities. Europe today experiences this cultural and identity split between acceptance and rejection, but we should not forget that if integration fails, outcasts will only fuel criminal behaviour and terrorism.

Since migration is here to stay (Ursula Von der Leyen as reported by Winiarska in this book, see also De Hass 2007), we need to learn from experience; scholars can help to develop better strategies and more constructive policies. This is what this book is about. It gathers a group of researchers who study the complex nature of the migratory movements and their impact on European societies. Migrants' adaptation to new cultural and working environments are analysed, together with the effects of their presence on the social, economic and political structures of destination countries. The authors' intent is to increase awareness of the effects that various migration waves, age groups and ethnic origins have had on European countries and the integration dynamics of immigrants, both as skilled and non-skilled workers and entrepreneurs.

The book incorporates a variety of perspectives and a multidisciplinary approach and has thus been divided into three parts and a large introduction.

We would like to thank Helena Winiarska of the European Commission for reminding us, in the introduction, what the EU has done to promote a comprehensive approach to migration, such as the provision of incentives and support for measures taken by Member States to facilitate the integration of legally resident third-country nationals. Furthermore, Winiarska clearly details the main axes of EU support: since 2016 the European Agenda on Migration has guided the work of the Commission, EU agencies and Member States. This has led to the development of an innovative EU migration infrastructure, with new laws and coordination and cooperation systems, as well as direct operational and financial support. Although there remains much to be done, the progress made over the past few years should not be underestimated and has helped the EU to diminish irregular border crossings into the EU and to save lives, rescuing 760,000 migrants at sea and over 23,000 migrants in the Nigerian desert since 2015. Despite these accomplishments, we should also keep in mind that there is no such thing as a single European migration policy, since each Member State retains its own right to determine volumes of admission for regular migrants coming from third countries to seek work.

In the first section of the book, titled *Immigrants and the Labour Market: Employment Opportunities and Challenges*, Aniko Bernat presents a chapter on the attitudes towards labour immigration in Hungary derived from comprehensive empirical research. The analysis focuses on the tension between two "desired public goods" in Hungary: the need for an immigrant labour force in order to alleviate labour shortages and foster economic growth, and the state's "zero immigration" policy, which has fomented xenophobia and anti-immigration attitudes in the native population. The analysis reveals a number of controversial or conflicting attitudes that embody cognitive dissonance. These controversial attitudes are widely shared by the Hungarian population and focus on the perceived essential need for workers versus the rejection of immigrants. The cognitive tensions that emerge could be reduced via appropriate information and *ad hoc* public strategies, but not much has been done so far. Overcoming labour shortages by involving a foreign-origin workforce would be a common good and serve the economy and thus society and its members in general, yet these macro level benefits are rejected in order to avoid challenging the comfort zone of an ethnically homogenous society.

The second chapter by Pedro Góis and José Carlos Marques offers a completely different prospect, that of a country, Portugal, which has increasingly contributed since the new millennium to European labour demand through highly skilled and less skilled emigrants, reflecting their positive integration process in several European countries. This chapter, using statistics and a large-scale survey questionnaire administered to Portuguese individuals that left the country, shows that high and low-skilled migrants display diverse characteristics due to differences in their migration resources and labour market integration processes, yet share some structural factors and constraints that call for integrating these two types of migration in a common analytical framework. Contemporary Portuguese migration is filling employment gaps in the European segmented labour market in both the highly skilled segment and in the low skilled segment. Both forms of labour mobility combine permanent forms of migration with movements that are temporary, circular and that can be described as "liquid migrations". Last but not least, we should keep in mind that Portuguese migration within the EU can be considered an internal free workforce movement which is creating a truly European labour market.

The second section, titled *Immigrants: An Economic Resource or a Burden?*, offers historical and economic insights on migrants' impact on host countries and their possible contribution to those countries' economies. The migration phenomenon, as was examined in the first part of this book, is strongly connected to destination countries' attitudes towards labour inputs and migrants' willingness to improve their living and working conditions. The contributions contained in this second part focus on European policies regarding the integration of immigrants, their involvement in destination countries' economic growth (and in their personal success) and their contribution to the welfare system sustainability, with particular reference to the Italian pension system.

Paolo Tedeschi's chapter addresses important issues relating to the arrival of migrants in the European Community countries in the 20 years after the Second World War. Those flows triggered novel social and economic problems (such as the housing issue) related to migrants' integration in the foreign labour market and civil society in view of their different languages and customs. Also, migrants' professional skills played a role in their integration path. In order to analyse these topics the European Economic Community (EEC) carried out two investigations in 1959–1961 and 1973, shedding light on immigrants' living conditions, in order to implement appropriate policies. The 1959–1961 survey was carried out in the main European destination countries (France, Belgium and Germany) and led to the adoption of the Commission Recommendation of 7 July 1965 by the Member States on the housing of workers and their families moving within the Community. It established that workers who were European Community citizens and regularly employed in the territory of another EEC Member State should enjoy the same rights and benefits as local workers.

The second EEC survey took place in 1973 and found that migrants did not choose their housing conditions, which were more a consequence of the existing political, economic and social systems' decisions. Thus migrants, in some cases, were discriminated both as workers and also as inhabitants in social and housing policies. As Tedeschi underlines, the housing solutions forced upon immigrants were part of "the machinery of social confinement and control, of making life insecure, and thus inhibiting or eliminating any demands which might be made". In successive years, the economic crises of the 1970s and the following end of the Golden Age highlighted other problems connected with immigration flows. Increasing economic difficulties, declining productivity and rising unemployment rates led to more restrictive and less generous immigration policies for non-EEC workers. In the case of Belgium, this created problems with new irregular migrants who were in direct competition with low-skilled native workers. The economic crisis increased discrimination and xenophobia.

Ultimately, what both EEC surveys underscored was that the housing problems of migrant workers were mainly affected by national migration policies. As a result, the real status of migrants (a relevant economic resource or social problem) depended on economic trends and only to a residual degree on cultural differences.

In the fourth chapter Patrizia Battilani and Francesca Fauri compare the history of Chinese immigrant entrepreneurs in Bologna and London and evaluate the economic and social similarities and differences between the two communities and entrepreneurial contexts. The aim is to investigate whether migrant communities coming from the same country share similar characteristics, or whether they tend to diverge depending on the country to which they have chosen to move. The result is that certain cultural and social features, such as the roles of the family and the community, which are strictly linked to the culture of the country of origin, tend to be preserved regardless of the immigrants' place of destination. Both in Bologna and London, for many decades (before the late 1930s in the UK, and up until the 1980s in Italy), the small original Chinese group came from mainland China and was comprised mainly of males who often married local women and formed a community located in a specific geographical area, engaged in (very different) selected businesses with low barriers to entry. In conclusion, Battilani and Fauri underline how Chinese immigrant entrepreneurs have tended to adapt to the market features of the destination society, and this has proven an important factor in accounting for their business success. Their adaptive integration efforts proved successful in the long run both in Bologna and London, and Chinese immigrants have represented an economic resource for both countries. Indeed, this conclusion is in line with what the international literature has stressed: migrant workers contribute to the economic and social development of both destination and origin countries (Massey et al. 1993; Massey 1999; Phillips and Massey 1999; Costant and Massey 2005).

In Chapter 5 Anna Attias and Donatella Strangio focus on the Italian pension system: the authors deal with the complexity and the different perspectives of the pension issue, highlighting the difficult demographic transition and its sustainability at the European level. The Italian case is one of the most emblematic in this context. The use of a Leslie mathematical model – applied to the pension system, closely linked to the labour market and demographics – emphasizes the impact of migration and the advantages and disadvantages and sustainability of the Italian pension system. Findings reveal that regular migrants play a crucial role in supporting the Italian pension system. This outcome stresses the importance of regulating and "controlling" migration in terms of worker flows by responding to demographic deficiencies that, in the Italian case, reflect a country strongly in need of younger workers.

The integration of migrant workers into the labour market is an essential requirement for the well-being of modern societies and migrant workers may be considered as an important resource. In this regard, the International Labour Organization's work on labour migration focuses on supporting Member States in the formulation and application of international labour standards, strengthening cooperation and dialogue between governments and social partners, providing technical assistance to countries of origin in the development of decent employment policies and programmes, and collaboration with destination countries in promoting the integration of migrants into the labour market (ILO 2015). The management of migratory flows requires interventions in terms of governance, anti-discriminatory integration and social protection policies aimed at ensuring decent work for migrants and better living conditions for them and their families.

Finally, the last section, entitled *Immigrant Networks, Well-Being and Education*, explores some aspects of the multifaceted social dimension of migrants' integration into the receiving country. The concept of integration embeds cultural, social, economic and political features, and "integration" is an umbrella term the boundaries of which are huge and blurred. In the field of migration studies, there is no agreement as regards either the term which may better describe the consequences of immigration or its outcomes. Alternative terms have been commonly and historically used – such as "adaptation", "accommodation", "acculturation" and "assimilation" (Mayo-Smith 1894a; 1894b; Simons 1901a; 1901b; 1901c; 1901d; Warner and Srole 1945; Park and Burgess 1969) – and none of them is value-free. Especially in the US, assimilation – defined as "a process of interpenetration and fusion in which persons and groups acquires the memories, sentiments, and attitudes of other persons or groups, and, by sharing their experience and history, are incorporated with them in a common cultural life" (Park and Burgess 1969: 735) – has been discarded for quite some time. The idea that migrants would be involved in a long-term, but linear, taken-for-granted and unilateral process of Anglo-conformity or Americanization (Gordon 1964) was charged with ethnocentric pretensions and fell openly into disrepute in the early 1990s (Glazer 1993). Although the concept of assimilation has later undergone a new revival, it has been redefined and softened (Alba and Nee 1993; Brubaker 2001). Assimilation can be in play, but it does not necessarily involve all dimensions nor do the latter develop at the same pace. For example, if the language spoken by natives moves "like an arrow" and is more likely to be acquired in a straight-line fashion, ethnic self-identity may vary over time "like a boomerang" in a reactive manner (Rumbaut 1997: 941). The linear process may also be interrupted by changing economic and political conditions – and follow an uneven and bumpy course (Gans 1992). Further, assimilation is no longer the only possible outcome, but – according to the segmented assimilation theory – is just one achievable result along with downward-mobility (assimilation into the oppositional culture of the streets and integration into the underclass) and selective patterns (upward mobility is consistent with the maintenance of cultural core elements of the ethnic community) (Portes and Zhou 1993).

The fact that immigrants' upward mobility may also occur in the case of assimilation resistance has been accepted by the new assimilation theory as well. This potential outcome is tangible as regards many successful immigrants engaged in starting a new business. The sociological literature on ethnic enclaves has demonstrated that ethnicity can be a crucial resource in particular segments of the labour market, such as self-employment and entrepreneurship (Portes and Jensen 1989; Portes 2010). Some ethnic groups may indeed take advantage of the ethnic resources rooted in their social capital (i.e. mutual trust, solidarity and reciprocity), which fosters the development of co-ethnic business networks and facilitates ethnic enterprise. According to the resource disadvantage theory, even if immigrants' choice of starting up a new business is sometimes a coercive option, due to the experience of persistent episodes of unemployment and/or discrimination in the mainstream labour market, entrepreneurship may be a profitable investment promoting upward social mobility.

Giancarlo Gasperoni and Debora Mantovani's chapter focuses on migrants engaged in launching a new business and sheds light on a crucial, but oft-overlooked topic placed in between the fields of migrant entrepreneurship and integration: the potential sources of financial assistance used by aspiring immigrant entrepreneurs. Sociological literature has stressed that financial resources are essential for setting up a new enterprise, but immigrants are at a disadvantage and face several challenges (more so than natives) to access credit. Migrants' limited availability of personal savings discourages banks from granting them loans, and their immigrant status is often responsible for episodes of prejudice and discrimination by lenders. The authors empirically explore potential sources of financial help to which some ethnic groups (Maghrebis, Chinese and Filipinos) residing in Italy resort to start a new business. The ethnic-based selection of cases – to which a control group of native Italians has been added – and the methodological approach applied – based on the non-directive "vignette" technique – have permitted the authors to: investigate in an in-depth manner respondents' value orientations shaping their search for financial support; compare immigrants' attitudes with natives'; examine immigrants' level of integration in the receiving society. Results reveal that cultural norms and values play an important role not only as regards immigrants' propensity to look for financial backing, but also where such help should be sought. Potential sources of financing also vary according to ethnicity: Chinese mostly rely on *blood* (family members), whereas Maghreb-origin immigrants are more similar to Italians: they resort to the market (*banks*) as a first step, which may suggest an ability to interact with the local credential system and be interpreted as a sign of integration in the receiving country. Filipinos are also quite inclined to resort to the market, but their proclivity to apply for loans is rather low, which is consistent with their traditionally lukewarm stance towards entrepreneurship.

Migration is usually experienced as an opportunity to achieve a better life and, even if migrants are often little satisfied with their lives in the destination countries, they tend to report higher levels of life satisfaction than their co-ethnic members left behind in the country of origin (OECD 2017). Nonetheless, migration is also a challenge and may threaten migrants' well-being, especially if it implies a fracture in family composition and only some family members decide to migrate. Indeed, migration tests family solidarity, since the geographical and physical distance may be responsible for family cohesion disruption; this aspect is particularly evident when parents decide to migrate and to leave their underage children to other family members' care.

This topic is extensively investigated by Francesca Tosi, who sheds light on an under-investigated dimension of migrants' integration: the well-being of transnational mothers, who – unlike fathers – are expected to provide their children not only with material and financial support, but also with emotional care. This different pattern of expected parental roles puts a lot of pressure on transnational mothers, who are often affected by feelings of guilt and distress. Resorting to the *Social Condition and Integration of Foreign Citizens 2011-2012* survey conducted by the Italian National Institute of Statistics (Istat), Tosi analyses Eastern European migrant women's subjective well-being, taking into account both physical and mental health dimensions, and compares transnational mothers with non-transnational mothers and childless women as well. Her main results reveal that, although migration allows mothers to provide financial and material support to their children left behind in the country of birth, transnational mothers are more likely to be affected by lower subjective physical and mental well-being; this outcome persists even when individual characteristics (socio-economic conditions and migration background) are held constant.

This final section ends with Eleonora Vlach's chapter dedicated to immigrants' offspring and their educational choices. Children of migrants are key actors to be considered when examining and assessing the degree of integration of foreign populations in a receiving country. In fact, they represent a crucial link between the ("old") country of origin and the ("new") country of destination (Foner 1997). Despite their origins, many children of immigrants – especially if they were born in the receiving country – share several features with their native peers, such as: a strong fluency in the language spoken by natives, an educational qualification formally recognised by the labour market but earned in the local education system, a good propensity to hang out with friends belonging to the majority group. In other words, immigrant-origin children are more likely than their parents to absorb attitudes and cultural values and norms of the "new" society. Education is undoubtedly a crucial element for immigrant-origin children: school is indeed a good vehicle of socialization and transmission of competencies. Nonetheless, sociological literature has often stressed that children of immigrants experience more challenges than their native peers at school. The former are more likely to drop out and to achieve worse educational grades than the latter, and these discouraging outcomes are often due to the widespread poverty and social exclusion experienced by immigrant populations.

Vlach aims to explore both students' propensity to continue their educational career at the end of compulsory schooling and – for those who decide to remain in the educational system – the type of track chosen (academic *versus* vocational). Her study focuses on four European countries (England, Sweden, Germany and the Netherlands), chosen for their migratory history and educational systems' features, and compares three different groups of students: natives, immigrant students born abroad and immigrant-origin students born in the country of investigation. Her analyses are performed on the *Children of Immigrants Longitudinal Survey in Four European Countries* and examine if, and to what extent, students' migratory experience and ethnicity affect educational decisions. Results point out that ethnic background plays a pivotal role both in the transition from compulsory to post-compulsory schooling and in selecting an academic track, whereas migratory experience's net effect is not statistically significant. This means that children of immigrants' educational trajectories are strongly shaped by factors, such as socio-economic origin and ethnicity. Finally, educational institutional features are important aspects as well: disadvantaged students gain more educational benefits in comprehensive school systems (England and Sweden) rather than in selective and curricula-based ones (Germany and the Netherlands).

A large part of the contributions included here originated, to some degree, within the international conference on "Migration from, to and within Europe: Economic and Social Opportunities and Costs", held at the Forlì Campus of the University of Bologna on 19–21 June 2019 and financed by Prof. Fauri's Jean Monnet Chair. Some of the texts, in a preliminary version, were presented and discussed by their authors. The fertility of the perspectives and the findings of those papers suggested the opportunity to develop those works for this volume. All chapters included in this book are the result of a strict selection process undertaken at the end of fruitful and vibrant discussions, which took place within the conference's scientific committee (composed of Gianmarco Ottaviano, Matteo Sanfilippo and the co-editors of the book) and by the publisher as well. The book aims to promote a debate among scholars of different disciplines (economic history, sociology and demography) in order to improve the understanding of the effects that different forms of migration from, to and within European borders have had and will continue to exert on economic and social change in the host countries.

References

Alba R. and Nee V. (1997). Rethinking Assimilation Theory for a New Era of Immigration. *International Migration Review*. 31(4): 826–874.

Brubaker R. (2001). The Return of Assimilation? Changing Perspectives on Immigration and its Sequels in France, Germany and the United States. *Ethnic and Racial Studies*. 24(4): 531–548.

Cipolla C.M. (1997). *Storia economica dell'Europa pre-industriale*. Il Mulino: Bologna.

Constant A. and Massey D.S. (2005). Labor Market Segmentation and the Earnings of German Guestworkers. *Population Research and Policy Review*. 24 (October): 489–512.

De Hass H. (2007). Turning the Tide? Development Will Not Stop Migration. *Development and Change*. 38(5): 819–841.

Fauri F. (2015). *The History of Migration in Europe: Perspectives from Economics, Politics and Sociology*. London and New York: Routledge.

Foner N. (1997). The Immigrant Family: Cultural Legacies and Cultural Change. *International Migration Review*. 31(4): 961–974.

Foreman-Peck J. (1995). *A History of the World Economy*. Havester: Hertfordshire.

Gans H.J. (1992). Second Generation Decline: Scenarios for the Economic and Ethnic Futures of the Post-1965 American Immigrants. *Ethnic and Racial Studies*. 15(2): 173–192.

Glazer N. (1993). Is Assimilation Dead? *The Annals of the American Academy of Social and Political Sciences*. 530: 122–136.

Gordon M. (1964). *Assimilation in American Life*. Oxford University Press: New York.

Hanson G.H. (2010). International Migration and the Developing World. In Rodrik D. and Rosenzweig M. (eds.). *Handbook of Development Economics. Vol. 5*. The Netherlands: North-Holland, 4363–4414.

Lucassen J. and Lucassen L. (2009). The Mobility Transition Revisited, 1500–1900: What the Case of Europe Can Offer to Global History. *Journal of Global History*. 4(4): 347–377.

Lucassen J. and Lucassen L. (eds.) (2014). *Globalising Migration History: The Eurasian Experience (16th–21st Centuries)*. Leiden and Boston: Brill.

Massey D.S. (1999). Why Does Immigration Occur? A Theoretical Synthesis. In Hirschman C., Kasinitz P. and DeWind J. (ed.). *The Handbook of International Migration: the American Experience* . New York: Russell Sage Foundation, 34–52.

Massey D.S., Arango J., Graeme H., Kouaouci A., Pellegrino A. and Taylor J.E. (1993). Theories of International Migration: A Review and Appraisal. *Population and Development Review*. 19(3): 431–466.

Mayo-Smith R. (1894a). Assimilation of Nationalities in the United States. I. *Political Science Quarterly*. 9(3): 426–444.

Mayo-Smith R. (1894b). Assimilation of Nationalities in the United States. II. *Political Science Quarterly*. 9(4): 649–670.

OECD (2017). *How's Life? 2017: Measuring Well-Being*. Paris: OECD.

Park R.E. and Burgess W.E. (1969). *Introduction to the Science of Sociology*. London: University of Chicago, 3rd ed.

Phillips J.A. and Massey D.S. (1999). The New Labor Market: Immigrants and Wages after IRCA. *Demography*. 36(2): 233–246.

Portes A. (2010). *Economic Sociology: A Systematic Inquiry*. Princeton: Princeton University Press.

Portes A. and Jensen L. (1989). The Enclave and the Entrants: Patterns of Ethnic Enterprise in Miami before and after Mariel. *American Sociological Review*. 54(6): 929–949.

Portes A. and Zhou M. (1993). The New Second Generation: Segmented Assimilation and its Variants. *Annals of the American Academy of Political and Social Science*. 530, Interminority Affairs in the U.S., Pluralism at the Crossroads: 74–96.

Rumbaut R.G. (1997). Assimilation and its Discontents: Between Rhetoric and Reality. *International Migration Review*. 31(4): 923–960.

Simons S.E. (1901a). Social Assimilation I. *The American Journal of Sociology*. 6(6): 790–822.

Simons S.E. (1901b). Social Assimilation II. *The American Journal of Sociology*. 7(1): 53–79.

Simons S.E. (1901c). Social Assimilation VII. Assimilation in the Modern World. *The American Journal of Sociology*. 7(2): 234–248.

Simons S.E. (1901d). Social Assimilation IV. *The American Journal of Sociology*. 7(3): 386–404.

Taylor A.M. and Williamson J.G. (1994). *Convergence in the Age of Mass Migration*. NBER Working Paper No. 4711.

Warner W.L. and Srole L. (1945). *The Social Systems of American Ethnic Groups*. New Haven: Yale University Press.

Part I

Immigrants and the labour market

Employment opportunities and challenges

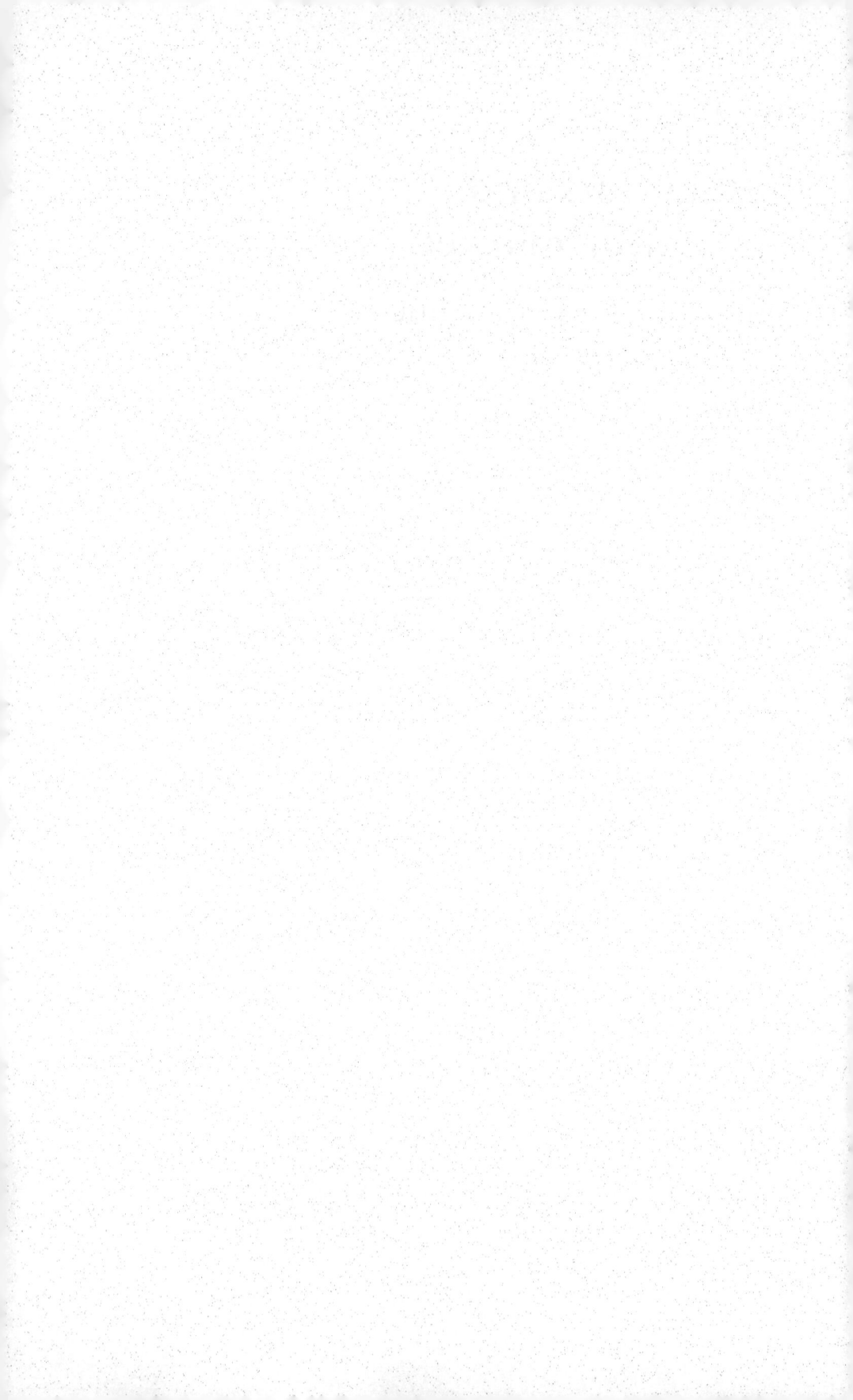

3 Hostility in times of labour shortage

Controversial attitudes towards labour immigration in Hungary

Anikó Bernát

Introduction

The chapter presents a segment of a comprehensive empirical research[1] that aimed to explore the attitudes and the underlying drivers behind the intense political and public discourse on migration in four Eastern European transition countries by applying both quantitative and qualitative methods (representative surveys, focus groups and expert interviews). The analysis finally revealed a number of controversial or conflicting attitudes or beliefs that are often similar to cognitive dissonances. This chapter is focusing on the controversial attitudes widely shared by the Hungarian population related to labour immigration, more precisely the conflicting attitudes around the demand for workforce and the rejection of immigrants, which is embedded in another, broader contradiction between the evaluation of immigration and emigration. These conflicting attitudes apparently lead to cognitive tensions that should be reduced and integrated into a more coherent framework at both macro and micro levels, i.e. in the political and public discourse as well as at the level of individual cognition.

The conflicting attitudes revealed by the empirical research connected to the classical cognitive dissonance theory of Leon Festinger (1957) that is basically referred to an internal psychological inconsistency of an individual, however such inconsistencies can also be examined at macro level. The cognitive tension can emerge from various situations, including the inconsistency between various mental attitudes and personal actions, and it leads to an uncomfortable psychological condition that motivates people to reduce the mental dissonance. There are two main approaches that can be applied to eliminate or reduce the tension: one is the modification of the cognition via changing behaviour or action, while the other is acquiring new information or opinions selectively. The term cognitive dissonance can also be defined a bit more broadly, beyond the strict definition and also embrace controversies, conflicting attitudes, facts, beliefs or behaviour that lead to a cognitive tension.

The reduction of the cognitive dissonances at macro, i.e. political level in Hungary explored in the empirical research apparently combined these two main reduction strategies by introducing legislative amendments that are facilitating the recruitment of foreign labour force from neighbouring countries of specific professions to alleviate labour shortage that is exempt from labour market testing, while communicating it as a "guest worker programme" that is not considered "true" immigration with integration claims of the migrants. Public level reduction strategies can, however, take more forms, and the research is focusing on societal aspects rather than the macro-political aspects.

Hungary has had scarcely any experience of migratory movements in its recent history. Before the First World War, it was a multinational, multi-ethnic country, but it became ethnically homogeneous after 1920, when it lost two thirds of both its territory and its population. Immigration of Hungarians from neighbouring countries was significant in the 1980–1990s, but that was Hungary's only relevant experience of immigration until the recent migration flow in 2015. The main waves of Hungarian emigration were influenced by the Second World War in general, the Holocaust in particular and the post-war occupation by the Soviet regime, as well as by the failed revolution of 1956.

As for current trends, inward migration remains at a very low level (whatever the government campaigns may suggest about the threat to Hungary of immigration). Taking the EU as a whole, Hungary is one of the countries with the lowest percentage of immigrants: the number of foreign citizens permanently resident in Hungary was 173,000 in 2019, or 1.8 per cent of the total population in 2017, only 7 out of 1,000 residents of Hungary were foreign citizens. The number of asylum seekers was around 2,000 between 2010 and 2012; this figure started to edge up in 2013–2014, peaking in 2015 at 177,135 asylum applications. Since then there has been a rapid decline, and by 2017 the level was again very low. It was not the official anti-immigration campaign itself that caused this decline, but rather its consequences – i.e. some very specific legislation, combined with a border fence as a physical barrier on the Serbian and Croatian borders. These moves have met the government's "zero-immigration" ideology.

Labour shortage as a prominent influencer of migratory movements

The analysis focuses on the tension between two "desired public goods" in Hungary: the need of an immigrant labour force in order to alleviate labour shortage and foster economic growth, and the state level "zero immigration" policy that is seemingly satisfying a large share of the population reflected by the high level of xenophobia. Labour immigration as a possible solution to labour shortage is a "no-go-zone" for Hungary according to the official, state-level, anti-immigration approach that has a strong effect on public opinion as xenophobia and anti-immigration attitudes are widespread in the Hungarian population. Hungary is one of the transitional countries that recently experienced massive economic growth combined with labour shortage (in the early 2020s up until the COVID-19 outbreak in early 2020). Labour shortage is a new phenomenon for Hungarian society after a long struggle with unemployment during the transition years in the 1990s and the prolonged economic crisis after 2008. However, labour demand could not be satisfied sufficiently by a mainly domestic labour supply for various reasons, among them the increasing emigration (which is also a new phenomenon for Hungary) that is mainly fuelled by the low-income level. On the other hand, labour shortage cannot be satisfied (officially) neither from external sources by labour immigration due to the strong anti-immigration campaign by the government (although there are some state supported programmes recruiting labour immigrants to specific sectors or companies mainly from neighbouring countries, but it is not communicated openly as it would not fit into the official state approach of zero immigration).

Aside from the demographic, economic and political factors, the labour shortage as a specific element behind migratory movements often remains hidden, albeit it is also relevant for both the immigrants and the host country. The increased emigration to the old Member States (EU-15) from Hungary and the other new Member States (EU-10) following enlargement of the EU in 2004, and then the economic crisis of 2008 (which intensified further after 2011), has had a macro-level impact on the labour markets of both the sending and the receiving countries (Hárs 2019). The beneficial effects in most of the host countries are well documented (Kahanec, Pytliková and Zimmermann 2016), but the impact on the countries of origin are mixed. Early results showed slightly increased wages and decreased unemployment rates (Brücker et al. 2009), but only in the short run; over the longer term, the demographic impact of the outflow of young and qualified workers, and the consequences of this for the domestic labour markets, with labour shortages in some occupations, would appear to be clearly negative for the sending countries. Moreover, the future prospects of the welfare systems of the sending countries would seem to be even more parlous, due to the aging population remaining behind (Kahanec 2013; Zaiceva 2014).

A shortage of labour has been a clear trend in Hungarian economy since 2012 (until March 2020, the start of the economic crisis caused by the COVID-19 pandemic). It is described by Köllő and Varga (2018) and confirmed by all relevant related employment and economic indicators. At the beginning of the period, increased labour shortages and the further upsurge in outward migration of Hungarians almost overlap (around 2011–2012), the two phenomena are often linked in public and policy discourse as cause and effect. And this is supported by the experiences of other EU-10 countries (mainly Poland and the Baltic countries) where the mass exodus of workers has been followed by reduced unemployment and increased labour shortages in those sectors (manufacturing, construction) that are most affected by outward migration. However, the Hungarian pattern is different: the emerging labour shortage and the increased outward migration have not reduced the rate of unemployment. Thus, both high levels of unemployment and labour shortages coexist in the current Hungarian labour market. This is primarily a consequence of structural tension and friction, and is mostly due to the mismatch between the qualifications of job seekers and employees and current labour market needs: outward migration is just a secondary driver of the labour shortage (Köllő and Varga 2018; Hárs 2019). Despite this evidence, the shortage of labour and outward migration are usually directly linked in both the public and political discourse.

Besides the anti-immigration policies and campaigns by the current Hungarian government, there are certain policies to attract migrant workers from non-EU countries, and lately there has been a growing number of immigrant guest workers in Hungary, mainly from neighbouring countries, but also from China, Vietnam or India. If we compare the figures for 2017 and 2018, we find that the number of people from third countries who applied for a residence permit with the aim of working in Hungary increased from 24,539 to 60,931 (National Directorate-General for Aliens Policing 2017–2018).

Conflicting attitudes around migratory movements and labour shortage

The general negative attitudes towards immigration and immigrants and the positive or neutral attitudes towards emigration and emigrants is set within the frames of the Hungarian attitudinal landscape in the past decades, which has been further confirmed by the empirical findings of the research (Bernat 2020). This chapter aims to highlight the contradictions in attitudes revealed by this empirical work, which are typical of cognitive dissonance.

A core dissonance stretches between the perceived relevance of immigration (less relevant) and emigration (highly relevant). This is in stark contrast to the dominance of immigration in political (and thus public) discourse, while emigration is rarely discussed and remains in the shadow. Although qualitative evidences confirm, that people are usually aware of the contradiction and find it awkward and embarrassing that the intensive immigration-focused governmental communication campaign hinders discussion of the real concern, which is emigration. Outward migration is understood as a multi-layered damage of society, described as the loss of people, who are absent from their families and social networks at the micro level, and from the Hungarian economy and society at the macro level.

The other main contradiction lies between the core attitudes toward inward and outward migration, where the assessment of immigration is rather negative, whereas emigration is viewed as positive or neutral, understandable when evaluated from the perspective of the emigrant, despite its negative impact at both the personal and the public (economic and social) level. A negative attitude toward immigrants also applies to asylum seekers and refugees, who are the most vulnerable groups of immigrants; but in general, their vulnerability is not a driver to accept or to empathize with them, but is rather another reason for threat. The comparison between the Hungarian refugees fleeing from communist Hungary during the revolution of 1956 and contemporary war refugees from the Middle East could be theoretically obvious, but cultural differences and the preference of homophily rather than heterophily makes it a rarely validated comparison.

The empirical research provided a wide range of arguments that serve to alleviate the obvious contradiction, such as stating that immigrants are more harmful than useful to Hungary in terms of their cultural and/or religious norms (they are lazy, littering, etc.); they are unable to work (due to lack of motivation, education, language or other skills); and immigrants are usually young, single males, often illiterate, which makes them equally useless and threatening, as these "typical" immigrants are often perceived as "outsiders" who want to dominate the locals (by forcing them to adopt their religion and norms) and as dangerous (abuse, terrorism). By contrast, emigrant Hungarians are perceived as skilled, competent, hardworking people with a cultural and religious background similar to that of the host society; and so it is impossible to draw any parallels between immigrants and emigrants in terms of competency, motivation and usefulness. And this is a key element in argumentation to sever the link between labour demand and (immigrant) supply: the negative stereotypes linked to third-country immigrant labour force make it unsuitable to fill in labour market gaps even though labour force is highly demanded in times of labour shortage. Overcoming labour shortage and boosting the economy by involving a foreign workforce would be a common good, would serve the economy and thus society and its members in general, but the macro level benefits are refused in order not to challenge the comfort zone of an ethnically homogenous society.

Another clear contradiction emerged from the discussion of the real goals of immigrants arriving in Hungary, which centred around the economic exploitation rather than the economic improvement of the host country. If immigrants come to work, they are perceived as wanting to exploit the Hungarian labour market, taking jobs away from the Hungarians and depressing wages and possibly also as an incompetent and demotivated workforce. But if they come to Hungary with no plans to work, then that is an even worse exploitation of the host country. In this case immigrants are perceived as "welfare tourists", exploiting the welfare state to get social benefits, aid and other state and NGO support; others, however, pointed out that in fact no welfare benefits are offered to them (and indeed, they are entitled to only very low general social benefits). One possible strategy to reduce this cognitive dissonance is the typical argument that even though they get no integration benefits, but only the general social benefits (which are inadequate also for Hungarian citizens), that still tempts them. Moreover, they are seen as those who are wasting donations (food donations thrown away), which further underlines the fact that they do not deserve any help.

This links via cultural argumentations to another contradiction: there seems to be an apparent acceptance of immigrants who want to work and who respect Hungarian culture, but anti-immigrant sentiment nonetheless surfaces if theory threatens to become reality. Although the labour shortage in a wide range of professions and jobs (both unskilled and skilled) is patently obvious, people often search for a short cut in the argument to demonstrate immigrants' inability to fill the labour market gap properly (see typical counter-arguments above); this often references the lack of personal skills and motivation, which often stem from cultural or religious differences. The acceptance of immigrant labour in some demanded, and often skilled jobs (such as IT, medical professions or skilled workers) is seemingly valid only at the general level, but not at a personal level, when it might become a reality.

Moreover, it was often mentioned in conjunction with the government's zero-immigration policy that there are "organized guest worker" programmes at the state level to target immigrants; these are becoming increasingly familiar to the public, in spite of a lack of official state information. This contradiction is reduced by arguing that labour immigrants are just "guest workers"; they will go home soon; they have no integration plans; and due to the "guest worker lifestyle", they are barely in contact with the locals and make no claims for social integration or social benefits. Moreover, they are mainly from neighbouring countries (Ukraine, Serbia), and are not "that kind" of "typical" (i.e. Muslim or other Asian or African, undesirable) immigrant – especially if they are ethnic Hungarians (which is often the case, because of the Hungarian minorities living in those neighbouring countries).

Conclusions

Migration is at the top of the political agenda recently both in Europe and Hungary. The specific context in Hungary builds up from the mix of a strong anti-immigration component (supported by an extremely intensive communications campaign) and an almost non-existent emigration component (which people tend to miss, as it is perceived as a much more relevant issue, with an impact on most families). It is further shaped by the anti-immigration sentiments of Hungarians that stem from the history of an ethnically homogenous society, characterized by a low level of immigration and balanced with a low level of emigration thanks to the EU-accession of Hungary. This combination offers a fertile soil for several conflicting attitudes or beliefs, often cognitive dissonances that are often reduced by arguments with limited validity. It is partly due to the fact that people often do not realize the contradictions between the opinions and statements they offer, and so the arguments to reduce cognitive dissonance are often unconsciously developed. That might be why the less well-elaborated arguments are often inadequate to hinder or explain the tension between contradictory attitudes, but as contradictions are often not realized it can help to limit the development of cognitive tensions in some cases.

Note

1 The chapter is based on the empirical research project "Those who come and those who go: Exploring cognitive dissonances around immigration and emigration in Hungary, Poland, Lithuania and Bulgaria", funded by the Friedrich-Ebert-Stiftung's regional project "Flight, migration, integration in Europe" (based in Budapest, Hungary). The cross-country project was coordinated by TÁRKI Social Research Institute (Hungary). The country-level research was carried out by Sova Harris (Bulgaria), Spinter Research (Lithuania), Insight Shot (Poland), and TÁRKI Social Research Institute (Hungary).

References

Bernat A. (2020). *Those Who Come and Those Who Go: Country Report Hungary. Migration Patterns and Attitudes toward Migratory Movements in Selected Post-Socialist Transition Countries. The Cases of Hungary, Poland, Lithuania and Bulgaria*. Budapest: Friedrich Ebert Stiftung.

Brücker H., Baas T., Beleva I., Bertoli S., Boeri T., et al. (2009). *Labour Mobility within the EU in the Context of Enlargement and the Functioning of the Transitional Arrangements*. Nuremberg: European Integration Consortium-IAB, CMR, fRDB, GEP, WIFO, wiiw.

Festinger L. (1957). *A Theory of Cognitive Dissonance*. Stanford: Stanford University Press.

Hárs Á. (2019). Increasing Outward Migration: Opportunities, Hopes and Labour Market Impacts. In Tóth I.Gy. (ed.). *Hungarian Social Report 2019*. Budapest: TÁRKI, 137–159.

Kahanec M. (2013). Labor Mobility in an Enlarged European Union. In Constant A.F. and Zimmermann K.F. (eds.). *International Handbook on the Economics of Migration*. Cheltenham: Edward Elgar, 137–152.

Kahanec M., Pytliková M. and Zimmermann K.F. (2016). The Free Movement of Workers in an Enlarged European Union: Institutional Underpinnings of Economic Adjustment. In Kahanec M. and Zimmermann K.F. (eds.). *Labor Migration, EU Enlargement, and the Great Recession*. Berlin and Heidelberg: Springer, 1–34.

Köllő J. and Varga J. (2018). Shortage and Unemployment. In Fazekas K. and Köllő J. (eds.). *The Hungarian Labour Market 2017*. Budapest: Institute of Economics, Centre for Economic and Regional Studies, Hungarian Academy of Sciences.

National Directorate-General for Aliens Policing (2017-2018). *Statistics for 2017 and 2018*, www.bmbah.hu/index.php?option=com_k2&view=item&layout=item&id=177&Itemid=1232&lang=hu

Zaiceva A. (2014). *Post-Enlargement Emigration and New EU Members' Labor Markets*. IZA World of Labor, No. 40.

4 Is talent divide a proper form with which to characterize contemporary migration flows?

Evidence from the Portuguese emigration within the European Union

Pedro Góis and José Carlos Marques

Introduction

Boundaries among social scientists within specific crosscutting domains, continuously challenge the possibility of getting a wide view of given issues. This is the case of migration studies, an area widely known to be interdisciplinary, gathering contributions from many social scientists whose disciplinary background is not always evident. For example, many practical and institutional boundaries separate those studying the so-called voluntary (economic migration) and forced migration (refugees), a frontier nowadays blurred with the mixed migration flows in migration studies. Other lines separate those studying international and internal migration as a field of study that does not always apply to areas like the European Union (EU). Is migration a word we need to use or should we move to the use of mobility as the emerging explanatory concept in regional studies or within the free movement areas? Around each specific topic, scientific events are organized, journals are published, theory is developed, leading to a clustering that disregards frequent communication with other sub-scientifically areas. The frontier, in many cases, become a (closed) border in between topics and disciplines. The same sub-disciplinary division happens with the study of highly skilled migration, when compared to the study of less skilled migratory movements. For some authors, highly skilled movements are a specific form of mobility whose particularities are better captured through the use of alternative concepts (Chiswick and Miller 2011; Ruhs and Anderson 2012). As pointed out by Vasey (2010: 157–158)

> there is a tendency to fall into the trap of reproducing an unhelpful dichotomy between highly skilled migrants (HSMs) and other less skilled migrants (or, more accurately, migrants working in less skilled roles). In a sense this is a replication of the duality at the heart of much debate about contemporary global migrations – that there is a small

> elite of highly skilled migrants (...) [and] an undifferentiated mass suitable only to fill the lowest echelons of the labour market, to do those jobs too dirty, dull or demeaning for the native workforce.

Albeit the reliance on simple dichotomies are becoming increasingly imprecise due to diversification of migration modalities (King 2002), the discussions around different types of migrants, such as highly skilled and less skilled, remain important to grasp the functioning of the political economy of international migration, being particularly relevant from an economic point of view (Chiswick and Miller 2011).

Regarding migration studies, the roots of the skill divide convention seem to be two sided: the first one can be expressed as policy determined and the second one as labour market derived (Fabbricotti 2016). Being, in our interpretation, complementary, both approaches to skill divide in migration research apply when looking to Portuguese intra-EU migration in recent decades.

The skill divided as policy determined

Within most advanced EU economies, mainly in central and Western Europe, a skill divide splits services occupations, intensifies the services and manufacturing sectors and reverberates upon migration patterns. The result is an escalating face-off between a "global hunt for talent" – claiming for a Brain Gain – and the recruitment of seasonal agricultural and manufacturing workers for the dirty, dangerous and demanding (DDD) jobs – trying to fill the gap within local labour markets. Authors like Didier Bigo and Elspeth Guild (2005) reveal how the dominant vision of labour migration policies in the European Union was formulated by opposing high skills migration to low skill migration. In their approach, they observe a skill divide splitting the framework for regulating migration into trade agreements between the EU and third countries (Bigo and Guild 2005) *vis-à-vis* third-country nationals (TCN) immigrants. The departing paradigm was a perspicuous skill divide topography. This division has been successively deepened through a regulatory framework intended to attract highly skilled workers and to constrain the possibility of low skilled workers from entering the EU labour market (Borjas 2001; Nieto, Matano and Ramos 2015). As pointed out by Geddes and Sholten (2016), the creation and sustention of these categories and, above all, the differentiation that is politically made between highly skilled migrants and low skilled ones determine the mobility opportunities of each one of these groups of migrants and shape their perception by the receiving societies (Van Mol and de Valk 2016).

There is a tendency to fall into the trap of reproducing a dichotomy between highly skilled migrants and migrants working in less skilled roles without giving due attention to the political and social causes of this sociological separation. The oil crisis of 1973–1974 had a considerable impact on the economic landscape of Europe reducing the need for labour and creating an idea of the immigration as redundant (Zimmermann 2005). Between the 1970s and the end of the 1980s the number of Greek, Italian, Portuguese and Spanish foreigners in Northern and Central European countries diminished (with the exception of Switzerland, where the number of Portuguese grew substantially; Marques 2008). The volume of immigrants in the European Economic Community (EEC-6 or EEC-9), however, kept rising, due to a low intensity chain migration and the related natural growth of migrant populations (Van Mol and de Valk 2016). In 1981 Greece and in 1986 Portugal and Spain join the EEC forming the EEC-12. The 1992 Maastricht Treaty's abolition of internal borders and the creation of Europe's Schengen Area, significantly facilitated intra-EU movements in the European Community-12 (Castles 2006a). At the same time, migrants' entrance into the EU became progressively restricted due to the unification of the European market, which imposed strict external border controls and visa regulations. Nevertheless, strict immigration policies were not universally applicable to all segments of migration, but mostly to low skilled migrants from third countries.

After the 1990s several Member States of the European Union changed their migration models and developed new modalities for the exclusive admission of skilled and highly skilled migrants in order to respond to labour shortages in specific segments of the labour market (Solimano 2008). The UK was the first European country to develop an open high-skill migration policy in the late 1990s. Other EU countries, such as the Netherlands or Germany, followed this policy in the early 2000s. In the mid 2000s the EU adopted the EU Blue Card scheme to attract the best and brightest of the world to the European Union countries (Triandafyllidou and Isaakyan 2014). These exceptions, within a general framework characterized by restrictive immigration policies, were aimed at responding to some labour market needs in fast growing economic sectors or specific professions (ICT, health, science). Accelerated or preferential procedures have been thus created, particularly in those countries or sectors where it has become necessary to fill specific skill gaps not occupied anymore by autochthonous workers or by long-term foreign residents. In general, these policies to attract highly qualified workers were considered an important means to support economic growth and avoid bottlenecks in national economies (Góis and Marques 2007). Public opinion never showed signs of rejection of these professionals, perceived in a positive way as expatriates and not as immigrants. These highly skilled workers were seen as knowledge brokers, key professionals in the health sector, producers of wealth, technological geeks, entrepreneurs in both their 'home' country and receiving societies. In contrast, channels for the entrance of lesser skilled immigrants had been made successively more restrictive. Contrary to the highly skilled migrants, the newcomers with low and medium levels of educational attainment and those low skilled already in the EU were portrayed as a societal burden in the popular discourse (Platonova and Urso 2012).

At least from the 1990s, highly skilled professionals are looked for by states and enjoyed a much greater level of *de facto* mobility than their unskilled compatriots. These policy developments were, however, mainly directed exclusively towards third-country nationals, since citizens and long-term foreign residents of an EU member country are covered by the *acquis communautaire* on the free movement of workers (Kahanec, Pytliková and Zimmermann 2016). For intra-EU-migrants, the non existence of constraints to intra-EU mobility has been framed by some authors as a distinctive feature of current migration flows in Europe (Favell 2008; Engbersen, Snel and De Boom 2013). Following the guest worker systems based on bilateral agreements that ended in the mid-1970s (Van Mol and de Valk 2016), a *de facto* south-north and east-west low skilled migratory flow within the Europe's Schengen Area was initiated from the 1990s onwards (Castles 2006a; 2006b; Kahanec, Pytliková and Zimmermann 2016). These skilled and low skilled migrations were economically visible at least from the end of the 1980s in different building and reconstruction sites, in the tourism sector, in the cleaning and personal services sector, and, from 2000s, as posted workers in construction sites around Europe (Darvas 2017; Batsaikhan, Darvas and Raposo 2018), or in industrial sites in a handful of European countries (Constant and Massey 2002; Van Mol and de Valk 2016; Pires 2019). Though, even for these intra-European migrants, the regulatory response to the labour market divide has been to treat qualified migrants more favourably in terms of entry and stay than their less qualified countrymen. The incomplete easing of mobility difficulties underscored the inequality of the EU migration regimes and its preference towards qualified migrants. A particular development at the EU level serves to illustrate how this labour market divide benefits from institutional and regulatory integration measures that help to shape patterns of highly skilled mobility and migration within the EU.

Europeanization of highly skilled mobility

The interaction between the changes of the labour market and the evolution of the European higher education system has been insufficiently studied, albeit the intention to increase the mobility of employees in Europe in order to complete the internal labour market has undoubtedly backed the evolutions in Higher Education in Europe. Mobility of students, common studies programmes (like Erasmus), and an EU-wide R&D area are, among others, major activities in spurring the labour market for higher education graduates. The so-called "Bologna Process" (which started in 1988) and the conception in 2010 of the European Higher Education Area (EHEA), established a convergent system of "cycles" of study programmes, increased the highly-skilled migration potential inside the European Union, and provided employers a certificate of equivalence of learning and knowledge. Today, one indirect consequence of being an EU Member State, a pillar of the

EU as a free movement space, is that their citizens (and long-term residents) can move with their skills and diplomas (Teichler 2019). Additionally, the Bologna Process has indirectly led to a growing pace of intra-European degree mobility and to a rising participation in student mobility through study or internship in another country, throughout programmes such as Erasmus, Leonardo da Vinci or Marie-Sklodowska Curie grants (Choudaha 2017; Teichler 2019).

These student mobility programmes are only one part of a wider strategy to allow for the intra EU mobility of the highly skilled. Others are diploma and postgraduate mobility and bilateral mobility programmes, mobility of researchers (Cairns 2014), and the recognition of diplomas of the regulated professions. The recognition of professional qualifications, unified through Directive 2005/36/EC, was intended to overcome the obstacle of "limited portability of professional qualifications" (Riemsdijk 2013: 52) throughout the EU. It allows for qualified professionals (mainly highly skilled ones) to enter the labour market of a country other than the one from which they received their professional or academic qualification, thus allowing them to transfer their human capital to another country. It constitutes an instrument that permits the matching of labour demands for specific professions or qualifications that exist in different countries with the supply of qualified migrants without cumbersome intermediation mechanisms. These regulations allow, for example, northern European countries (Germany, UK, France, among others) to mitigate their necessity of health workers and engineers, among other qualified workers.[1]

The skill divided as a result of the segmented labour markets

Known as the labour market segmentation (LSM) theory, both in its economic and in its institutional variants, LSM recognizes the existence of dualism as a structural feature of labour markets (Doeringer and Piore 1971). According to this classic theory, a share of the high-skilled migrants occupies the same place as the native worker and competes against them in the primary labour market, while low-skilled migrants continue to occupy the secondary labour market. For these authors the segmentation is associated with demand-side factors (demand fluctuation in the labour market) more than with supply-side (personal characteristics of the migrant workers) (Piore 1979). Moreover, for LSM the segmentation of the labour market is one of the drivers of the demand for foreign labour force that consequently determines the allocation mechanism of immigrants to specific segments of the national labour market. Segmented labour market theories help to explain the power in the skill divide perspective regarding labour migration into the European Union (Piore 1970; 1975; Doeringer and Piore 1971; Leontaridi 2002).

The sectors of the labour market identified by the segmented market theory are nowadays more complex than initially envisaged by the proponents of this theory. The division between a primary and a secondary labour market based, among others, on the conditions of security and salary offered in each segment, is currently less clear than it was during the golden age of Fordism.[2] This is particularly true for the integration of migrants in different segments of the country's labour markets. Contrary to previous periods, migrants (both highly and low skilled ones) are being integrated in labour intensive jobs, under frequently precarious conditions and fulfil vacancies that cannot be filled with the host countries labour force.

The construction of a European Labour Market (or of a transnational European Labour Market) has been constrained by the existence of institutional frameworks (labour regulations, mobility opportunities and welfare provisions) with different degrees of embedment in national and transnational settings (Geddes 2003; Geddes and Scholten 2016). The tensions between the national determinants of the labour market (including salary differentials, welfare access and fiscal inclusion) and the European wide politics towards the creation of a common labour market (the Europeanization of the labour market) fostered the development of specific intersections between the functioning of particular segments of national labour markets and transnational EU wide provisions. Thus, the economic peripheries of the EU Member States tend to become origin countries while central economies tend to be recipients of intra EU migration. It is worth mentioning that the level of "Europeanization" of national labour markets varies substantially between EU Member States and even more in the interior of States between economic activities. For young, well-qualified, transnationally mobile individuals the Europeanization of the labour market provides new opportunities. Nevertheless, according to Verwiebe and Eder (2006), transnational mobility creates new career chances in the upper segments of the labour market, but, on the other hand, also increases the risks of having to integrate oneself into the lower end of the income hierarchy. Thus, the traditional notion of labour market segmentation, which describes a situation in which native-born workers do not compete with the immigrant labour pool for jobs, is outdated when referring to the EU migrants inside the European Union. EU migrants can compete, at least in theory, with natives and between each other for both low and high skill jobs. In practice, they interact in distinct frameworks and with different intensity levels. It is therefore necessary to integrate in the contemporary analysis of labour market segmentation, especially when applied to the native-migrant labour relations, the several processes that have contributed to changes in labour market segmentation: technological change (Hoos, Manning and Salomons 2009), the evolution of flexible labour market structures (Rubery and Piasna 2015), and changes in the skill supply (McCollum and Findlay 2015).

The EU's Posted Workers (Directive 96/71/EC and Directive 2018/957) is one of these arenas of intersection in which "negotiations and collective agreements in the national or transnational arenas of industrial relations" (Mense-Petermann 2019) leads to specific outcomes in regard to labour mobility. Since the 1990s posting of workers has been a specific form of workforce cross-border mobility in the European Union. Within the framework of free movement of services, as one of the essential principles of the EU single market, the main goal is to ensure that companies and entrepreneurs can offer their services in another EU state without the necessity to set up their company seats there. In 2015, there were around 2 million work postings in the EU (European Commission 2016). This figure indicates the number of Portable Document A1 (PD A1) that were issued – a statement indicating that a worker pays social security contributions in another EU country. According to Mussche, Corluy and Marx (2016: 3), the free movement of services, that frame the directives on posted workers, is shaping a hybrid European labour market in which "permanent type mobility is greatly complemented with high levels of short-term service mobility", that answers specific needs of the national labour markets in the EU. These posted workers would make up 0.65 per cent of the labour force and 0.9 per cent of total employed people in the EU28 in 2015 (European Commission 2016). Poland, Germany and France counted as the main sending countries, while Germany, France and Belgium were the main receiving countries.

As seen above, the formation of this incomplete European Labour Market is thus influenced by structural factors (regulations on the free movement of people or on the free movement of services) and by conjunctural factors that define the conditions under which the matching of workers and jobs occurs (salaries, fiscality, access to welfare provisions, economic crisis in specific regions, networks of migrants, organizations dependent on migrant labour, etc.). The mentioned institutional frameworks are examples of the impact that different developments have on the constitution of an EU labour market and on shaping intra-EU migration. There is still a need for studies that shed greater insights on this relationship, as well as on the influence of other processes in the constitution of the contemporary intra-European migratory system. One of the variables that deserves a thorough scrutiny is the effect that an increasing share of tertiary-educated migrants among total migration, common in most traditional immigration countries in Europe, have on the development of the labour market segmentation. It remains to be seen if the skill divide continues to be distorted by de-skilling (due to the inability to transfer their skills and qualifications) or up-skilling processes experienced by EU national migrants or if their migration leads to the deskilling of highly skilled migrants already living in the country. It also needs further research to know if migrants in low-skilled jobs are seen as "learning migrants" (who learn new skills and acquire human capital through training and experience abroad) (Baláž et al. 2019) and thus became qualified migrants with enhanced mobility capital that can impact on their migration aspirations.

In light of these considerations, the remainder of this chapter aims at testing the hypothesis that Portuguese contemporary migration is filling employment gaps in the European segmented labour market simultaneously in the highly skilled segment and in the low skilled segment. In doing so, our chapter intends to provide an insight on two questions: firstly, in which EU national labour market segments are the contemporary Portuguese migrants mainly concentrated?; and, secondly, is this talent divide a proper form with which to characterize Portuguese contemporary migration flows inside the EU? Our research on the contemporary Portuguese migration within the European Union has shown the simultaneity of low and high skill migration flows to a different number of destination countries (Peixoto et al. 2019; Marques et al. 2020). These results need now to be complemented with an in-depth analysis of the labour market insertion processes of these migrants, such as the one carried out below.

Methods, results and discussion

Portugal witnessed a strong upsurge concerning intra-EU migration over recent decades. High skilled and less skilled mobility coexisted in the new migratory period (Marques et al. 2020). The data analysed in this chapter results from a large-scale survey (n = 6,086) applied to Portuguese individuals who left the country in the new century and was carried out during the research project "Back to the Future: New Emigration and the Portuguese Society (REMIGR)". A structured questionnaire with a series of close-ended questions was used for interview schedules. A caveat and disclaimer are that this sample, although robust, does not mean automatically a representative sample. In questionnaires like this one, the sample of people asked is ideally a representative microcosm of the target population, with each demographic group represented at their respective share. Unfortunately, in migration studies, surveys that fulfil this requirement are uncommon due to the lack of data on which to build the population universe and to extract a representative sample from this population. This is the case of Portuguese contemporary emigration and even more accurately with the Portuguese intra-EU migration where departure registers do not exist and immigration statistics regarding EU citizens are scarce in many EU Member States.

Labour market integration of migrants in selected EU countries: Germany, France, Luxembourg and the UK

Europeanization has changed the speed and scale at which migratory movements occur inside the EU (Fligstein 2000). The skill divide in migrant labour, defined as the diverging admission practices depending on the individual migrants' skill levels, is a consequence of a broader segmentation of the labour markets rather than a pre-existent explanatory policy framework as the Portuguese intra-EU migration is able to demonstrate. EU workforce is still characterized by a large skill divide, both between and within countries. In our empirical analyses, we consider different destination labour markets for Portuguese intra-EU migratory flows. From the data presented, we argue that Europeanization has created simultaneously a strong regional demand for skills and talents in certain labour markets while keeping the need for low or medium skill workers in traditional labour markets for Portuguese emigrants. The skill-divide is thus still present in Portuguese contemporary emigration, albeit the configuration of different skill levels is currently more diverse than in past migratory flows. We will show this structural trend trough the example of contemporary Portuguese emigration to the UK, Germany, France and Luxembourg.

The analysis of our data shows that although high and low skilled migrants display diverse characteristics because of differences in their migration resources, migration and labour market integration processes, there are some common structural factors and constraints that call for integrating these two types of migration in a common migratory framework.

As in previous migration flows, post-2000 migrants to the studied countries were predominantly employed[3] (54.4% of the emigrants), or unemployed (23.1%) before emigration.[4] This shows that an important part of this emigration had been motivated by a weak labour market integration (unemployment or underemployment). A share of Portuguese migrants seems to simply follow economic opportunities. This is a valid assumption for those in lower-skilled and insecure job sectors, but also for highly skilled migrants (e.g. nurses or scientists). Data on the labour status at the time of the survey confirm the importance of economic reasons for recent Portuguese emigration to each one of the countries. Particularly significant is the positive development of the employees and the marked decrease of the unemployed,[5] a regular feature of labour migration flows.

Relevant in the data gathered in the Remigr project is also the number of those that stated they were students before emigration (15.8%). For the majority of them, migration to another country was connected with a mobility from inactivity to activity due to the integration in labour market of the destination country, as can be confirmed by the reduction of those that continue to be students in either one of the observed countries (6.5% in the sum of all countries). For those young migrants the transition from the educational system to the labour market was not completed in Portugal, but in a foreign country, thus demonstrating that an international transition to the labour market allowed these migrants to enlarge their labour market opportunities to other EU countries. The development of a space of free circulation and the institutionalization of a common policy on diploma and qualification recognition through the Bologna Process acted as accelerators of this mobility and, at the same time, allowed a faster integration into the foreign labour market, specifically into the primary labour market for those with the required qualifications (Góis et al. 2016; Marques et al. 2016).

The opportunity to get access to an enlarged labour market also facilitated the adjustment of the occupational structure of the highly qualified to their initial qualifications. In some cases, they experienced a sort of major deskilling or brain waste because their acquired skills and knowledge remained completely unused in the country of destination. This becomes evident if we look at the evolution of the insertion of higher qualification holders in professions corresponding to their level of education.[6]

With emigration, holders of a higher education degree show, in all countries, an increase in the mismatch between their qualification and their profession that intensifies the situations of overqualification verified before emigration. The continuation of their permanence leads to a decrease in the percentage of mismatches in all countries, albeit in France and Luxembourg it continues to be higher than before migration. The reduction is particularly significant in migrants that went to the other two countries, indicating that they were mostly affected by the constraints of the national labour market (due to career blockages, precarity, underemployment, etc.) and were particularly successful in transferring their qualifications to a foreign labour market thus taking advantage of the existent economic opportunities. Overall, this path of professional insertion, marked by an initial phase of downward professional mobility, followed by upward mobility is in line with what was observed in other Portuguese migratory flows. The difference is that in previous migratory flows this occupational mobility was mainly experienced by the less skilled migrants since the most qualified were not only in smaller numbers, but they were either at the origin or at the destination country active in professions close to their academic background.

A more detailed look at the occupational group where migrants currently work supports the distinction of two different migrants profiles: one working in highly skilled occupations (managers, professionals and technical professional, ISCO-08 skill levels 3 and 4), and another employed in medium skilled occupations (craft workers and operators, and service and sales workers, skill level 2 and 1). These two profiles vary across the country where they live. While migrants in France and Luxembourg work predominantly in medium skilled occupations,[7] migrants in Germany and the UK work largely in highly skilled professions (respectively, 74.9% and 71.8%). These diverse profiles of migrants' integration in the labour market of each country are, obviously, an outcome of distinct qualification profiles of the migrants that went to each one of these countries and of differential degrees of adjustment between qualification and professional occupation

Table 4.1 Mismatch between level of education of the highly skilled and their professional group in Germany, France, Luxembourg and the UK (%)

	DEU	*FRA*	*LUX*	*UK*	*Total*
Profession in Portugal	17.7	24.1	22.7	18.7	19.5
First profession in host country	15.7	40.9	38.3	27.8	28.4
Actual profession in host country	12.0	26.4	28.7	13.6	16.0

Source: Survey of Portuguese Abroad - Project REMIGR.

in the studied countries. In Germany and the UK the large majority of the highly skilled work in an occupation that matches their skill level (85.6% and 88.0%, respectively, while in France and Luxembourg this percentage is, correspondingly, 73.6% and 71.3%). Imperfect matching of skills to the labour market could be a result of a multitude of factors, like: a) "matter of choice related to compensating advantages"; b) "voluntary short-term strategy to enter the labour market"; c) the action of a desperate move due to long periods of unemployment (Ordine and Rose 2011); or d) a result of a mismatch between type of qualifications and the needs of the labour market. The available data did not allow each of these hypothesis to be pursued, but we believe that while factors a), b), and c) could have been important in the initial phase of the migrant's integration in the host labour markets, factor d) is responsible for the maintenance of the mismatch between qualifications and jobs in which migrants currently work.

Migration process, circulation and return

At the beginning of the twenty-first century the growth of the Portuguese national product started the slowdown, leading to rising budget deficits and increasing unemployment. After 2008 this negative economic behaviour was further aggravated by the 2007–2008 global financial crisis and by the Eurozone debt crisis that started in 2009 (Amaral 2010; Baldwin and Giavazzi 2015). From 2000 to 2013, the unemployment rate grew from 4.9 per cent to 16.4 per cent. Faced with an unfavourable economic situation and with rising unemployment it is no surprise that economic motivations were presented as the main reason for leaving the country by 41.0 per cent of the respondents to our survey. The specific economic causes that lead to emigration are, however, slightly different in each of the studied countries. While emigrants to France mentioned that the most important motives for leaving were being unemployed (14.9%) and low career opportunities (14.7%), emigrants to Luxembourg pointed to low salaries (16.4%) and unemployment (13.1%), emigrants to Germany and to the UK referred mainly to low opportunities to develop a professional career (respectively, 34.7% and 39.1%). The greater relevance that emigrants in Germany and in the UK attributed to low career perspectives is related to their higher educational profile when compared with emigrants to the other two countries. Despite these differences, it is clear that strict economic motivations (unemployment, low salary) are, in all three cases, combined with motivations associated with some idea of the desired development of migrant's professional biographies, and with the pursuance of post-materialist values (expressed as the motivation for new experiences).

Two other reasons for migration point to differences between the migration flows to each one of the studied countries. The first is to study motives that were particularly important for Germany and the UK showing thus that these countries play an important role as a destiny for graduation,

Table 4.2 Motivations for migration to Germany, France, Luxembourg and the UK (%)

	DEU	*FRA*	*LUX*	*UK*	*Total*
Economic motives	34.8	40.5	42.0	42.4	41.0
Family motives	5.1	12.9	10.5	4.2	6.8
Study motives	11.5	6.6	3.1	10.8	9.2
Look for new experiences	21.2	15.0	14.3	16.3	16.5
Didn't have future in Portugal	21.3	21.9	26.2	21.0	21.8
Other	6.1	3.1	3.9	5.1	4.7
Total	100.0	100.0	100.0	100.0	100.0
(N)	(750)	(1,014)	(621)	(2,868)	(5,253)

Note: Multiple response question: percentages based on responses.

Source: Survey of Portuguese Abroad - Project REMIGR.

and mainly post-graduation. The second, and most expressive, were family reasons (reunification, accompanying family), indicating that part of the emigration to France and Luxembourg is supported by a network of family members in that country or that it is an outcome of a family migration process (respectively, 40.5% and 42.0% migrated with a partner or other family member). In Germany and the UK, the percentage of migrants that indicate this reason for migration is substantially lower showing that migration to these countries is less supported by a network of family members and more based on an individual migration strategy (respectively, 55.6% and 53.4% of migrants to these two countries migrated alone). This is confirmed by questions on the reasons for migrating to each country and on the migration strategies followed. The presence of family members or friends (either for a long time or recently arrived) influenced the decision of 48.2 per cent of migrants to choose France as the destination country, of 54.8 per cent to choose Luxembourg, of 25.6 per cent to choose Germany and of 24.4 per cent to opt for the UK.

The influence of family and friends (the migration network) in the migration process played an important role in different Portuguese migratory movements, contributing (with varying degrees of intensity and productivity) for the construction and maintenance of specific migratory flows. In the emigration movements to the countries under study, networks also played a relevant role, although assuming variable configurations according to specificities of each destination country (and, by extension, of the characteristics of migrants that went to them). While in the flow to France and Luxembourg the migration network was an important reason to choose this country as destination (in particular for low-skilled migrants), in the flow to Germany and the UK, the action of relatives and friends already living in the country played a minor influence in selecting it as the migration destination. This seem to be in line with the weakening of the network of family and friends and with the emergence of more individualized forms of migration proposed by the concept of liquid migration (Engbersen 2012). Migration paths of current migrants were, according to this perspective, freed from the constraints of the network (e.g., of destination countries, and occupation sectors) and thus prone to select between a greater diversity of destination countries and labour market opportunities. The differential action of migratory networks in the studied countries and, within them, for different migrant groups points to the contextual nature of the migratory network effect. That is, networks are not real entities able to pursue actions regardless of the national, economic and social context in which they exist. Only when they transmit opportunities for inclusion in specific functional systems (in the labour market, for example) (Bommes 2011) do they become productive and are valued as such by immigrants. The data from our survey suggest that the family network was particularly useful for emigrants that went to France or Luxembourg while it was less helpful for emigrants that went to Germany or the UK who had to rely mostly on friends already living in the country.

A significant part of the surveyed (40.3%) already had, before entering one of the studied countries, one (or more) migratory experiences. The percentage is slightly lower for migrants who went to France (32.2%) or Luxembourg (34.8%), than for migrants to Germany (56.4%) or the UK (40.9%). Despite these differences it is possible to state that for a substantial number of individuals migration was already part of their working or studying lives. The highly qualified show a higher participation rate in prior migratory movements (52.5%, against 22.1% of the less qualified), essentially due to the fulfilment of study or training periods in another country. Thus the biographies of a considerable number of emigrants have already been marked by some moments of stay abroad, which enable them to acquire a "mobility habitus" (Cairns 2014) that influenced their decision about further migratory movements. In fact, 61.8 per cent of the respondents who had some study or training period abroad stated that this experience influenced their decision to reside abroad. They are therefore part of a "new generation of mobile Europeans" (Saar 2016: 2) for which stays abroad are an integrative part of their professional life.

Temporality of migration

These data corroborate, albeit to a limited extent, that contemporary migratory processes are often heterogeneous, circular and varied in terms of duration (Robertson 2014). Although circular and temporary migratory forms have, with different intensities, already been present in different migratory movements of the past, the development of modern transport and communication technologies has further facilitated the temporal heterogeneity of migrations (Robertson 2014). In addition, in the case of European Union countries, the deepening of an institutional context favourable to free movement has made cross-border mobility an integral part of the social, economic, political and cultural lives of many citizens (Cairns et al. 2017), allowing, thus, the intensification of non-permanent migratory forms. This is true, as signalled behind, both for highly skilled and for lesser skilled migrants, albeit the forms by which this frequent mobility is accomplished varies between these two migrant groups.

We can observe the development of less permanent forms of migration through the analysis of a set of questions on migrants' future projects. One of these regards the intention to return or stay in the host country. The intentions of staying in the host country can, even when recognizing the frequent discrepancy between these and their effective implementation, be classified through a continuum that goes from the intention of returning to Portugal to the intention of staying in the host country. In the questionnaire applied, besides these two extreme options, emigrants could indicate their intention to emigrate to another country, or that they did not yet have defined plans. The answers obtained a point to the prevalence of stay intentions (33.7%) followed by indecision regarding future migration projects (31.7%). Migrants living in France, Luxembourg and the UK more often indicate that they wish to remain in the country, while emigrants in Germany express greater uncertainty about their future migration (34.6%). The uncertainty regarding the migratory project is high in all studied countries (varying between 23.7% in France, 32.1% in Luxembourg and 34.1% in the UK) and particularly among the highly qualified migrants (34.0%, against 28.2% among the lesser qualified).

This strategic uncertainty regarding future intentions is one characteristic of the liquid migration pointed forward by Engbersen (2012) and can be framed in a strategy that Eade (2007) called "intentional unpredictability". This strategy allows emigrants to keep their migratory options open and respond to any opportunities that arise in the country of origin, in the country where they currently reside, or in any other country. As Eade (2007) acknowledges, the lack of definition of the future may indicate the adaptation of migrants to an increasingly flexible, deregulated and transnational labour market. The uncertainty regarding the future migration project seems to be present even in those who said they wish to remain in the country where they are currently residing. When asked about the expected length of stay in the country, a high percentage of respondents (46.6%) were unable to define the expected period of stay. And, reflecting probably their working conditions and their unstable labour relations, the lesser skilled migrants were particularly indecisive on their indented period of stay in the host country (63.3%, against 35.6% for the highly skilled).

The case of posted workers

Since 2005, emigration from Portugal has intensified. The development of different forms of short-term migratory movements, as well as the frequent interconnections between permanent (more than one year) and repeated temporary movements (up to six months), appear in this context as one of the most striking features of Portuguese emigration. Some of these migratory flows are substantially different from the traditional forms of Portuguese emigration, because Portuguese companies, which take advantage of free movement options within the EU, are promoting the mobility of their workers and widening their operational markets. A specific case that exemplifies the increasing temporality of current migration flows and, simultaneously, shows the gradual constitution of the European-wide labour market for, mainly, low skilled workers is the case of posted workers who work in construction, maintenance, logistic and agriculture as a result of Portugal's membership of the European Union. This type of migratory outflow is substantially different from traditional forms of Portuguese emigration since Portuguese companies acted as subcontractors for big European construction companies that used free movement within the European area to their advantage by promoting the mobility of Portuguese workers (Góis and Marques 2018). The downside of the high-skill bias of the EU migration policies is that they lead to a larger underground economy for low-skilled labour from TCN. Public services, such as construction, entertainment, healthcare and domestic work, are jobs which national workers often refuse to take on. Employers operating in countries subscribing to skill-selective policies, like the UK, Germany, Luxembourg and France, among others, find it increasingly difficult to recruit lower-skilled migrants on the legal labour market. As employers' demands for lower-skilled immigrants are not being catered to by official policy, they sub-contract temporary work via posted workers intra-EU migrants.

This allowed, since mid-1990s, Portuguese construction companies to benefit from the differential in labour costs that existed between Portuguese and other European construction workers (Baganha and Carvalheiro 2002). Objective data on posted work is scarce in Portugal but data on the issuing of the Portable Document A1 (or the previous E101 certificate) show a continuous declining trend between 2010 and 2011 as a result of the economic crisis in some of the main destination countries of Portuguese posted workers, followed by a sharp increase in 2013, a new decline in 2015, stabilization in 2016 and again a rise in the two last available data for 2017 and 2018.

This temporary, but continuous, provision of labour services throughout the EU is an insight in how transnational labour regulations function to promote the efficient matching of the demand for labour in specific sectors and countries with the existent supply of workforces available in other countries. This type of labour mobility complements other forms of short and long term mobility modelling a "typically European labour market that is driven by diversity" (Mussche, Corluy and Marx 2016: 2) in which highly skilled and lesser skilled migrants respond to opportunities that emerge in different national contexts. The data presented in this chapter show that

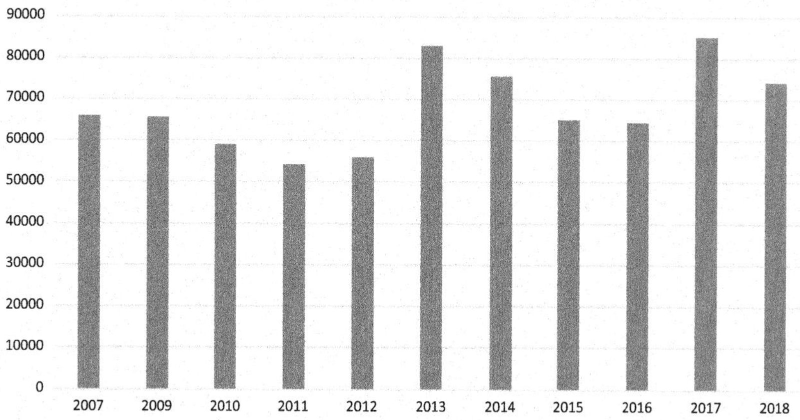

Figure 4.1 Number of A1 Portable Documents issued by Portugal, 2009-2018
Source: European Commission (2011; 2012); Pacolet and De Wispelaere (2014; 2015; 2016); De Wispeleare and Pacolet (2017a; 2017b; 2018); De Wispelaere, De Smedt and Pacolet (2019).

Portuguese migration, as other intra-EU migration flows, is, also, a function of prevailing organizational differences of the national labour markets that depend on the existence of a transnational labour market that allows migrants inclusion in specific segments of the labour market, and thus continuously contributes to the sustention and expansion of this transnational labour market. Through this process northern European countries manage to recruit (formally or informally) from crises affected regions labour forces that contribute to resolve constraints (which are increasingly structural) in their labour markets.

Conclusions

The emigration from Portugal has been continuous for many decades, but its rhythm and termini varied, assuming different migratory cycles (Marques and Góis 2016; Góis and Marques 2020). One of the distinguishing characteristics of Portugal is the pattern of migratory cycles very dependent on the interaction of internal economic conditions and the receptivity of migratory destinations. The change of rhythm and destinations is a demonstration of the plasticity and adaptability of Portuguese emigrants to a labour market beyond national borders. The intra EU migration is only a part of Portuguese contemporary migration but an important share in the last decades (Peixoto et al. 2016) complemented by north-south migrations towards African countries and Brazil. The main reasons for this trend are the demand and the relative ease of access of Portuguese workers of working age to employment; family ties or active social networks with Portuguese established throughout Europe; relative geographical proximity and ease of mobility in the region of free movement within the European Economic Area; the recognition of academic qualifications obtained in Portugal in the European system, higher salaries and, last but not least, the lowest travel costs when compared with other more distant geographical regions. The labour market is no longer just national. Portuguese emigrants in different sectors and professions are now taking on a new connection with a European labour market. This connection to a transnational labour market implies a competition with workers of other nationalities.

The development of different forms of short-term migratory outings, as well as the frequent interconnections between permanent and temporary movements, appears in this context as one of the most striking features of Portuguese emigration. Another novelty of the recent Portuguese emigration, when compared to past migratory movements, is the progressive higher qualification of the labour force involved. The intensification of the country's integration into the European migration system has produced new job mobility opportunities now available as short-term migration opportunities (posted workers) or more permanent opportunities for both low-skilled workers and highly skilled workers (Góis and Marques 2006; Peixoto et al. 2016).

Regarding the evolution of the internal migration within the European Union there is currently a mismatch between labour demand and supply. This mismatch is not fully visible in statistics due to the informality of those migratory flows. This results in an emerging new divide, one splitting the EU migrants along skill, education and occupational levels, rather than nationality. A major consequence of the so far "incomplete European integration" is that recruitment in low or highly skilled professions simultaneously considers local/national labour markets, labour markets of other EU Member States and labour markets of non-EU countries depending on the availability in the labour market and labour costs. In certain professions this will induce an intra-EU temporary or permanent migration or, when labour is not available (or it is too costly), will induce migration from third countries.

The number of incoming TCN that coincide, in some cases, with high levels of unemployment, and especially of long-term unemployment in EU countries, are signs of this divergence. It appears that Europeans are willing in insufficient numbers to move from one country to another. Country-specific labour shortages are not immediately visible when looking to intra-EU migration. However, it is interesting to note here that, contrary to government assessments and EU migratory policies of what shortages they should respond to, it is the shortage of low skilled workers, which generates most of the intra-EU movements. The UK example suggests shortages in both public and private sectors for highly skilled and low skilled professionals. Portuguese migrants filled shortages in health services, in construction, in seasonal agriculture, food sector, hotels and restaurants.

Similarly to labour migration flows from Central and Eastern European countries, Portuguese contemporary migration combines permanent forms of migration with movements that are temporary, circular and that can be described as "liquid migrations" (Engbersen, Snel and De Boom 2010; Peixoto et al. 2016). There is some expectation that network factors, intermediary agents such as global employment sites such as Linkedin or Glassdoor, social networks and social media, recruiters, universities and others will enlarge intra EU labour migration over time, creating a truly European Labour Market. In the UK food industry, at the farms level, some growers already recruit directly in Portugal, some use recruitment agencies and some labour is supplied directly at the farm gate. In this case, different channels are used to fulfil the specific labour needs of a specific labour market regarding scarce low skilled work. In the UK or Germany health sector the same recruitment strategy is directed towards nurses and doctors, generating a new north-south branch of the intra-EU migration industry. Differences in salaries and career prospects between countries make a huge difference and allow for a highly-skilled drain from south to north (in a way a sort of brain/skilled drain of human capital).

Notes

1 For example, between 1997 and 2018 (and mainly between 2010 and 2018), 26,545 migrating professionals received a positive decision on the recognition of their professional qualification obtained in Portugal. Most of them in the UK (51.1%), Belgium (9.4%), and Germany (6.8%), and in professions in the health sector (58.2%) (source: https://ec.europa.eu/growth/tools-databases/regprof/).

2 It should be noted that this distinction between a primary and a secondary labour market has been criticized by several authors, and that Gordon (1995) has proposed considering these two segments as two typical ideal forms located at the end of a continuum characterized by the diversity of work situations more than as two discrete sets of jobs.

3 About 51.4% of emigrants to Germany, 53.9% to France, 65.7% to Luxembourg, and 52.8% to the UK.

4 Respectively, 22.2%, 21.3%, 16.3%, and 25.7%.

5 Employed and unemployed account, respectively, for 82.8% and 4.85% of emigrants to Germany, 83.9% and 5.9% of those who went to France, 79.7% and 10.0% of emigrants to Luxembourg, and 87.1% and 2.4% of emigrants to the UK.

6 We use here the relationship between ISCO-08 major groups and four ISCED-97 levels of education described by ILO, assuming that the professional groups of Managers, Professional, and Technicians and Associate Professional require skills usually obtained through the frequency of a higher educational institution. Thus the insertion of tertiary level graduates in one of these professional groups signify a match between qualification and professional occupation, while the insertion in a professional group that require a lower level of education signifies an mismatch due to overeducation (ILO 2012).

7 In France 66.4%, and in Luxembourg 71.0%, work in medium skilled occupations.

References

Amaral L. (2010). *Economia Portuguesa. As últimas décadas*. Lisboa: Fundação Francisco Manuel dos Santos.

Baganha M. and Carvalheiro L. (2002). Uma europeização diferenciada: o sector da construção civil e obras públicas. In Reis J. and Baganha M.I. (eds.). *A economia em curso. Contextos e mobilidade*. Porto: Afrontamento, 63–86.

Baláž V., Williams A.M., Moravčíková K. and Chrančoková M. (2019). What Competences, Which Migrants? Tacit and Explicit Knowledge Acquired Via Migration. *Journal of Ethnic and Migration Studies*. doi: 10.1080/1369183X.2019.1679409.

Baldwin R. and Giavazzi F. (eds.) (2015). *The Eurozone Crisis: A Consensus View of the Causes and a Few Possible Remedies*. London: Centre for Economic Policy Research.

Batsaikhan U., Darvas Z. and Raposo I.S.G.A. (2018). *People on the Move: Migration and Mobility in the European Union*. Brussels: Bruegel.

Bigo D. and Guild E. (2005). *Controlling Frontiers: Free Movement into and within Europe*. Aldershot: Ashgate.

Bommes M. (2011). Migrantennetzwerke in der funktional differenzierten Gesellschaft. In Bommes M. and Tackle V. (eds.). *Netzwerke in der funktional differnzierten Gesellschaft*. Wiesbaden: VS Verlag, 241–259.

Borjas G.J. (2001). Does Immigration Grease the Wheels of the Labor Market. *Brookings Papers on Economic Activity*. (1): 1–51.

Cairns D. (2014). *Youth Transitions, International Student Mobility and Spatial Reflexivity. Being Mobile?*. Basingstoke: Palgrave Macmillan.

Cairsn D., Cuzzocrea V., Briggs D. and Veloso L. (2017). *The Consequences of Mobility. Reflexivity, Social Inequality and the Reproduction of Precariousness in Highly Qualified Migration*. Basingstoke: Palgrave Macmillan.

Castles S. (2006a). *Back to the Future? Can Europe Meet Its Labour Needs through Temporary Migration?*. Oxford: International Migration Institute.

Castles S. (2006b). Guestworkers in Europe: A Resurrection?. *International Migration Review*. 40(4): 741–766.

Chiswick B.R. and Miller P.W. (2011). Educational Mismatch: Are High-Skilled Immigrants Really Working in High-Skilled jobs, and What Price They Pay if They Aren't. In Chiswick B.R. (ed.). *High Skilled Immigration in a Global Labor Market*. Washington: American Enterprise Institute, 111–154.

Choudha R. (2017). Three Waves of International Student Mobility (1999–2020). *Studies in Higher Education*. 42(5): 825–832.

Constant A. and Massey D.S. (2002). Return Migration by German Guest-Workers: Neoclassical versus New Economic Theory. *International Migration*. 40(4): 5–39.

Darvas Z. (2017). *Could Revising the Posted Workers Directive Improve Social Conditions?*. Presentation to the Conference of Think Tanks on the Revision of the Posted Workers Directive: European Parliament.

De Wispelaere F. and Pacolet J. (2019). *Posting of Workers. Report on A1 Portable Documents Issued in 2018*. Luxembourg: DG Employment, Social Affairs & Inclusion, Publications Office of the European Union.

De Wispelaere F. and Pacolet J. (2017a). *Posting of Workers. Report on A1 Portable Documents Issued in 2016*. Luxembourg: DG Employment, Social Affairs & Inclusion, Publications Office of the European Union.

De Wispelaere F. and Pacolet J. (2017b). *Posting of Workers. Report on A1 Portable Documents Issued in 2017*. Luxembourg: DG Employment, Social Affairs & Inclusion, Publications Office of the European Union.

De Wispelaere F. and Pacolet J. (2018). *Posting of Workers. Report on A1 Portable Documents Issued in 2016*. Luxembourg: DG Employment, Social Affairs & Inclusion, Publications Office of the European Union.

Doeringer P.B. and Piore M.J. (1971). *Internal Labor Markets and Manpower Analysis*. Lexington: Heath.

Eade J. (2007). *Class and Ethnicity: Polish Migrant Workers in London: Full Research Report*. ESRC End of Award Report, RES-000-22-1294. Swindon: ESRC.

Engbersen G. (2012). Migration Transitions in an Era of Liquid Migration: Reflections on Fassmann and Reeger. In Okólski M. (ed.). *European Immigrations: Trends, Structures and Policy Implications*. Amsterdam: Amsterdam University Press, 91–105.

Engbersen G., Snel E. and De Boom J. (2010). "A Van Full of Poles": Liquid Migration from Central and Eastern Europe. In Black R., Engbersen G., Okólski M. and Pantîru C. (eds.). *A Continent Moving West? EU Enlargement and Labour Migration from Central and Eastern Europe*. Amsterdam: Amsterdam University Press, 73–88.

Engbersen G., Snel E. and De Boom J. (2013). Liquid Migration: Dynamic and Fluid Patterns of Post-accession Migration Flows. In Black R., Engbersen G., Okólski M. and Panţîru C. (eds.). *Mobility in Transition: Migration Patterns after EU Enlargement*. Amsterdam: Amsterdam University Press, 115–140.

European Commission (2011). *Posting of Workers in the European Union and EFTA Countries: Report on E101 Certificates Issued in 2008 and 2009*. DG Employment: Social Affairs & Inclusion.

European Commission (2012). *Posting of Workers in the European Union and EFTA Countries: Report on A1 Portable Documents Issued in 2010 and 2011*. DG Employment: Social Affairs & Inclusion.

European Commission (2016). *Posting of Workers – Report on A1 Portable Documents Issued in 2015*. DG Employment: Social Affairs & Inclusion.

Fabbricotti A. (ed.) (2016). *The Political Economy of International Law*. Cheltenham: Edward Elgar Publishing.

Favell A. (2008). The New Face of East-West Migration in Europe. *Journal of Ethnic and Migration Studies*. 34(5): 701–716.

Fligstein N. (2000). The Process of Europeanization. *Politique européenne*. (1): 25–42.

Geddes A. (2003). *The Politics of Migration and Immigration in Europe*. London: Sage.

Geddes A. and Scholten P. (2016). *Politics of Migration and Immigration in Europe*. London: Sage.

Góis P. and Marques J.C. (2007). *Estudo prospectivo sobre imigrantes qualificados em Portugal / Prospective Study on Qualified Immigrants in Portugal*. Lisboa: ACIDI, I.P.

Góis P. and Marques J.C. (2009). Portugal as a Semiperipheral Country in the Global Migration System. *International Migration*. 47(3): 19–50.

Góis P. and Marques J.C. (2018). Retrato de um Portugal migrante: a evolução da emigração, da imigração e do seu estudo nos últimos 40 anos / Portrait of a Migrant Portugal: The Evolution of Emigration, Immigration and Migration Studies in the Past 40 Years. *e-cadernos ces*. (29): 125–151.

Góis P. and Marques J.C. (2020). Portuguese Intra-EU Migration: The Dynamics of an Ongoing Migration Process. *Racial and Ethnic Studies*. doi: 10.1080/01419870.2020.1772989.

Góis P., Marques J.C., Candeias P., Ferreira B. and Ferro A. (2016). Novos Destinos Migratórios: a Emigração Portuguesa para o Reino Unido. In Peixoto J., Oliveira I.T.D., Azevedo J., Marques J.C., Góis P., Malheiros J. and Madeira P.M. (eds.). *Regresso ao Futuro: A nova Emigração e a Sociedade Portuguesa*. Lisboa: Gradiva, 71–108.

Gordon I. (1995). Migration in a Segmented Labour Market. *Transactions of the Institute of British Geographers*. 20(2): 139–155.

Goos M., Manning A. and Salomons A. (2009). Job Polarization in Europe. *American Economic Review: Papers & Proceedings*. 99(2): 58–63.

ILO (2012). *International Standard Classification of Occupations (ISCO-08), Volume I: Structure, Group Definitions and Correspondence Tables*. Geneva: International Labour Organization.

Kahanec M., Pytliková M. and Zimmermann K.F. (2016). The Free Movement of Workers in an Enlarged European Union: Institutional Underpinnings of Economic Adjustment. In Kahanec M. and Zimmermann K.F. (eds.). *Labor Migration, EU Enlargement, and the Great Recession*. Berlin: Springer, 1–34.

Leontaridi M. (2002). Segmented Labour Markets: Theory and Evidence. *Journal of Economic Surveys*. 12(1): 103–109.

Marques J.C. (2008). *Os Portugueses na Suíça: Migrantes Europeus / Portuguese in Switzerland: European Migrants*. Lisboa: Imprensa de Ciências Sociais.

Marques J.C., Candeias P., Góis P. and Peixoto J. (2020). Is the Segmented Skill Divide Perspective Useful in Migration Studies? Evidence from the Portuguese Case. *Journal of International Migration and Integration*. doi.org/10.1007/s12134-020-00757-2.

Marques J.C. and Góis P. (2016). Structural Emigration: The Revival of Portuguese Outflows. In Lafleur J.-M. and Stanek M. (eds.). *Old Routes, New Migrants: Lessons from the South-North Migration of EU Citizens in Times of Crisis*. Heidelberg: Springer, 65–82.

Marques J.C., Góis P., Candeias P., Ferreira B. and Ferro A. (2016). A emigração recente de Portugueses para França. In Peixoto J., Oliveira I.T.D., Azevedo J., Marques J.C., Góis P., Malheiros J. and Madeira P.M. (eds.). *Regresso ao Futuro: A nova Emigração e a Sociedade Portuguesa*. Lisboa: Gradiva, 109–139.

McCollum D. and Findlay A. (2015). "Flexible" Workers for "Flexible" Jobs? The Labour Market Function of A8 Migrant Labour in the UK. *Work, Employment and Society*. 29(3): 427–442.

Mense-Petermann U. (2019). Theorizing Transnational Labour Markets: A Research Heuristic Based on the New Economic Sociology. *Global Networks*. 20(3): 410–433.

Mussche N., Corluy V. and Marx I. (2016). *The Rise of the Free Movements: How Posting Shapes a Hybrid Single European Labour Market*. Bonn: IZA Discussion Paper nº 10365.

Nieto S., Matano A. and Ramos R. (2015). Skill Mismatches in the EU: Immigrants vs. Natives. *International Journal of Manpower*. 36(4): 540–561.

Ordine P. and Rose G. (2011). *Educational Mismatch and Wait Unemployment*. Bologna, AlmaLaurea Inter-University Consortium: Alma Laurea Working Papers 19.

Pacolet J. and De Wispelaere F. (2014). *Posting of Workers: Report on A1 Portable Documents Issued in 2012 and 2013*. Luxembourg: DG Employment, Social Affairs & Inclusion, Publications Office of the European Union.

Pacolet J. and De Wispelaere F. (2015). *Posting of Workers: Report on A1 Portable Documents Issued in 2014*. Luxembourg: DG Employment, Social Affairs & Inclusion, Publications Office of the European Union.

Pacolet J. and De Wispelaere F. (2016). *Posting of Workers: Report on A1 portable documents issued in 2015*. Luxembourg: DG Employment, Social Affairs & Inclusion, Publications Office of the European Union.

Peixoto J., Candeias P., Ferreira B., Oliveira I.T., Marques J.C.L. et al. (2019). New Emigration and Portuguese Society: Transnationalism and Return. In Pereira C. and Azevedo J. (eds). *New and Old Routes of Portuguese Emigration*. IMISCOE Research Series. Cham: Springer International Publishing, 49–72.

Peixoto J., Oliveira I.T.D., Azevedo J., Marques J.C., Góis P. et al. (2016). *Regresso ao futuro: a nova emigração e a sociedade portuguesa*. Lisboa: Gradiva.

Piore M.J. (1970). Jobs and Training. In Beer S.H. and Barringer R.E. (eds.). *The State and the Poor*. Cambridge: Winthrop Press, 53–83.

Piore M.J. (1975). Notes for a Theory of Labour Market Stratification. In Edwards R.E.A. (ed.). *Labour Market Segmentation*. Lexington: Heath.

Piore M.J. (1979). *Birds of Passage: Migrant Labor and Industrial Societies*. Cambridge: Cambridge University Press.

Pires R.P. (2019). Portuguese Emigration Today. In Pereira C. and Azevedo J. (eds.). *New and Old Routes of Portuguese Emigration: Uncertain Futures at the Periphery of Europe*. Cham: Springer International Publishing, 29–48.

Platonova A. and Urso G. (eds.) (2012). *Labour Market Inclusion of the Less Skilled Migrants in the European Union* . Brussels: IOM.

Riemsdijk M.V. (2013). Obstacles to the Free Movement of Professionals: Mutual Recognition of Professional Qualifications in the European Union. *European Joumal of Migration and Law*. 15(1): 47–68.

Robertson S. (2014). *The Temporalities of International Migration: Implications for Ethnographic Research*. Institute for Culture and Society. Occasional Paper Series 5, https://doi.org/10.4225/35/57a969210f1a0.

Rubery J. and Piasna A. (2015). Labour Market Segmentation and Deregulation of Employment Protection in the EU. In Piasna A. and Myant M. (eds.). *Myths of Employment Deregulation: How It Neither Creates Jobs nor Reduces Labour Market Segmentation*. Brussels: ETUI, 43–60.

Ruhs M. and Anderson B. (eds.). (2012). *Who Needs Migrant Workers? Labour Shortages, Immigration and Public Policy*. Oxford: Oxford University Press.

Saar M. (2016). Individualisation of Migration from the East? Comparison of different socio-demographic groups and their migration intentions. *Studies of Transition States and Societies*. 8(3): 45–59.

Solimano A. (ed.) (2008). *The International Mobility of Talent: Types, Causes and Development Impact*. Oxford and New York: Oxford University Press.

Sumption M. and Young R. (2014). Immigration and the Health-Care Workforce in the United Kingdom since the Global Economic Crisis. In Siyam A. and Dal Poz M. (eds.). *Migration of Health Workers: WHO Code of Practice and the Global Economic Crisis*. Geneva: WHO, 97–107.

Teichler U. (2019). Bologna and Student Mobility: A Fuzzy Relationship. *Innovation: The European Journal of Social Science Research*. 32(4): 429–449.

Triandafyllidou A. and Isaakyan I. (2014). *EU Management of High Skill Migration*. RSCAS Global Governance Programme Policy Briefs 2014/04.

Van Mol C. and De Valk H. (2016). Migration and Immigrants in Europe: A Historical and Demographic Perspective. In Garcés-Mascareñas B. and Penninx R. (eds.). *Integration Processes and Policies in Europe: Contexts, Levels and Actors*. Cham: Springer International Publishing, 31–55.

Vasey D.H. (2010). *A Complex Work of Migration: Knowing, Working and Migrating in the Southwest of England*. PhD Dissertation in Geography: University of Exeter.

Verwiebe R. and Eder K. (2006). The Integration of Transnationally Mobile Europeans in the German Labour Market. *European Societies*. 8(8): 141–167.

Zimmermann K.F.O. (2005). *European Migration: What Do We Know?* Oxford: Oxford University Press.

Part II

Immigrants

An economic resource or a burden?

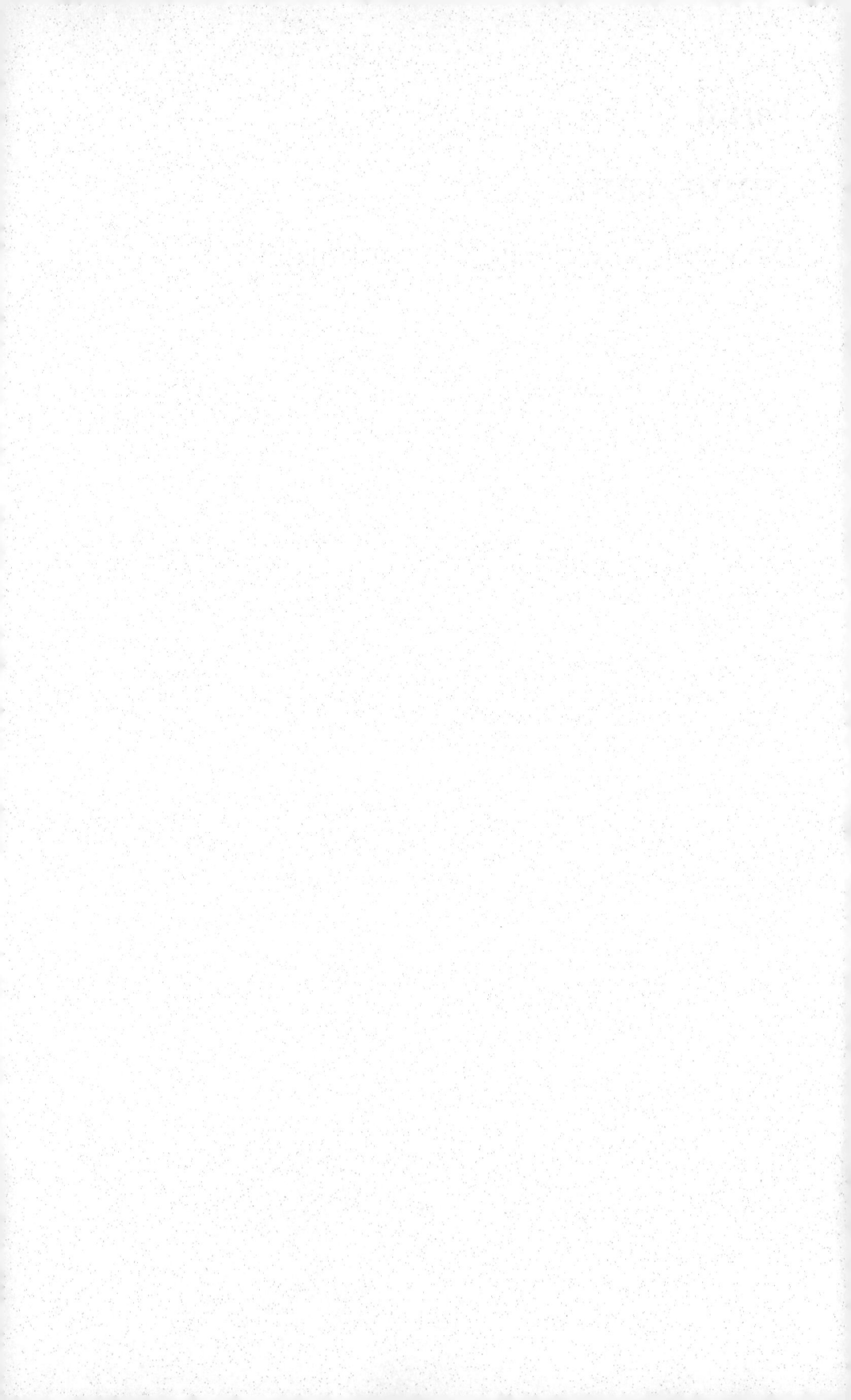

5 An economic resource or a social problem?

European institutions and migrants from the 1950s to the 1970s: the case of Belgium

Paolo Tedeschi

Introduction

The aim of the article is to show the evolution of the attitudes of the European institutions concerning migration from the first steps of the integration process to the end of the 1970s, thus from the very positive economic trend characterizing the Golden Age to the strong negative effects of the two oil shocks (1973 and 1979) modifying rules and attitudes of the European governments.[1]

The chapter in particular indicates the main effects of immigration on Belgian policies. The example of one of the founders of the new Europe, which received a lot of migrants in proportion to the native population (they progressively increased from 4.3% in 1947 to 8.9% in 1981) might indeed help better understand the relationship between European institutions and European countries hosting migrants.[2] It is in fact important to note that European institutions did not have the possibility to actually force the national government to bide by the immigration rules, which were progressively established by the European Coal and Steel Community (ECSC) and, later, by the European Economic Community (EEC).

Since the birth of the European integration process, the debates and discussions concerning migrants have been based on the evaluation of the economic and social advantages and costs that migrants represented for the host countries: the arrival of thousands of foreign workers in fact represented a fundamental input of manpower for the development of some local industrial enterprises, mines and humble/low paid services. At the same time, it created relevant social problems related to the difficult integration of migrants' families in their new countries. The difficult question was: do migrants represent a relevant and indispensable economic resource for the host country or, on the contrary, do they quickly become a critical social problem which can eliminate all economic benefits for the host country?

European institutions and national governments had to find the correct answer because economic development needed foreign workforce but it was also necessary to avoid dangerous social conflicts in a context, the cold war, where social problems meant an increase of the consensus for the political parties allied with the USSR. Therefore, during the period under consideration, European institutions had to find a compromise between those who wanted to liberalize the labour market in the European Common Market and those who, on the contrary, wanted to put strong limits to the circulation of workers (even if they were EEC citizens, in particular coming from Italy).

These problems obviously concerned Belgium too: Belgian mines needed a foreign workforce and they in fact asked for immigrants since the early post-world period, when the idea of European economic integration was simply a "romantic project" drafted by some members of the European Federalist Movement or by a think tank such as the European League of Economic Cooperation (ELEC) (Dumoulin and Dutrieue 1993; Becherucci 2018). As the Belgian case immediately clarified, the integration of migrants was not a simple process because of the strong cultural differences existing between natives and foreigners reinforced by the local people' s fear of losing their jobs (or see their wages reduced) due to the arrival of new workers accepting inferior work conditions. Besides, in a context where the poorest local citizens had lots of problems to find somewhere to live, it was very difficult to host migrants in decent houses and this clearly favoured the creation of ghettos reserved to foreign workers where inhabitants did not consider respecting the law a priority. These hard life conditions favoured the birth of criminal organizations and also the exploitation of a part of migrants. Furthermore, discussions concerning these issues started when the Belgian government deemed it important not to admit that problems related to the distribution of foreign workers among Belgian provinces increased the existing division between the Flemish and Walloon communities.

This chapter illustrates the different types of migrants arriving in the EEC countries: clearly, the different migrants' professional skills modified their economic impact as well as the possible replacement of native workers. It is also evident that the migrants' political orientation was relevant: no countries welcomed people favouring the development of pro-USSR political movements or people organizing strikes to obtain better wages and modify contractual clauses. Migrants' habits and their knowledge of the language used in the host country also influenced the duration and likelihood of attaining a successful integration process. All these variables obviously affected the final answer to the question on the real importance of foreign labour and the actual benefit for the host countries to invest in their accommodation.

In order to better evaluate the debate about the impact of migrant workers, this chapter will show the results of two surveys which were organised by the European institutions and concerned the problem of migrants' accommodation in EEC countries (Tizzoni 2020). These surveys were carried out on behalf of the European Commission in 1959–1961 and 1974–1975 and allowed European institutions to assess how politicians, public officers, entrepreneurs and workers weighed up the migrants' habits, their accommodation and also their level of integration in their host country. The organizers' aim was to better understand the needs of migrants and citizens so as to provide some suggestions and advice to EEC countries. Finally, the difference emerging between the two surveys allows us to emphasize the effects of the changes in economic conditions: in the first survey, the people who answered were living during the Golden Age which was characterized by a great improvement of the quality of life of ECSC/EEC citizens; in the second one, people had to face the negative effects of the oil shock, that is the first great social and economic crisis affecting European countries after the Second World War.

More attention will be given to Belgian answers, but opinions coming from other EEC countries will be considered too: they in fact illustrate that there were no relevant differences between Belgian and other countries' comments. All answers indirectly allow us to discern how these people considered foreign workers, whether they considered them as a fundamental resource (and hence it was important to increase the efforts to foster their integration) or they thought it would be better to reduce or stop the flow of migrants because they created more problems than benefits.

Finally, this work underlines how the positive decisions and the mistakes made in the period under consideration could have allowed European institutions to improve the rules concerning future immigration waves, such as those that took place from the last two decades of the nineteenth century. However, European leaders' short historical memory and the related progressive reduction of European development aid to migrants' native countries made that experience almost useless and the same mistakes were repeated.

The impact of immigrants on new Western European societies and economies

The different types of migrants and their economic relevance

ECSC and EEC policies concerning immigrants had to solve problems relating to the different juridical status of people asking for a job and an accommodation in the ECSC/EEC host countries: European institutions' main aim was the elimination of all obstacles avoiding the free circulation of communitarian workers and also the provision of a decent accommodation. This also meant the integration of ECSC/EEC principles and rules into the national legislation concerning labour rights and the welfare of migrant workers and their families.[3] There were in fact different types of migrants and so there existed different rules: people coming from Italy (a founding member of the new little Europe with six adherent countries)[4] or from the Belgian, Dutch and French former colonies (sometimes, they were not able to remain in their native countries because they had previously worked with the "Europeans" and so they were considered as traitors by their compatriots) (McDonald 1965; Simon and Noin 1972; Simon 2002). The latter were evidently favoured: they had in fact the support of the European institutions, they could make good use of their studies in the same educational system of their host country and so they usually had a good knowledge of its language, customs and habits.

Other migrants came from the countries signing with the ECSC/EEC members (and moreover with the "Western world" formed by the USA and its allies) some relevant military and economic agreements as in the case of Portugal, Greece and Turkey, all member countries of the NATO (Pereira 2012; Santos 2017). These migrants were allowed to enter the ECSC/EEC countries because their arrival reduced the pressure on the labour market at home and, as it happened for the Italian migrants, the remittances to their families increased the local GDP. These effects gave a high strategic value to the migrants' presence in the host countries: the improvement of the quality of life in their native countries in fact reduced the consensus for revolutionary political movements related to the USSR.

There were also some migrants running away from countries ruled by dictators (e.g. the people coming from Spain) and other forms of authoritarian government (as it happened for people arriving from Eastern Germany, from the former German territories and from the Eastern European countries under Red Army occupation): they were normally considered refugees because they were able to demonstrate that they had been persecuted for their political opinions and at the same time they could become "guest workers" (Dreyfus-Armand 1999; Dufoix 2002; Dumoulin and Goddeeris 2005; Łukasiewicz 2017; Sanz Lafuente 2018). They *de facto* represented, during the 1950s, most of the refugees living in the ECSC/EEC countries. However, their impact on public opinion and on the labour market of the host country was normally the same as the impact of economic immigrants: few people really distinguished the two different juridical conditions and, moreover, the entrepreneurs' attitude was the same towards people arriving from Southern or Eastern Europe. Migrants and refugees were victims of the same exploitation because they usually represented the workforce with the weakest contractual power.

However, this was not true for everyone: more protection granted by European institutions meant more security against exploitation (Italian workers' conditions were less difficult and have strongly changed for the better since the Commission Recommendation of 7 July 1965) and, at the same time, more professional skills obviously allowed immigrants of all kind to find a better job (most high skilled refugees quickly obtained a job corresponding to their know-how). A great number of immigrants normally had to accept a first contract for a fixed time, but when the contract expired, they were free to work where their skills were asked for. During the 1950s and 1960s migrants benefited from a labour market becoming wider and richer in all ECSC/EEC countries (only Southern Italy continued to export its workforce): immigrants needed a job and their host countries needed their work: so, migrants became imperative for European economic development.

They guaranteed both high professional skills (in particular political refugees were employed as engineers and scientists) and low cost workforce for the cheap and humble jobs (servants, garbage collectors, etc.). They represented the essential workforce for mines, iron and steel factories, construction companies (as in the case of most of the migrants arriving from the Italian Mezzogiorno and other Southern European regions): their presence allowed lots of industrial sectors to increase their production and favoured the European economic expansion of the 1950s and 1960s which was called the Golden Age. In particular during the 1950s migrants allowed mainly Western European enterprises to obtain the workforce they needed without increasing labour cost: they paid migrants average wages and they did not have to increase them to attract new workers. These enterprises increased their earnings to invest in the renovation of their plants and machinery and they progressively became more productive and competitive. Besides, migrants and their families expanded demand both in their host countries and in their native ones through remittances sent to their families: in the case of Italian migrants this implied the general growth of Italian consumption and of the quality of life which was called "the economic miracle". This positive economic trend concerned all migrants' native countries and the related demand growth also increased the sales of ECSC/EEC products, which had already taken advantage of the growth of local demand. The immigrants' demand of local goods increased during the 1960s when real wages progressively soared; demand also increased for the traditional clothes, books, music records and in particular food coming from their native countries (e.g. Italian pasta and pizza or North African couscous).

Concerning the Belgian case, after the Second World War Belgium needed immigrants to maintain its position as one of Europe's leading industrialized nations: foreign workers fuelled the existence of most of the enterprises operating in the Belgian mining, textile, iron, steel and building sectors. In the early 1950s the demand for a new workforce was particularly strong in the coal industry and in the building sector: foreign workers could not find a job in other sectors and there were some exceptions only in the steel and quarrying industries. After 1957 the recruitment of foreigners extended beyond the coalmines, gradually spreading to the metal industry and construction: in any case, foreign miners were permitted to seek work in other productive sectors after a five-year contract. The coal industry had to look abroad to find new labour for other reasons: after the disaster in the coalmine of Marcinelle where 262 miners were killed and exactly half of them were Italian, new migrants coming from extra-ECSC countries substituted Italian workers who left the mining sector. The heart of the Belgian economy in fact depended on immigrants: the local workforce did not want to accept the dangerous and unhealthy jobs in the coalmines.[5] In the early 1960s new workers for the Belgian industries were also recruited from Turkey and Morocco, whose governments signed special bilateral agreements with the Belgian government: European migrants were not enough to meet the needs of the Belgian industry because the improvement in the quality of life in Southern Europe had reduced the need to emigrate to be employed in the toughest and most humble jobs.[6]

The positive economic conjuncture of the Golden Age helped lots of migrants to improve their social conditions: they could find better and better-paid jobs and buy a house. Some migrants became entrepreneurs and most of them traded products coming from their native countries: they also printed newspapers in their native language which gave relevant information about practical matters, including the reunification of families (to the husband abroad). Other migrants organized spaces for dancing and music, allowing the expatriate community to maintain a link with their native culture and moreover to socialize with compatriots: this also facilitated the development of support networks which were very useful to find new jobs and to obtain solidarity in order to face a situation of discrimination or disadvantage.

As happens in all ECSC/EEC host countries migrants had a relevant impact on certain aspects of Belgian economic and social life: migrants' families, especially the youngest generations who studied in Belgium, influenced Belgian lifestyle in terms of food, music, sport, agronomics, sociability etc. When the process of integration had a good result migrants' children studied in Belgian schools, became Belgian citizens and participated in Belgian public life, occasionally (and increasingly) assuming central roles in political and economic institutions. In these cases, the fundamental economic resource for the Belgian economic development progressively became an important part of the new Belgian society.[7]

During the Golden Age the decisive factors in shaping this positive course of integration were, firstly, migrants' professional skills and related job prospects and, secondly, the availability and standard of accommodation. Highly skilled migrants obviously had more opportunities than others even if it was possible that, in the first phase of their life in Belgium, they had to accept jobs having a profile and a remuneration lower than their professional level guaranteed to Belgian citizens. In a context where the process of integration was in any case very difficult, some other favourable variables were represented by the special protection granted by the European institutions to Italian migrants and, for French-speaking migrants coming from Africa, the possibility to use their language to work in Wallonia and Brussels. These advantages also kept their relevance after the oil shocks and the ensuing negative economic trend: high professional skills and a very good knowledge of French granted the possibility of being one of the few incoming migrants being accepted during the economic crisis.

The problem of migrants' accommodation and health assistance

In order to evaluate the actual social and economic impact of foreign workers it was also necessary to consider how to provide migrants' lodging and health assistance and how to face the related costs. These costs were fully or partially borne by the host countries depending on the agreement signed with the countries of origin. In a social and economic context characterized by a great increase of social security costs (Locatelli 2014), all ECSC/EEC countries had to choose whether to improve the migrants' quality of life or save this money for services concerning native citizens. However, they were all aware that poor and miserable migrants' lodging implied further social costs such as the cost of controlling the spreading of dangerous infectious diseases like tuberculosis (which obviously did not distinguish between natives and foreigners).

While destination countries had to manage the arrival and integration of migrants European institutions often supported their effort. It was in fact necessary to avoid the over-exploitation of migrants through excessively low wages and overly priced accommodation in order not to disrupt the local market and cause a real decrease in salaries and higher rents for local citizens. This clearly explains why some native workers had a hostile attitude towards migrants who were accused of stealing jobs from unskilled ECSC/ EEC citizens. This was not the case since foreign workers did not replace native workers, but they integrated the workplaces which most ECSC/EEC citizens refused, as entrepreneurs knew well. The representatives of the trade unions, on the contrary, pointed out that these jobs were refused because they were low paid: so, immigrants were surely essential for economic development, but only because they allowed factories to keep low labour costs. Trade unions in particular noted that the precarious migrants' living conditions clearly showed how foreign workers were exploited: if they were so essential and important for the improvement of factory production and productivity, they should receive better wages and accommodation.

Besides, both European trade unions and European institutions affirmed that it was very dangerous to create separate buildings for migrants because this *de facto* provoked their segregation in real *ghettos*: however, the strategic political choice of developing lodgings in the outskirts of the main industrial towns was implemented in all ECSC/EEC countries. This had a double negative effect: it limited the integration of migrants' families in the host country because they were isolated from the natives or they lived with the poorest ones; it favoured the birth of violent gangs, which "recruited" some young migrants who were angry because of their low and precarious incomes. So, new *ghettos* became the land where the law was not respected: this reduced the quality of life of all honest people living in these new neighbourhoods and it obviously increased suspect and negative stereotypes about migrants' attitudes and the real possibility of their being integrated into the countries which hosted them. This happened, for example, in the main industrial towns in West Germany and Belgium (Espahangizi 2004; Tedeschi and Tilly 2018) and in particular in France: the creation of new French *bidonvilles* crowded with migrants (and the related social problems with natives living in the outskirts of the great towns) obliged the French parliament to establish, at the end of the 1950s, special funds supporting Islamic migrant families and to promulgate, in 1964 and 1965, special laws limiting the growth of shanty towns (Gastaut 2004).

To improve integration, public institutions had to assign lodgements to immigrants in different districts of the industrial towns and, at the same time, they also organized public spaces where they could meet their compatriots. As a result, they had to learn the language and customs of the country where they worked and lived, but they could continue to maintain a link with their traditional habits.[8] All these policies implied a great cost for public institutions: the European Social Fund organized some vocational training courses allowing migrants to improve their professional skills and their knowledge of the language used in their host country, but the country had to pay half the cost (Laffan 1983; Mechi 2006). Moreover, the building of new lodgements and the creation of all utilities related to the new neighbourhoods (as potable water, electricity, telephone lines and sewage) and the related services (in particular new places in public schools, healthcare facilities and new police stations) increased public costs: so the arrival of migrants represented a relevant cost for native citizens and this obviously influenced the perception related to the economic relevance of foreign workers. Moreover, a part of the public opinion also thought that public investments concerning migrants' accommodation strongly influenced taxation (which increased) and subsidies for poor natives (which decreased): this was not true because the returns granted by migrants' work normally overcame all the costs related to their presence in the host country. Yet from a political point of view, the governments' economic benefit was reduced by the risk of a lessening of consensus and votes by native citizens.

All these problems obviously existed in Belgium too: the strong migration flows in some Belgian towns (in particular Brussels, Charleroi, Mons and Liège) created tensions around the provision of accommodation for migrants and complicated the relationship between migrants and local inhabitants. Migrant workers were in fact joined by their wives and families and this favoured the growth of the number of foreigners: at the same time, the problem of low wages and exorbitantly high accommodation costs increased. The initial segregation of migrants into camps (which were previously used for war prisoners) ended with the birth of the ECSC, but it was followed by the confinement of foreign workers to very definite residential areas in the crumbling parts of industrial towns. Other forms of socio-economic exclusion (school dropout, social and cultural marginalization and female unemployment) reinforced the migrants' sense of alienation and isolation which was favoured in Belgium (and in the Netherlands too) by the *pilarization*, that is the division of people depending on their religion, customs and political ideas. Migrants' spatial and social segregation related to their different habits in particular concerned the migrants' waves of the 1960s and early 1970s including lots of non-white and non-Christian manual workers from outside Europe. These immigrants encountered challenges that white Christian Europeans as Italians did not have to face: they in fact were helped by a migrant network built before the Second World War and, obviously, were granted better protection as citizens of an ECSC/EEC country, in particular since 1965. On the contrary, for non-European Muslims who formed the majority of the new immigrant waves during the 1960s and 1970s the natives' prejudices were stronger because the cultural differences were greater and they were not compensated for by the advantage related to the knowledge of the French language, as happened for some communities (e.g. the Moroccan one) (Morelli 2004; Tedeschi and Tilly 2018).

During the 1950s, European institutions realized that the cost of migrants' accommodation could create a negative prejudice about foreigner workers among the local population: at the same time, they also recognized that precarious lodgements favoured migrants' illegal behaviours and the natives' negative perception of foreign inflows. Therefore, the European institutions suggested that Belgian communities and factories receiving migrants created workers' villages including accommodation, schools and leisure areas for dancing or playing sports. The ECSC in particular financed the building of new houses for migrants: starting with the first ECSC experimental programme of 1954, the new houses for migrant miners and workers had to be built to attract immigrants' families: this allowed the improvement of the living conditions of the workforce in the two industrial sectors of the ECSC. After eight years, in 1962, about 72,000 houses were built and they were low cost rented to coal and steel workers and after redeemed by the latter at particularly favourable conditions. The coal crisis and then the oil shocks strongly reduced the programme in the following years: however, at the end of 1979 the houses built were 155.413 and 60 per cent were built in West Germany, 20 per cent in France, 5 per cent in Belgium, more than 4.5 per cent in Italy and more than 10 per cent in the other five ECSC/EEC countries (Leuvrey 1990; Mechi 2000). However, it was evident that, without the full collaboration of national governments, the risk to build low quality accommodation and enact an arbitrary distribution was high. Besides, native families without accommodation did not appreciate new houses for migrants: furthermore, to achieve economies of scale it was necessary to build at least 25 houses in the same area and this sometimes created tensions and discussions in the neighbourhood where migrants arrived in great number.

Other problems related to migrants' health assistance: it was in fact partially (sometimes fully) paid by Belgian mutual aid societies. Only when migrants (and obviously refugees) were able to find a regular job and support themselves, were they able to pay their welfare contributions. Furthermore, the cost of police patrolling and surveillance had to be strengthened: it was in fact necessary to avoid conflicts between natives and foreigners (who were accused of stealing or in some cases being some kind of "strike breakers" reducing workers' contractual power) and also among foreigners coming from different countries (or belonging to the same) because of behavioural problems caused by the burden of debts and alcohol abuse (with the possibility of violence against family members, especially women) (Morelli 2004; Tilly and Tedeschi 2018). This growth of public expenses, related to the inflow of migrants, implied that, if the European institutions pushed to increase the reception of migrants (influenced by the Italian government that aimed at reducing the unemployment rate), they had to contribute as they did for the housing: however, excluding the money related to the High Authority fines for companies that did not respect the ECSC rules, all the money arriving from European institutions was paid by the richest ECSC/EEC countries, that is, countries hosting migrants. This obviously means that West Germany, which built most workers' houses, had to pay more than other ECSC/EEC countries. The Belgian government, which had to face strong migration flows, also had serious financial problems managing the migrants' issue, especially when, after the end of the Golden Age, tax revenues decreased and it was necessary to spend more to stop the migrants' arrival and to continue the relatively efficient model of integration existing before: so, the policies concerning migrants became more relevant in the political debate, in particular where foreign workers and their families represented a significant percentage of the inhabitants (De Biolley 1994).

Finally, as happened in all ECSC/EEC countries, the costs related to the accommodation of the migrants obviously depended on their number and also on the actual demand of their professional skills existing in the labour market. Therefore, during the Golden Age, when enterprises increased their dimension and output for a growing labour market, demand increased, allowing the arrival of lots of foreign workers who initially had a low wage level and poor accommodation, but a feasible perspective of improving their quality of life. Furthermore, they had a job (even if poorly paid) and their demand of goods and services (and their families' too) progressively increased, favouring the growth of the host country GDP, that is the general wealth and wellness. On the contrary, after the oil shock, when the economic crisis strongly increased the number of the unemployed, migrants lost their job and the new inflows had few, if any, possibilities to find a job. This obviously reduced the foreigners' earnings and increased the violation of laws in their residential areas: social problems related to the presence of migrants (in particular the new ones) overcame the advantage for the national GDP and justified the restrictions and the stop of the migration flows (with the related increase in the number of illegal entries into ECSC/EEC countries).[9] For the ECSC/EEC public opinion, which also included the sons or nephews of the waves of migrants of the 1950s (and before), the presence of migrants became a social problem, which undermined the advantages. This is what clearly emerges from the comparison of the two surveys carried out by the European Commission whose members simply wanted to know how to correctly evaluate the needs of factories and citizens in the destination countries.

European institutions' aid for host countries: how to evaluate the needs?

The first survey during the "economic miracle"

European institutions had to help the ECSC/EEC member countries to solve the problems related to the reception and integration of migrants: during the Golden Age the positive economic trend favoured the flow of migrants toward Western Europe. The limited financing guaranteed by European institutions did not represent a problem.

To fully understand the impact of migrants and, in particular, the problem of accommodation, a first survey was launched pursuant to a proposal by the Belgian representative at a meeting of the ministers concerning housing issues. He justified the survey on the basis of the influence of housing on the migrants' adjustment prospects to the host country. The failure of adjustment brought along in fact very serious social and human consequences and, moreover, relevant economic effects. Unintegrated jobless people could easily become manpower for outlaw organizations belonging to the local traditional underworld or could be taken on by the Soviet intelligence. On the contrary, the immigrant work helped the local companies, which suffered the lack of local workforce and, in general, it progressively increased the sales of goods and services. The survey was carried out in France (in Paris), Belgium (in Liège) and West Germany (in Westphalia) over the 1959–1961 period; the results were debated inside the Commission by some representatives of the Six (Tizzoni 2020).

The survey illustrated the migrant workers' answers concerning their work conditions and their accommodation: it also included the comments of Belgian and German opinion leaders who stressed that the different cultural and social background of migrant workers hampered their integration and prevented them from getting better housing conditions; on the contrary, the interviewed workers stressed that their accommodation was better than they had in their native countries and that their poor housing conditions were merely the consequence of their low salaries. In Belgium many personalities deemed as positive the spatial segregation of foreigners according to their countries of origin. German opinion leaders remarked that building national "ghettos" could hamper the integration of foreigners: migrants had to establish better relations with native people and hence they had to improve their knowledge of language and local traditions. If this was not easy for people coming from former German regions, it was evident that for Italian migrants the adjustment problems were more important: the survey in fact indicated that Italian workers had great difficulty in assimilating the German way of life and it also suggested that the use of Italian chefs to prepare the workforce meals could improve the Italian workers' health and quality of life. The survey confirmed that Western Germany guaranteed foreigners better life and work conditions than other ECSC/EEC countries, but integration remained very difficult, for German-speaking migrants as well.[10] The French report showed a better situation and underlined that in a lot of cases the migrants' skills, tenacity and human qualities enabled them to acquire, by their own means (that is without waiting for the hypothetical intervention of an official service), decent housing capable of sheltering them and their families: the result concerning the French case was strongly influenced by the strict control and selection of migrants that French authorities made in that period: they *de facto* chose most of the foreign workers who entered the French labour market.[11]

The first survey led to the adoption of the Commission Recommendation of 7 July 1965 to the Member States on the housing of workers and their families moving within the Community. It established in particular that workers who were ECSC/EEC citizens and who were regularly employed in the territory of another ECSC/EEC Member State could enjoy the same rights and benefits as local workers in all matters relating to access to housing. Besides, it established "the abolition of all discrimination on the grounds of nationality, in particular with regard to the criteria for the allocation of rental housing, the granting by the public authorities of loans, bonuses, subsidies, tax concessions or other advantages provided by state housing assistance, including access to property" (Tizzoni 2020).

These rules clearly had a relevant impact on national legislations and they increased the cost of housing for the EEC member countries. So, one year later, the six were asked to provide updates about the implementation of the recommendation: in spite of the efforts to achieve better housing conditions for foreign workers, the negative bias against their supposed difficult adjustment to the host countries was reaffirmed. The Dutch representative declared that the adaptation to the host country and especially to the way migrants were "housed" was quite difficult: he in fact indicated that foreign workers coming from Southern Europe tended to group together by nationality and they continued to be strongly influenced by their own culture and lifestyle. This meant that European institutions had to modify the rules or agree to finance the construction of new buildings in the host countries in order to share out migrants in different areas.

The second survey during the oil shock crisis

In the following years, French economic problems, the crisis of the Belgian coal sector and the increase of the EEC budget share spent on the Common Agricultural Policy, did not allow European institutions to significantly increase the aid for migrants. Furthermore, in the 1970s, the oil shocks strongly increased the number of jobless people in all Western European countries. The solution was a restriction of work permissions for migrants coming from extra ECSC/EEC countries, even though special agreements were signed with some African or Asian countries. Most migrants were not able to keep a job (or to find a new one) and they were compelled to work in illegal activities: public opinion obviously began to perceive their presence as a social problem. European institutions did not increase financial aid for host countries and so they could not criticize the partial closing of frontiers (Berlinghoof 2017). This created problems, as in the Belgian case with new irregular migrants: the number of foreigners was in fact reduced, but it was impossible to fully stop the migration flow and the negative social consequences. The new immigrants who arrived during the downturn had no regular work permits and were in direct competition with low-skilled native workers in the labour market. As a result, the economic crisis not only increased discrimination and xenophobia, but it heightened protectionism around local workers making migrants very vulnerable. Low-skilled immigrants generally worked in precarious positions in industrial and service companies, which were most exposed to the negative effects of the recession. Therefore they were often the first to be dismissed, thus increasing the number of jobless people. Depending on the agreement signed by their native country they could access some subsidies, but if their presence was illegal they obviously received nothing with the related negative effects on their quality of life (and of their families).

During this worst economic conjuncture (in 1974–1975), a second survey took place involving all the ECSC/EEC members. The survey aimed at challenging the stereotypes on migrants and their housing habits, and migrant workers in all nine EEC countries were interviewed. Firstly, the interviews proved as untrue the prejudice that migrants accepted uncomfortable housing either because they did not want anything better, or because what they were getting in the host country was in any case better than they had in their native country. On the contrary, observing the housing market, it appeared that migrants did not choose their housing conditions: the latter were the manifest consequence of the decisions taken by the existing political, economic and social system. Hence, migrants were discriminated as workers and also in social and housing policies. Furthermore, the housing set aside for foreigners, or rather the housing which their marginal position constrained them to occupy, was part of "the machinery of social confinement and control, of making life insecure, and thus inhibiting or eliminating any request which might be made" (Tizzoni 2020).

Both the surveys displayed that the European citizens' attitude towards the housing problems of migrant workers mainly depended on national and communitarian migration policies. Consequently, the ECSC/EEC tried to influence national social housing policy and avoid the fact that foreign workers were entitled to a "limited" right to housing. Besides, the housing policy concerning the migrants' accommodation was strictly linked to the goals of boosting industrial productivity and improve social control. During the early 1960s, foreign workers were considered responsible for their poor housing conditions: natives thought that migrants saved money in order to help their relatives at home or in order to return to their country of origin as soon as they could. As a result, they did not invest in improving their accommodation in the host country and were reluctant to change their habits because they simply wanted to set aside the necessary capital to go back to their "real" home. In Belgium some migrants actually had this aim, but a significant part of them had a very different one: for example, if they had children who went to school and were educated as ECSC/EEC citizens, the perspective of returning to the native country was postponed until retirement. Besides, migrants who were able run a shop or other autonomous activities (as a vehicle repair shop, a restaurant etc.) were proud of their new living conditions and they went back their native country only for holidays. Furthermore, lots of migrants progressively discovered that they were no longer Italian, Spanish, Moroccan, Turkish etc., even if they were not really Belgian: so they preferred to live where their daughters/sons grew up, studied and found a job. Finally, during the negative economic trend related to the oil shocks, migrants working in Belgian factories knew that in their native country there were no jobs, so, they remained in Belgium even if they had to accept a new low-paid job and poor accommodation.

While the survey made in the early 1960s was affected to a large extent by the migrant workers' perception shared by European elites, the survey made in the 1970s shed a light on the segregation and discrimination of migrant workers. This referred to foreigners' housing conditions and so it commented on the limited results of the European institutions' intervention in such a field. It also underlined what foreigners suffered at work and at home and its analysis became more relevant because, during the negative economic trend, the number of jobless people increased and consequently also the occasion to profit from migrant workers, especially newcomers and irregular ones.

The experience made during the analysed period and in particular during the 1970s, allowed European officers working on migrant policies to verify that it was necessary to spend more money to reduce migration flows and to prepare the host countries to organize good migrants' accommodation. This was the only way to be sure to reduce the social problems related to migrants. If European institutions spent more money in favour of the social and economic cohesion in ECSC/EEC countries, it would be possible to reduce the number of economic migrants arriving from the Common Market countries. The same goal could obviously be achieved if European development aid improved the quality of life in the poorest African and Asian countries. Furthermore, if European institutions helped ECSC/EEC countries to give decent accommodation to migrants (and refugees), it would be possible to decrease the main risks related to the building of *ghettos*, that is the difficult integration in the host country and the growth in the number of thieves and dangerous outcasts.

The surveys were also used to evaluate and reduce the real cost of migrants' integration: it was a complex calculation (Dupaquier and Laulan 2006), which had to consider how communitarian and national leaders thought to finance all projects that could improve the foreigners' social and economic conditions (in their native countries or in the host ones) and, thus reduce migrant flows. The increase in GDP in poor nations favoured in fact the purchase of local and European goods and services. Excluding radical positions (which went from halting migrant flows to paying all expenses related to their arrival by an increase in the public debt), there existed some proposals which did not distress the communitarian and national budgets. They were based on the "Déclaration solennelle sur l'identité européenne" of 1973 and defined a new European model of economic and social cohesion including policies in favour of the improvement of the "well-being of all" (Déclaration sur l'identité européenne 1973). For example, it was possible to reduce the budget for the armed forces (an argument strongly debated during the 1970s and later) and/or to increase taxes on all pure *rentiers*' revenues, that is people and financial institutions that did not invest their money in the productive and commercial companies. However, none of these proposals was taken into consideration and national governments continued to face migrants' problems without a specific communitarian budget, which, on the contrary, existed for productive sectors such as agriculture or heavy industry. Finally, during the 1980s, the neoliberal ideology arriving from the USA and the UK as well as the lack of cohesion between European trade unions facing the de-industrialization process, stopped all new European policies aimed at solving the main problems emerging from the surveys.[12]

Conclusions

The European institutions' attention to migrant flows from the 1950s to the 1970s allowed all the social and economic problems related to the arrival of people with different language, religion and habits in most of the ECSC/EEC member countries to be brought to the fore. During the Golden Age the problems outweighed the advantages: as it was forseen when the EEC was established (Molinari 1958), the availability of thousands of migrants represented one of the most relevant factors favouring the excellent results of the European Common Market. Most foreign workers *de facto* shaped a new European identity demonstrating that the integration process was difficult but not impossible (Milza 1994). Only in the 1970s, when the two oil shocks strongly reduced work availability in Western Europe, the problem of the migrants' presence became important and favoured measures limiting immigration in ECSC/EEC countries. Accordingly, the real status of migrants (relevant resource or social problem) in particular depended on the economic trend and only for a residual part on the cultural differences. If European institutions and national governments had decided to invest to reduce migration flows and to guarantee better migrants' accommodation, then the process of integration could have become sustainable and migrants would really have been an economic resource for all and not only for the people exploiting them.

However, European leaders, distracted by new political and economic theories attributing more importance to market rules and a strong reduction in public expenditure, forgot the experience made from the 1950s to the 1970s: they in fact repeated the same mistakes into the new millennium. Therefore, few investments were made in favour of the poorest backward regions and countries: moreover, an excessive tolerance was allowed for people offering foreign workers a very low wage and bad accommodation. So, migrants continued to be discriminated against in their workplaces and in their social life (Nys and Beauchesne 1992; Miles and Thränhardt 1995; Borraccetti 2018). The correct answers to the question about the actual migrants' usefulness and the proposals to solve the related problems (through financial aid to economic backward areas) kept "blowing in the wind" and they did not influence European leaders, in particular after the new 2008 economic crisis and the new conflicts in Mediterranean areas, which strongly increased the number of migrants and refugees travelling towards the "European fortress".[13]

Acknowledgements

The author thanks Elisa Tizzoni (University of Pisa) for her precious suggestions and advice: she in particular gave some fundamental information concerning the surveys carried out by the European Commission.

Notes

1 A wide bibliography exists about the economic, sociologic, and juridical aspects of the ECSC/EEC labour market from the 1950s to the 1970s: see, among others, Dahlberg (1967-68); Tapinos (1974); Collins (1975); Boehning (1972; 1973); Werner (1986); Romero (1991; 1993); Grassi (1994); Goedings (2000); Varsori (2000); Garson and Loizillon (2003); Hansen (2003); Lucassen, Feldman and Oltmer (2006); Taccolini (2006); Messina (2007); Caruso, Pleinen and Raphael (2008); Blanco Sio-Lopez and Tedeschi (2015); Fauri (2015a); Penninx and Garcés-Mascarena (2015); Laschi, Deplano and Pes (2017); Comte (2016; 2018); Fauri and Tedeschi (2018). See also note 10 and the documents in the European Commission Historical Archives (ECHA): CEAB 1, n. 1649–73, CEAB 7, n. 1316, 1484, 1863 (free circulation of workforce, 1953–63), CEAB 4, n. 634, 720, 948–949, 1166, 1168, CEAB 7, n. 1402, 1485, 1607–1608 (social security for migrant workers, 1953–1968).

2 A wide bibliography exists about migrations flows to Belgium from the 1950s to the 1970s: see, among others, Clémens, Vosse-Small and Minon (1953); Martens (1976); Tricot 1979; Bastenier (1992); Phalet and Swyngedouw 2003; Morelli (2004); Martiniello, Rea and Dassetto (2007); Tilly (2015); Tedeschi and Tilly (2018). See also note 4.

3 A wide bibliography exists about the harmonization of communitarian and national regulations in the ECSC/EEC countries from the 1950s to the 1970s (in particular about the social policy): see, among others, the main European documents as CECA (1957a; 1957b; 1963); CEE (1966; 1968); Recommandation de la Commission aux Etats membres concernant l'adoption d'une liste européenne des maladies professionnelles (1962) and also European Social Charter (1966); Gui (1975); Masini (1975).

4 A wide bibliography exists about the Italian migrants in other ECSC/EEC countries: see, among others, Clémens, Vosse-Small and Minon (1953); Livi Bacci (1972); Morelli (1988; 2016); Dumoulin (1989); Besana (2002); Blanc-Chaleard (2003); Beyers (2005); Colucci (2008); De Clementi (2010); Cumuli (2012); Fauri (2015b); Ventresca (2017). See also ECHA, CEAB 1, 1680 (Italian workers in Belgian mines, 1955–1956).

5 The improvement of miners' safety in fact represented the first case of intervention for European institution (Leboutte 2005).

6 Besides the references in the note 2, see Vincineau (1984); Khoojinian (2006); Akgunduz (2008).

7 Besides the references in the notes 2, 4, and 6, see Perrin and Poulain (2002); Van Ingelgem (2014); Tedeschi (2017).

8 Lots of documents concerning the problem of migrants' accommodation were drafted by the High Authority of the ECSC. A special working group for the building of "The Workers' Houses" started its activity in Luxembourg on 28 October 1952 and prepared a survey about the migrant workers' houses dimensions and structures. See ECHA, CEAB 1, n. 1625, 1817, 1849, CEAB 13, n. 3, 6–8. About the ECSC financial helps for building houses for workers from 1952 to 1968 also see: CEAB 1, n. 669, 1790, 1816–1832, 1834–1852.

9 Illegal migrants also arrived in ECSC/EEC countries during the Golden Age and they normally found a job even if they were low-paid: however, after the first oil shock and the strong reduction of the migration flows their number increased as well as the social problem related to the lack of work. See Leman (1995); Martini and Lutz (2014).

10 About migrants' living conditions in West Germany also see: Dreyer (1961); Boehning (1970); Korte (1985); Herbert and Hunn (2001).

11 About migrants' living conditions in France also see: Stoetzel (1954); McDonald (1969); Spire (2005).

12 About changes in the ECSC/EEC social policies arriving during the 1970s and 1980s and their effects, see, among others, Papademetriou (1978); Boehning (1983); Caire (1992); Magnusson and Strath (2001); Bussière, Dumoulin and Schirmann (2006).

13 A wide bibliography exists about the European institutions policies concerning the regulations of the migration flows and the migrants' accommodation (as well as refugees' one) from the 1980s to the early new Millennium: see, among others, Callovi (1992); Geddes (2000; 2003); Düvell and Jordan (2002); Bendel (2005); Parsons and Smeeding (2006); Koff (2008); Chou (2009; Schain (2009); Parkes (2010); Boswell and Geddes (2011); Kaunert and Léonard (2012); Novotný (2012; Roos (2013; Collett (2015).

References

Akgunduz A. (2008). *Labour Migration from Turkey to Western Europe, 1960-1974. A Multidisciplinary Analysis*. London: Ashgate Publishing Company.

Bastenier A. (1992). *L'Etat belge face à l'immigration: les politiques sociales jusqu'en 1980*. Sybidi Paper No. 10, Louvain-la-Neuve.

Becherucci A. (2018). Le proposte della Conferenza sociale del Movimento europeo di Roma del 1950 sull'organizzazione e la tutela del lavoro migrante in Europa. In Laschi G., Deplano V. and Pes A. (eds.). *Europa in movimento. Mobilità e migrazioni tra integrazione europea e decolonizzazione, 1945-1992*. Bologna: Il Mulino, 71–99.

Bendel P. (2005). Immigration Policy in the European Union: Still Bringing Up the Walls for Fortress Europe? *Migration Letters*. 2(1): 20–31.

Berlinghoof M. (2017). Labour Migration: Common Market Essential or Common Problem? The EC Committees and European Immigration Stops in the Early 1970s. In Calandri, E., Paoli S. and Varsori A. (eds.). *Peoples and Borders: Seventy Years of Migration in Europe, from Europe, to Europe (1945-2015). Journal of European Integration History*. Special issue: 155–176.

Besana C. (2002). Accordi internazionali ed emigrazione della mano d'opera italiana tra ricostruzione e sviluppo. In Zaninelli S. and Taccolini M. (eds.). *Il lavoro come fattore produttivo e come risorsa nella storia economica italiana*. Milano: Vita e Pensiero: 3–17.

Beyers L. (2005). Italians in Belgium since the 1970s: A Unique Process of Changing Positions and Identities. *Studi Emigrazione/Migration Studies*. XLII(160): 762–785.

Blanc-Chaleard M.C. (2003). *Les italiens en France depuis 1945*. Rennes: PUR.

Blanco Sio-Lopez C. and Tedeschi P. (2015). Migrants and European Institutions: A Study on the Attempts to Address the Economic and Social Challenges of Immigration in EU Member States. In Fauri F. (ed.). *The History of Migration in Europe: Perspectives from Economics, Politics and Sociology*. London: Routledge, 126–153.

Boehning W.R. (1970). *The Social and Occupational Apprenticeship of Mediterranean Workers in West Germany*. Canterbury: University of Kent Centre for Research in the Social Sciences.

Boehning W.R. (1972). *The Migration of Workers in the United Kingdom and the European Community*. Oxford: Oxford University Press.

Boehning W.R. (1973). *The Economic Effects of the Employment of Foreign Workers: With Special Reference to the Labour Markets of Western Europe's Post-Industrial Societies*. Paris: Working Document, OECD, Manpower and Social Affairs Directorate.

Boehning W.R. (1983). Regularising the Irregular. *International Migration*. 21(2): 159–174.

Borraccetti M. (ed.) (2019). *Labour Migration in Europe, Vol. 1: Exploitation and Legal Protection of Migrant Workers*. London: Palgrave Macmillan.

Boswell C. and Geddes A. (2011). *Migration and Mobility in the European Union*. Basingstoke: Palgrave Macmillan.

Bussière E., Dumoulin M. and Schirmann S. (eds.) (2006). *Milieux économiques et intégration européenne en Europe occidentale au XXe siècle. La crise des années*

1970. De la conférence de La Haye à la veille de la relance des années 1980. Bruxelles: Peter Lang.

Caire G. (1992). *L'Europe sociale. Faits-Problèmes-Enjeux.* Paris: Masson.

Callovi G. (1992). Part II: Western Europe: New, Old and Recast of Immigration Questions in the Post-Cold War Period. Regulation of Immigration in 1993: Pieces of the European Community Jig-Saw Puzzle. *International Migration Review.* 26(2): 353–372.

Caruso C., Pleinen J. and Raphael L. (eds.) (2008). *Postwar Mediterranean Migration to Western Europe: Legal and Political Frameworks, Sociability and Memory Cultures.* Frankfurt am Main: Peter Lang.

CECA (1957a). *Rapport sur la migration et la libre circulation des travailleurs dans la Communauté.* Luxembourg: CECA.

CECA (1957b). *Obstacles à la mobilité des travailleurs et problèmes sociaux de réadaptation.* Luxembourg: CECA.

CECA (1963). *CECA 1952-1962. Résultats, limites, perspectives.* Luxembourg: CECA.

CEE (1966). *La libre circulation de la main d'œuvre et le marché du travail dans la CEE.* Bruxelles: CEE.

CEE (1968). *Décision, Règlement No. 1612/68 et Directive relatifs à la libre circulation des travailleurs à l'intérieur de la Communauté.* Bruxelles: CEE.

Chou M.H. (2009). The European Security Agenda and the "External Dimension" of EU Asylum and Migration Cooperation. *Perspectives on European Politics and Society.* 10(4): 541–599.

Clémens R., Vosse-Small G. and Minon P. (eds.) (1953). *L'assimilation culturelle des immigrants en Belgique. Italiens et Polonais dans la région liégeoise.* Liège: Vaillante-Carmanne.

Collett E. (2015). The Development of EU Policy on Immigration and Asylum: Rethinking Coordination and Leadership. *Migration Policy Institute-Policy Brief Series,* www.migrationpolicy.org/research/development-eu-policy-immigration-and-asylum-rethinking-coordination-and-leadership.

Collins D. (1975). *The European Communities. The Social Policy of the First Phase. Volume 1: The European Coal and Steel Community 1951-70; Volume 2: The European Economic Community 1958-72.* London: Robertson.

Colucci M. (2008). *Lavoro in movimento. L'emigrazione italiana in Europa, 1945-57.* Roma: Donzelli.

Comte E. (2016). La rupture de 1955 dans la formation du régime européen de migrations. *Relations internationales.* 166(2): 136–158.

Comte E. (2018). *The History of the European Migration Regime: Germany's Strategic Hegemony.* London: Routledge.

Cumuli F. (2012). *Un tetto a chi lavora: mondi operai e migrazioni italiane nell'Europa degli anni Cinquanta.* Milano: Guerini.

Dahlberg K.A. (1967-68). The EEC Commission and the Politics of the Free Movement Labour. *Journal of Common Market Studies.* 4(6): 310–333.

De Biolley O. (1994). *La vie politique des communes bruxelloises. L'argument immigré dans les campagnes communales (1970-1988).* Louvain la Neuve: Academia.

De Clementi A. (2010). *Il prezzo della ricostruzione: l'emigrazione italiana nel secondo dopoguerra.* Roma-Bari: Laterza.

Déclaration solennelle sur l'identité européenne (1973). *Bulletin des Communautés européennes.* 12: 127–130.

Dreyer H.M. (1961). Immigration of Foreign Workers into the Federal Republic of Germany. *International Labour Review*. 84(1-2): 1–25.

Dreyfus-Armand G. (1999). *L'exil des républicains espagnols en France: de la Guerre civile à la mort de Franco*. Paris: Albin Michel.

Dufoix S. (2002). *Politiques d'exil. Hongrois, Polonais et Tchécoslovaques en France après 1945*. Paris: PUF.

Dumoulin M. (ed.) (1989). *Mouvements et politiques migratoires en Europe depuis 1945: le cas italien*. Louvain la Neuve: Ciaco.

Dumoulin M. and Dutrieue A.M. (1993). *La Ligue Européenne de Coopération Economique (1946-1981). Un groupe d'études et de pression dans la construction européenne*. Bern: Peter Lang.

Dumoulin M. and Goddeeris I. (eds) (2005). *Intégration ou représentation? Les exilés polonais en Belgique et la construction européenne*. Louvain-la-Neuve: Academia Bruylant.

Dupaquier J. and Laulan Y.M. (eds.) (2006). *Immigration/Intégration: un essai d'évaluation des coûts économiques et financiers*. Paris: L'Harmattan.

Düvell F. and Jordan B. (2002). Immigration, Asylum and Welfare: The European Context. *Critical Social Policy August*. 22(3): 498–517.

Espahangizi R. (2014). Migration and Urban Transformations: Frankfurt in the 1960s and 1970s. *Journal of Contemporary History*. 49(1): 183–208.

European Social Charter (1966). *European Social Charter "Research 1966" by the Council of Europe. Recommendations of the Committee of Ministers: Reports from the Social Committee of the Special Representative for Refugees and Surplus Population*. Strasbourg: ESC.

Fauri F. (2015a). European Migrants after the Second World War. In Fauri F. (ed.). *The History of Migration in Europe: Perspectives from Economics, Politics and Sociology*. London: Routledge, 103–125.

Fauri F. (2015b). *Storia economica delle migrazioni italiane*. Bologna: Il Mulino.

Fauri F. and Tedeschi P. (eds.) (2018). *Labour Migration in Europe Volume I: Integration and Entrepreneurship among Migrant Workers – A Long-Term View*. London: Palgrave Macmillan.

Garson J.P. and Loizillon A. (2003). *Changes and Challenges – Europe and Migration from 1950 to Present: The Economic and Social Aspects of Migration*. In a conference jointly organized by the European Commission and the OECD Brussels, 21-22 January.

Gastaut Y. (2004). Les bidonvilles, lieux d'exclusion et de marginalitè en France durant les trente glorieuses. *Cahiers de la Méditerranée*. (69): 233–250.

Geddes A. (2000). *Immigration and European Integration. Towards fortress Europe?*, Manchester: Manchester University Press.

Geddes A. (2003). *The Politics of Migration and Immigration in Europe*. London: Sage Publications.

Goedings S. (2000). Labour Market Developments, National Migration Policies and the Integration of Western Europe, 1948-1968. In Leboutte R. (ed.). *Migrations and Migrants in Historical Perspective. Permanencies and Innovations*. Bruxelles: Peter Lang, 311–329.

Grassi V. (1994). Le politiche migratorie nei principali paesi dell'Europa occidentale dal secondo dopoguerra agli anni '80. *Affari sociali internazionali*. (2): 57–80.

Gui L. (1975). La convenzione europea per la sicurezza sociale dei lavoratori emigranti. In *50 anni di studi nella rivista "Previdenza Sociale" dell'Istituto Nazionale della Previdenza Sociale*. Roma: INPS, 315–317.

Hansen R. (2003). Migration to Europe since 1945: Its History and Its Lessons. *The Political Quarterly*. 74(1): 25–38.

Herbert U. and Hunn K. (2001). Guest Workers and Policy on Guest Workers in the Federal Republic: From the Beginning of Recruitment in 1955 until Its Halt in 1973. In Schissler A. (ed.). *The Miracle Years: A Cultural History of West Germany, 1949-1968*. Princeton: Princeton University Press, 187–218.

Kaunert C. and Léonard S. (2012). The Development of the EU Asylum Policy: Venue-Shopping in Perspective. *Journal of European Public Policy*. 19(9): 1396–1413.

Khoojinian M. (2006). L'Accueil et la stabilisation des travailleurs immigrés turcs en Belgique, 1963-1980. *Cahiers d'Histoire du Temps Présent*. (17): 73–116.

Koff H. (2008). *Fortress Europe or a Europe of Fortresses? The Integration of non-European Union Immigrants in Western Europe*. Bruxelles: Peter Lang.

Korte H. (1985). Labor Migration and the Employment of Foreigners in the Federal Republic of Germany since 1950. In Rogers R. (ed.). *Guests Come to Stay: The Effects of European Labor Migration on Sending and Receiving Countries*. Boulder: Westview Press, 29–49.

Laffan B. (1983). Policy Implementation in the European Community: The European Social Fund as a Case Study. *Journal of Common Market Studies*. XXI(4): 389–408.

Laschi G., Deplano V. and Pes A. (eds.) (2017). *Europa in movimento. Mobilità e migrazioni tra integrazione europea e decolonizzazione, 1945-1992*. Bologna: Il Mulino.

Leboutte R. (2005). Coal Mining, Foreigners Workers and Mine Safety: Steps Towards European Integration. In Berger S., Croll A. and La Porte N. (eds.). *Towards a Comparative History of Coalfield Societies*. Aldershot: Ashgate, 219–237.

Leman (1995). *Sans documents: les immigrés de l'ombre. Latino-américains, polonais et nigérians clandestins*. Bruxelles: De Boeck.

Leuvrey B. (1990). Quelle politique sociale pour l'Europe du Plan Schuman? Critiques et propositions de l'Assemblée Commune de la CECA (1952-1955). In *Lettre d'information des historiens de l'Europe contemporaine*. 5(1–2), 105–119.

Livi Bacci M. (ed.) (1972). *The Demographic and Social Pattern of Emigration from Southern European Countries*. Florence: Matematic-Statistical Department of the University of Florence and Italian Committee for the Study of Population Problems.

Locatelli A.M. (2014). The Social Security Cost in the European Integration. In Bussière E., Dumoulin M. and Schirmann S. (eds.). *Economies nationales et intégration européenne. Voies et étapes*. Stuttgart: Franz Steiner Verlag, 14–154.

Lucassen L., Feldman D. and Oltmer J. (eds.) (2006). *Paths of Integration: Migrants in Western Europe (1880-2004)*. Amsterdam: Amsterdam University Press.

Łukasiewicz S. (2017). Central and Eastern European Cold War émigrés in the European Integration Process. In Calandri E. Paoli S. and Varsori A. (eds.). *Peoples and Borders: Seventy Years of Migration in Europe, from Europe, to Europe (1945-2015). Journal of European Integration History*. Special Issue: 139–154.

Magnusson L. and Strath B. (eds.) (2001). *From the Werner Plan to the EMU: In Search of a Political Economy for Europe*. Bruxelles: Peter Lang.

Martens A. (1976). *Les immigrés. Flux et reflux d'une main-d'œuvre d'appoint. La politique belge de l'immigration de 1945 à 1970*. Brussels-Louvain la Neuve: EVO-Presses universitaire de Louvain.

Martini M. and Lutz R. (2014). Illegal Mediterranean Migrations to Western Europe after World War II. *Journal of Modern European History*. 12(1): 80–83.

Martiniello M., Rea A. and Dassetto F. (eds.) (2007). *Immigration et intégration en Belgique francophone, État des savoirs*. Louvain-la-Neuve: Academia Bruylant.
Masini C.A. (1975). I regimi generali obbligatori di vecchiaia per i lavoratori dipendenti nei paesi membri della CEE. In *50 anni di studi nella rivista "Previdenza Sociale" dell'Istituto Nazionale della Previdenza Sociale*. Roma: INPS, 657–689.
McDonald J.R. (1965). The Repatriation of French Algerians, 1962-63. *International Migration*. III(1): 146–157.
McDonald J.R. (1969). Labor Immigration in France, 1946-1965. *Annals of the Association of American Geographers*. LIX(1): 116–135.
Mechi L. (2000). L'action de la Haute Autorité de la CECA dans la construction des maisons ouvrières. *Journal of European Integration History*. VI(1): 63–85.
Mechi L. (2006). Les États membres, les institutions et les débuts du Fonds Social Européen. In Varsori A. (ed.). *Inside the European Community: Actors and Policies in the European Integration 1957-1972*. Baden-Baden: Nomos, 95–116.
Messina A.M. (2007). *The Logics and Politics of Post-WWII Migration to Western Europe*. Cambridge: Cambridge University Press.
Miles R. and Thränhardt D. (eds.) ()1995. *Migration and European Integration: The Dynamics of Inclusion and Exclusion*. London: Pinter Publisher.
Milza P. (1994). Les migrants dans la formation de l'identité européenne. In Girault R. (ed.). *Identité et conscience européennes au XXe siècle*. Paris: Hachette, 47–64.
Molinari A. (1958). Manpower and the Common Market. *BNL Quarterly Review*. XI(46): 484–510.
Morelli A. (1988). L'appel à la main d'œuvre italienne pour les charbonnages et sa prise en charge à son arrivée en Belgique dans l'immédiat après-guerre. *Revue Belge d'Histoire Contemporaine*. XIX(1–2): 83–130.
Morelli A. (ed.) (2004). *Histoire des étrangers et de l'immigration en Belgique de la préhistoire à nos jours*, Brussels: EVO.
Morelli A. (ed.) (2016). *Recherches nouvelles sur l'immigration italienne en Belgique*, Bruxelles: Couleur Livres.
Nys M. and Beauchesne M.N. (1992). La discrimination des travailleurs étrangers et d'origine étrangère dans l'entreprise. *Courrier hebdomadaire du CRISP*. XV(1381–1382): 1–78.
Novotný V. (ed.) (2012). *Opening the Door? Immigration and Integration in the European Union*. Brussels: Belgium Center for European Studies.
Papademetriou D.G. (1978). European Labor Migration: Consequences for the Countries of Worker Origin. *International Studies Quarterly*. 22(3): 377–408.
Parkes R. (2010). *European Migration Policy from Amsterdam to Lisbon*. Baden-Baden: Nomos.
Parsons C.A. and Smeeding T.M. (eds.) (2006). *Immigration and the Transformation of Europe*. Cambridge: Cambridge University Press.
Penninx R. and Garcés-Mascarena B. (eds.) (2015). *Integration Processes and Policies in Europe: Contexts, Levels and Actors*. Cham: Springer.
Pereira V. (2012). *La dictature de Salazar face à l'émigration. L'État portugais et ses migrants en France (1957-1974)*. Paris: SciencesPo Les Presses.
Perrin N. and Poulain L. (2002). *Italiens de Belgique. Analyse socio-démographiques et analyse des appartenances*. Louvain la Neuve: Académia-Bruylant.
Phalet K. and Swyngedouw M. (2003). Measuring the Immigrant Integration: The Case of Belgium. *Studi Emigrazione/Migration Studies*. XL(152): 773–803.

Recommandation de la Commission aux Etats membres concernant l'adoption d'une liste européenne des maladies professionnelles (1962). *Journal Officiel des Communautés*. 80: 31 août.

Romero F. (1991). *Emigrazione e integrazione europea 1945-1973*. Roma: Edizioni Lavoro.

Romero F. (1993). Migration is an Issue in European Interdependence and Integration: The Case of Italy. In Milward A.S., Lynch F.M.B., Romero F., Ranieri R. and Sørensesn V. (eds.). *The Frontier of National Sovereignty: History and Theory 1945-1992*. London: Routledge, 33–57.

Roos C. (2013). *The EU and Immigration Policies: Cracks in the Walls of Fortress Europe?*. Hampshire: Palgrave Macmillan.

Santos Y. (2017). Entre l'Atlantique et l'Europe: l'émigration et le difficile rapprochement entre le Portugal et les pays de la CEE 1945-1968. In Calandri E., Paoli S. and Varsori A. (eds.). *Peoples and Borders: Seventy Years of Migration in Europe, from Europe, to Europe (1945-2015)*. *Journal of European Integration History*. Special issue: 17–36.

Sanz Lafuente G. (2018). Job Promotion and Labour Turnover among Spanish Workers in West Germany, 1960-1973. In Fauri F. and Tedeschi P. (eds.). *Labour Migration in Europe Volume I: Integration and Entrepreneurship among Migrant Workers – A Long-Term View*. London: Palgrave Macmillan, 43–70.

Schain M.A. (2009). The State Strikes Back: Immigration Policy in the European Union. *The European Journal of International Law*. XX(1): 93–109.

Simon G. and Noin D. (1972). La migration maghrébine vers l'Europe. *Cahiers d'outre-mer*. XXV(99): 241–276.

Simon J. (ed.) (2002). *L'immigration algérienne en France: de 1962 à nos jours*. Paris: L'Harmattan.

Spire A. (2005). *Étrangers à la carte. L'administration de l'immigration en France (1945-1975)*. Paris: Grasset.

Stoetzel J. (1954). *Français et immigrés: nouveaux documents sur l'adaptation. Algériens, Italiens, Polonais: le service social d'aide aux immigrants*. Paris: PUF.

Taccolini M. (2006). *La costruzione di un'Europa del lavoro. La Commissione per gli affari sociali dalle origini all'applicazione del Trattato di Roma (1953-1960)*. Milano: Franco Angeli.

Tapinos G. (ed.) (1974). International Migration: Proceedings of a Seminar on Demographic Research in Relation to International Migration held in Buenos Aires, Argentine (5-11 March 1974). Paris: CICRED.

Tedeschi P. (2017). Changer la Belgique en devenant Belges, changer son pays en y retournant: notes sur l'influence des émigrants aux XIXe et XXe siècle. In Figeac M. and Bouneau C. (eds.). *Circulation, métissage et culture matérielle (XVIe-XXe siècles)*. Paris: Classiques Garnier, 357–372.

Tedeschi P. and Tilly P. (2018). Notes on the Economic and Social Impact of the Migration Flows in Belgium from the Post-World War II to the New Millennium: Some Case Studies. In Fauri, F., Tedeschi P. (eds.). *Labour Migration in Europe Volume I: Integration and Entrepreneurship among Migrant Workers – A Long-Term View*. London: Palgrave Macmillan, 71–108.

Tilly P. (2015). From Economic Integration to Active Political Participation of Immigrants: The Belgium Experience from Paris to Maastricht Treaty (1950-1993). In Fauri F. (ed.). *The History of Migration in Europe: Perspectives from Economics, Politics and Sociology*. London: Routledge, 217–229.

Tizzoni E. (2020). Migrazioni e questione degli alloggi nella Cee tra anni Sessanta e Settanta. Due inchieste della Commissione europea, *Studi Storici*. LXI(1): 165–191.

Tricot A. (1979). *Les immigrés et la question du logement à Bruxelles*. Bruxelles: IEV.

Van Ingelgem G. (2014). Entre exotisme et tradition: Bruxelles et ses restaurants italiens dans la deuxième moitié du XX siècle. *Food History*. XII(2): 39–66.

Varsori A. (ed.) (2000). *Il Comitato Economico e Sociale nella costruzione europea*. Venezia: Marsilio.

Ventresca R. (2017). Italian Migration Policies at the Beginning of the European Integration Process: Fruitless Attempts?. In Calandri E., Paoli S. and Varsori A. (eds.). *Peoples and Borders: Seventy Years of Migration in Europe, from Europe, to Europe (1945-2015). Journal of European Integration History*. Special issue: 57–76.

Vincineau M. (1984). *Les traités bilatéraux relatifs à l'emploi et au séjour en Belgique des travailleurs immigrés*. Bruxelles: Centre socio-culturel des immigrés de Bruxelles.

Werner H. (1986). Post-War Labour Migration in Western Europe: An Overview. *International Migration*. 24(3): 543–557.

6 Chinese immigrant entrepreneurs in Italy and England

The cases of Bologna and London

Patrizia Battilani and Francesca Fauri

Introduction

Business success has been a common characteristic of Chinese people overseas. Their entrepreneurial achievements are based not only on family and kin-group solidarity, but also often on their being hard working, thrifty, risk taking, frugal and high savers (Macke 1992). Chinese entrepreneurs are well known for their capacity to maximize efficiency and profit through a strategy of working longer hours and offering lower prices than their competitors.

The present study is going to compare the history of Chinese immigrant entrepreneurs in Bologna and London and evaluate the economic and social similarities and differences between the two Chinese communities and enterprises. In particular, we aim to investigate whether migrant communities coming from the same country share similar characteristics everywhere, or whether they tend to diverge depending on the country they have chosen to move to. Do migrant entrepreneurs operate their businesses in accordance with the mentality and culture prevailing in the country of origin or in the country of destination? The incoming community's adaptability to the market features of the destination society might or might not be an important factor in accounting for its business success.

There are several differences between Bologna and London. The first is a medium-sized city, which began to industrialize at the turn of the twentieth century; the second is a large capital city, which after initially focusing on manufacturing businesses during the eighteenth-century industrial revolution, subsequently specialized in banking and finance. Furthermore, the first two waves of immigration have affected the two countries in different periods. Very few Chinese moved to Italy until the First World War, and none of those that did settled in Bologna. Immigration to that city began during the interwar years, with the arrival of the first peddlers and the establishment of the first Chinese community in Bologna, some years after Milan's Chinese community had taken shape. This second wave of immigration lasted until the 1980s, when a new generation of Chinese moved to Italy in virtue of Deng Xiao Ping's Open Door policy. In the United Kingdom, on the other hand, the number of Chinese immigrants started to rise at the turn of twentieth century, and they established a large community at Limehouse in London, a neighbourhood which remained a lively, welcoming place for immigrants up until the 1930s. The second wave of Chinese immigration to the UK started after the Second World War, when an increasing number of Chinese people emigrated from Hong Kong to the United Kingdom, and a new Chinese community took shape in London. Finally, a third wave of immigration was witnessed following the introduction of the aforesaid Open Door policy.

Due to the lack of common features characterizing the two cities, any possible similarities in the two communities of Chinese immigrants established therein can only be accounted for by the country of origin's prevailing culture, mentality and practices. Sociological studies have indicated that when immigrants are faced with a disadvantage, namely their preclusion from the mainstream capitalist economy, they often respond by creating their own form of capitalism (Portes 1981). While it is incontrovertible that "for any business to start there must be a demand for the goods and services it offers", our research shows that not all Chinese businesses were developed "to fill an ethnic niche, itself a structural condition the immigrant businessmen are eager to exploit", and that not all of the businesses that were set up by the first Chinese immigrants were "purveyors of culinary and cultural products" (Bun and Hui 1995: 524).

In the case of both Bologna and London, for many decades (before the late 1930s in the UK, and up until the 1980s in Italy), the small original Chinese community came from mainland China, was comprised mainly of male immigrants[1] who often married local women and formed a community located in a specific geographical area, engaged in selected businesses: in Bologna, these comprised peddling various wares and producing leatherette bags or ties and in the case of London, the Chinese immigrants were typically involved in the seafaring sector, or ran laundries and restaurants. As we shall see, in Bologna this wave of immigrant Chinese entrepreneurs saw them contributing towards the expansion of the "leather district" together with many small Italian entrepreneurs, and together they reaped the same benefits and faced the same challenges. In London, on the other hand, Chinese businessmen specialized in a niche/ethnic market strictly related to seafaring and to Chinese customers working on the ships (in the beginning at least). In both cities, Chinese immigrants chose activities with low barriers to entry.

After the Second World War, the influx of Chinese immigrants to the United Kingdom began to change. The vast majority of the Chinese coming to London had emigrated from the rural areas of Hong Kong. They took advantage of the ethnic niche related to the restaurant and catering business. However, by the end of the last millennium, the Chinese in Britain had not entered all areas of the labour market for various reasons, but tended to be "segregated" in the catering business in the main (Pang 1996;; Pang and Lau 1998).

In the case of Bologna, large influxes of Chinese immigrants began only in the 1990s as a consequence of the aforesaid Open Door policy. They set up many family businesses in the buoyant service sector. However, they also engaged in the labour intensive manufacturing sector. In this case they followed the pattern of "ecological succession" whereby openings for ethnic businesses emerge when the existing native business group no longer reproduces itself fast enough, thus creating opportunities for nascent immigrant entrepreneurs (Aldrich 1975). Indeed, in the Italian case Chinese immigrants took over shops and small firms sold by their former owners, and strived to generate whatever marginal profit there was left.[2]

The third wave of Chinese immigrants has since strengthened the similarities between the two entrepreneurial communities, which showed a growing interest in services. This is partly because barriers to entry into this sector are generally low, and little start-up capital is required.

In conclusion, we found that there were some striking differences between the Chinese communities that have settled and developed in Bologna and London, such as their business specialization and economic integration process. However, they also shared a number of similar characteristics such as the role played by the family and the community and the preference for sectors with low barriers to entry.

Chinese immigrant entrepreneurs in Bologna: from the creation of a leather and leatherette district to the development of the service sector

The Chinese in Italy arrived in three different waves of immigration. The first "wave" (1850–1915) actually saw just a few people move to Italy from China: students and priests studying and teaching at the Chinese college in Naples, diplomats and their families based in Rome, and a few sailors. Moreover, economic and diplomatic relations between the two countries remained rather scant up until the First World War (Battilani and Fauri 2018; Strangio 2020). In 1869, when the Suez Canal opened, for the first time the Italian ports became popular for ships sailing from Europe to the Far East. However, the Italian shipping companies only started scheduled services in the 1880s (Lloyd Triestino introduced regular services to Singapore and Hong Kong in 1880, and to Shanghai in 1881). The first permanent Chinese delegation did not settle in Italy until 1902. Thus it is no surprise to find that according to the 1911 Italian Population Census, only 39 Chinese men and six Chinese women lived in Italy at that time. Of these, only 20 had been in the country for more than three months.

The second wave of immigration occurred during the interwar period, when a moderate number of Chinese economic migrants arrived from France, from England, along the Trans-Siberian route and through the ports of Genoa and Venice. They spread throughout Italy, working as street vendors of ties and fake pearls. Their presence started to be noticed as from 1926 in various different cities (Milan, Turin, Bologna and Ancona), although their numbers never exceeded a few hundred. According to the Population Census, they numbered 331 in 1931 and 531 in 1936. With 77 Chinese in 1931, and 175 in 1936,[3] Milan had the largest such community in Italy, and the city soon became a reference point as well as a required stopover for most Chinese immigrants (Cologna 1997; 2005; 2014).

The third and most recent wave started in the 1990s and followed the introduction of the Open Door policy by Deng Xiao Ping. This wave was much larger than the previous two, as you can see in Table 6.1. Chinese communities spread throughout Italy, starting a number of different businesses ranging from manufacturing to service provision. Since the 1920s Milan has had the largest Chinese community in Italy, and up until the 1990s Bologna was ranked second.

Bologna is a medium-sized city less than 200 kilometres from Milan. During the twentieth century she developed as a centre for mechanical engineering and cooperative enterprise, becoming one of the richest metropolitan areas in Italy. Since the interwar years, and above all after the Second World War, Bologna has witnessed the flourishing of many small and medium-sized enterprises specializing in the production of machinery and other mechanical items constituting the backbone of its economic fabric. In the favourable economic context of post-war Italy, enterprises specializing in food processing, leather goods and clothing were also successful. With the addition

Table 6.1 Chinese immigrants living in Bologna, Milan and Italy as a whole (1911–2015)

Year	*Bologna*	*Milan*	*Italy*
1911	0	4	45
1921	0	3	164
1931	3	77 (100)	331
1936	8	175 (300)	531
1951	40*	300*	2,046
1961	80*	400*	
1971	200*	277	2,133
1981	170*	194	1,494
1986	219	580	4,466
1991	400	983	7,585
2001	1,404	10,296	46,887
2006	1,995	14,039	144,885
2011	2,861	20,852	209,934
2015	3,389	28,360	265,820

Source: The Municipal Registry Offices of Milan (1979–2015) and Bologna (1986–2015); Population Census (1911–1981); Istat (1961–2015).

*Our estimate is based on the number of Chinese family identified by different sources.

to the aforementioned small and medium-sized companies, Bologna saw the growth of cooperative enterprises that were to become the second pillar of the city's enduring economic structure.

The city could count on solid institutions, a shared work ethic, the informal transmission of knowledge and educational institutions deeply entrenched in the urban fabric (the university and many technical colleges). Bologna also enjoys considerable political stability: left-wing parties have governed the city from 1945 to the present, except for one short period between 1999 and 2004. In keeping with this political orientation, the city has promoted an image of itself based on the idea of social mobility and cohesiveness. In a nutshell, all the factors characterizing the industrial district model found fertile ground and enabled the completion of industrialization (Battilani 2020). Chinese immigration to Bologna took shape in this context. In this section we shall analyse this immigration using Chamber of Commerce and Municipal archival material in addition to oral history field work we ourselves have carried out. Twenty-five interviews were conducted with descendants of the first migrants, and with others who arrived in Bologna on subsequent waves of immigration.[4]

The second wave of immigration and the building of Bologna's Chinese community

No Chinese settled in Bologna during the first wave of migration to Italy, when only diplomats, students and sailors came and went. The original Chinese community only started to take shape at the end of the 1930s, with the second wave of immigration. According to the local newspapers, Chinese people first appeared in the city as street vendors, specialized in fake pearls, in 1926 (Corriere della Sera 1926). Later, they regularized their status by obtaining trading licenses, as witnessed by the Municipal archive's documentation.[5]

The immigrants of the second wave had a number of things in common. They all came from the province of Wenzhou, leaving their villages at a young age (between 16 and 25).[6] In general, their parents were peasant farmers and their departure was part of an overall strategy designed to increase the family's wealth and aimed at providing a source of investment for the farm's activities. In this context, the departure of certain sons was expected to lead to improvements in the living standards of the family as a whole.[7] This explains the endurance of family ties over the decades and the persistence of remittances, even when migrants never returned home. The help given to all relatives emigrating from China, regardless of their degree of kinship, bears witness to the strength of such kinship. The majority of these migrants spoke the Cingtian dialect and were illiterate, and therefore the ones who had been to primary school and could speak Mandarin became a reference point for the migrant community, as they could help others write letters, fill in applications, and so on.[8]

In Bologna, the first Chinese-Italian marriage was celebrated in 1938, two months before the introduction of the Fascist racial laws prohibiting mixed marriages. At the beginning of the 1940s the Chinese community comprised six Chinese-Italian couples (although some of them were not officially married), three of which had children, and 10 to 15 young men.[9] In Bologna, as elsewhere, street vendors soon rose up the value chain, and started to manufacture silk ties and leatherette bags in small workshops in the city. By 1942, there were ten such families according to the Bologna Chamber of Commerce's records. At that time, Italy had already signed the Tripartite Pact (27 September 1940) making China one of its enemies. As a consequence, about 147 Chinese, most of whom were unmarried, were placed in internment camps.[10] However, they were released in September 1943 following Italy's change of military alliance. From then on, the Chinese living in Italy shared the wartime experiences of the rest of the Italian population.[11] They were evacuated to avoid Allied bombings, and were sent to prison charged with conspiracy against the occupying government; however, there is no evidence that they were involved in the partisan movement.[12]

Economic recovery after the war was not an easy time, and consequently many Chinese took the opportunity offered by the UNRRA refugee programme to return home to China in 1946. Also some Cino-Italian families based in Bologna returned home. However, Bologna's Chinese community continued to exist, and by the mid-1950s it comprised at least 15 men and ten families, three of whom had come back from China after Mao Tse Tung came to power.[13]

During the 1950s, the Italian economy rapidly moved through a phase in its development that has since been called the Economic Miracle. Bologna's involvement in this 'economic miracle' consisted principally in the development of a variety of engineering companies and the flourishing of leather and clothing workshops. At that time, Chinese immigrants became part of the larger artisan community prospering in the city, and continued to specialize in the production and sale of leatherette bags. It is no coincidence that it was Tong Ling Sin, a Chinese immigrant who had arrived in Italy in the 1930s, who became the leather workshops' representative in Bologna's post-war Crafts Association in 1946 (Brini 1978). Due to the success of the first immigrants, others decided to settle in the area. Many came directly from China through the immigration chain. As a rule, brothers, nephews, sons or fathers came to Italy to be reunited with other family members already working and residing in the country. Until the mid-1960s, very few Chinese women arrived in Italy. The newcomers were welcomed by their relatives, and the entire community helped them set up their own businesses, which usually consisted of bag-manufacturing workshops. The community network provided the basic knowledge, and lent the capital, required to start up a workshop. This would explain why all of these immigrants entered the same business sector. The community had accumulated skills, expertise and contacts in the bag-manufacturing industry, which could then be shared with newcomers. Interestingly, each separate family set up its own workshop. When sons married, they left their father's workshop to set up their own businesses. In this way, each company usually remained relatively small.[14]

Chinese workshops were part of a larger leather and leatherette district which had developed in Bologna after the Second World War, and which included Italian craftsmen and women too, of course. The production system mainly comprised home workers who were usually women living either in the city itself or in the surrounding countryside. The larger workshops usually relied upon a network of salesmen travelling all over Italy, while the smaller ones sold their products to wholesalers. In the late 1960s, this district comprised some 300 workshops and small enterprises; at least 70 of them were run by Chinese immigrants.[15]

During the 1960s, some of these businesses grew in size. One of the most important such companies was the Umberto Sun Company which exported to other European countries and to Asia. In the 1970s, more Chinese enterprises were able to export, including "Asia" (owned by Tchen Chih Kuang), "Walmoda" (owned by Wu Manuela, Lin Sergio and Tse Chiu Hing Daniel) and "Orientale" (owned by Tong Long Sin).[16]

However, no Chinese entrepreneur was able to develop national brands. During the last two decades of the twentieth century, a number of Bologna-born entrepreneurs from the bag district became very active in the national market through their own brands: Mandarina Duck (set up in 1977), Furla (in 1927) and Borbonese (dating back to the 1950s). Their success was largely due to innovative communication strategies focusing on the creation of a recognizable style and a public image of glamour, charm and elegance. Despite the fact that some Chinese entrepreneurs registered their brands, none of them made the required investment in design and advertising to guarantee a share of the national market.[17]

From the late 1970s onwards, bag manufacturing became increasingly less economically viable. National brands had increased their market shares, while the room for local production had shrunk. In this context, many Chinese entrepreneurs shifted their specialization: some moved up the production chain and became wholesalers of raw materials (for both the fashion and furniture industries), while others changed sector completely as we will see in the next section.

The first generation of Chinese entrepreneurs managed their businesses by developing Chinese-Italian networks within Italy. Bologna's Chinese community has close relations with Milan, Rome and Florence.[18] Until 1971, the lack of diplomatic relations between Italy and the People Republic of China made it impossible to implement transnational business strategies. Even when the Chinese immigrants' companies started to export their products, they were never able to build privileged business relations with the home country. Furthermore, having supported the Kuomintang (the Chinese Nationalist Party), most migrants obtained Taiwanese passports after Mao Tse Tung's rise to power, even if their original families lived in mainland

China. Therefore, the transnational ties of immigrants were based more on kinship than on national identity. They kept sending remittances to China for a long time, and continued to welcome and help relatives arriving in Italy or elsewhere in Europe. However, these connections never went beyond the private sphere in the form of transnational business. Travel to the People's Republic was almost impossible for them, not to mention dangerous. None of them managed to do so before they reached their old age, that is, following Deng Xiao Ping's launch of the Open Door policy. Travelling to Taiwan was easier, and prominent members of the Chinese community, such as Umberto Sun (Sun Chin Yen Lin) went there frequently.

> Every year [my father] went to Taiwan for a month [...]. Chiang Kai-shek's son was still there.[19] I met him when I went along with my father. It was between December 1968 and January 1969. It was the only time I went there. [My father] attended a sort of refresher course.[20]

In Bologna, the Chinese immigrants recognized Umberto Sun (Sun Chin Yen Lin) as a key figure who managed public relations with Bologna's municipal authorities and with Taiwanese representatives in Italy, on behalf of the entire community. He was an eclectic entrepreneur who arrived in Bologna in 1937 as a street vendor, and then went on to set up his own workshop four years later. After the war he married an Italian woman he met after they had both been evacuated. In 1958, while his wife and two sisters-in-law successfully ran the workshop, he set up a company delivering gas cylinders to people's homes, and then in 1968 he bought a building in the hills near Bologna which was eventually converted into a poultry farm, once again run by his wife. In 1970 he opened the first Chinese restaurant in Bologna (Chamber of Commerce Archive). Designed for an Italian clientele, the restaurant's food was a combination of Chinese and Italian cuisine. Finally in 1978 he set up a company that specialized in traditional Chinese medicine (Chamber of Commerce Archives).

Despite his political connections with Taiwan, Umberto Sun never developed any real international business operations. The only enterprise which was the result of his travels to Taiwan was the medical treatment centre. However, in 1983 he set up a small import-export company with the aim of providing supplies to Chinese restaurants. At that time China had already modified its stance towards Western countries.

In conclusion, from the end of the Second World War to the 1970s, the first generation (of the second wave) of Chinese immigrants set up several family businesses producing leatherette bags, all of which were fully integrated into the local economic fabric. At first, Chinese workshops and homes were situated in the city centre, basically along four streets. Then from the 1960s on, most of them moved to the immediately surrounding area in the northern part of the City (the *Bolognina* district), where a recreational facility was also set up (the "China Club") around 1960–1961.

This centre became the meeting place for Chinese immigrants and their families on occasion of important celebrations such as the Chinese New Year, marriages and the likes.[21] The centre also had facilities for the preparation of Chinese food.

> There was a beautiful kitchen where they cooked everything, so that even before the first Chinese restaurant had opened we ate Chinese food there, at the China Club.[22]

Although they constituted a cohesive community, the Chinese did not form an enclave. We must not forget that most were Chinese-Italian families in which the wives had, and maintained, links with the local community. Many Italians continued to live in the neighbourhood where the Chinese immigrants were concentrated. No Chinatown took shape. Moreover, the production chain was of a Chinese-Italian character. First of all, they bought the raw materials, and sold their products, through the same wholesale companies[23] that provided their services to Italian entrepreneurs. Secondly, the home workers, together with part of the factory workers, were Italian. Between the 1950s and 1970s, Chinese immigration to Bologna was one of social and economic integration.

The third wave of Chinese immigration to Bologna and the coexistence of several generations

In the 1980s, the ties among Chinese immigrants became weaker. The second generation of the second wave of immigrants was completely integrated into the social and economic fabric of the city, and had developed its own relationships. This generation did not speak Mandarin and had little knowledge of Chinese culture. Very few of them continued their parents' businesses; some had the opportunity to go to university and subsequently built careers as white-collar workers.

From the late 1980s, the increasing openness of the Chinese economy fostered immigration flows to Italy which grew in size. The newcomers were literate and had grown up in Communist China. On the whole they preferred not to join the existing Chinese associations because of their different political views from those of the original immigrants (the latter were Nationalist Chinese connected to Taiwan).

During the third wave of immigration, Milan remained the preferred destination of the majority of such Chinese immigrants, followed by the province of Florence (and particularly the city of Prato where an important textile and fashion district developed). Bologna became one of the many Italian cities with a significant presence of Chinese immigrants.

Also in Bologna the newcomers had little in common with the previous ones except for the desire to look for better employment. They never joined the China Club, which closed down in the 1970s.[24] Gradually the (Chinese)

Table 6.2 Percentage of Chinese-born entrepreneurs per sector of activity in the province of Bologna in 2014

	Entrepreneurs born in China	*Total entrepreneurs*	*% born in China*
Agriculture, fishing and forestry	2	11,768	0.0%
Food processing and beverages	2	1,582	0.1%
Textiles, fashion-wear and leather	**364**	1,349	**27.0%**
Mechanical engineering	14	9,532	0.1%
Other manufacturing activities	3	5,511	0.1%
Utilities	0	747	0.0%
Building	10	15,560	0.1%
Wholesaling and retailing	**375**	28,629	**1.3%**
Transport	1	4,979	0.0%
Catering	**536**	7,314	**7.3%**
Real estate	20	13,555	0.1%
Services to people	116	3,608	**3.2%**
Architectural firms	9	978	0.9%
Sporting and recreational activities	10	822	**1.2%**
Other services	48	24,905	0.2%

Source: Bologna Chamber of Commerce, List of registered enterprises in 2014.

Evangelical Churches became the new meeting places for the Chinese community, where activities for children and youngsters were organized, along somewhat similar lines to the Italian Catholic Parish Centres.[25] Newcomers were also fairly active in setting up new types of association, such as Associna which promotes the Chinese-Italian identity and the exchange of the knowledge gathered over time by its members.[26]

Despite the many differences in their social and political attitudes, newcomers displayed a similar propensity for work and entrepreneurship. At the time of the third wave of immigration, Bologna's economy was going through a process of partial de-industrialization, moving away from manufacturing towards the service sector. Only mechanical engineering continued to play a pivotal role in the local economy: the area is still referred to today as 'packaging valley'. In other sectors, many businesses closed down or moved operations to countries with lower labour costs. Chinese entrepreneurs never became active in the mechanical engineering sector, but continued to set up clothing and leather companies, whereas few Italian entrepreneurs continued to operate in these industries, as can be seen from Table 6.2.

> In 1990, my grandparents arrived in Italy and started to produce clothes [...]. I came to Bologna in 1998 when I was 10 years old. My parents were already here [...]. They made women's clothes [...]. I went to school until the age of 18 [...]. Then the mechanical engineering company where I had done my internship closed, so I went to work with my father. We didn't think about selling up. Customers arrive directly [...] from Bologna and

> the surrounding areas. They are Italian. Now I'm helping in my Mum's workshop ... one day I will set up my own [...]. Usually Mum does everything in the workshop [...]. Customers give us the final models and the pieces already cut to size, and we have to sew them together according to the customers' instructions [...]. There are about 10 employees who never change. The one who has been with us for the least length of time has been here 5 years. In many cases, husband and wife work together. It works better with couples. We prefer hiring couples.[27]

However, some of the new arrivals found work in the service sector, as barkeepers, retailers, wholesalers, hairdressers. These new areas of employment reflected the transition of Bologna's economy towards the service industry.

> My uncle was in Crespellano (in the province of Bologna). My parents came to Italy around 2000, when I was 7-8 years old ... to work with my uncle who ran a bag workshop. Then he closed it to open a bar.[28]
>
> I arrived in Italy when I was 18 (in 1993). I had relatives here ... in Prato where I stayed for two years. I worked in a firm producing clothes [...]. I came to Bologna to work as a waitress at the Golden Dragon [a Chinese restaurant] [...]. Then I worked in a nursing home, then at McDonald's. Then I started my own business as a street vendor, which I did for less than three years [...]. Little by little I put aside some savings. I was lucky, It does not take much money to start this business. To open a restaurant would have been much more expensive. Then I decided to leave this job to be a wholesaler. If you know the right people you can move into this sector, where the work is less tiring. I originally had a warehouse, but I had a lot of expenses and then I closed everything. Now I show customers a sample, if they like it, I have it made and delivered.[29]

The move towards the service sector involved not only new immigrants but also some of those entrepreneurs who had arrived during the second wave of Chinese immigration to Italy. As mentioned before, since the 1980s many bag manufacturers have closed down their businesses and moved toward the service sector. Of the first five Chinese restaurants opened in Bologna between 1970 and 1983, four were set up by entrepreneurs coming from the leather sector and with no previous catering experience.[30] Other Chinese entrepreneurs set up food shops or travel agencies.[31]

> Yes, we all worked in the bag workshop, which remained in operation until 1989. Then the whole family moved to Rome to open a restaurant [...]. Instead, I remained in Bologna. I worked as an interpreter and tour guide. Then for two years I ran a restaurant in Mestre. After that I returned to Bologna again where in 1998 I opened a travel agency.[32]

A group of bag producers moved up the value chain and set up import-export companies: Umberto Sun set up a new import-export undertaking in 1983, while Dick Ting started to work in Hong Kong on behalf of Italian clients looking for buyers for their products. After a trip to Taiwan in 1982, Wu King Mascarino returned to Italy with the intention of starting a business importing and exporting Chinese goods.[33] Some of them started to work with mechanical engineering companies in Bologna, selling equipment in China.

At that time the transnational network of Chinese immigrants became a genuine, invaluable asset. Their ability to speak both Italian and Chinese, and to manage a dual network of contacts, enabled them to set up new businesses.

> I closed down my firm and started up a new business [...]. My new activity originated from the fact that Italian companies had asked me to accompany them to China [...]. China was a really closed country. I went. This experience gave me the idea of representing Italian companies in China, in the regions where I could count on my own contacts ... Northern and Central China. I never went to the South.[34]
>
> In 1988-1989 [my father] got the first contracts. He sold industrial equipment. I remember a plant designed to produce coagulated and coated fabrics. The whole plant [...]. He also sent engineers and specialists there. This was his job until 1995. All kinds of industrial equipment.[35]

During the 1990s, Chinese companies (based in China) started to export the products processed by the industrial equipment they had imported in previous years.

> Having sold industrial equipment to produce synthetic fabric and imitation leather in China, my father really understood that world [...]. All our China-based suppliers were of Italian origin [they derived from the first Italian companies set up there]. Then people working there started their own businesses. Now there are many companies producing leatherette in China. Most of them are quite small. We work with the top companies in order to guarantee high-quality products to our customers.[36]

Their prices were very competitive. The Italian companies stopped buying from the traditional wholesalers and tried to get materials directly from China. As a consequence, the Italian wholesalers who had traditionally supplied Bologna's leatherette district, were crowded out by a new generation of import-export companies, and one by one they closed down.

> Many of my Chinese clients who used to produce bags subsequently became wholesalers. They bought the synthetic fabrics directly from

> China and there was no longer any room for us [the Italian traditional wholesalers]. I lost a lot of money. Suddenly no one bought my products any longer.[37]

In conclusion, the history of Bologna's Chinese immigrants is characterized by an important change which took place during the 1980s and 1990s: the newcomers had grown up in Communist China and had a different cultural and political background; foreign relations between Italy and the People's Republic of China had greatly improved, and consequently travelling became easier, as did the development of transnational businesses. Bologna was de-industrializing, and new opportunities for immigrants emerged in the service sector as well as in the declining manufacturing sectors which local entrepreneurs no longer intended to invest in. Despite these changes, Chinese immigrants continued to display a strong propensity towards entrepreneurship: during the second wave of immigration, they focused on the emerging labour intensive industries; the third wave of immigrants, on the other hand, invested in the services as well as in traditional manufacturing industry that local entrepreneurs no longer saw as an attractive prospect for investment.

Chinese immigrant entrepreneurs in London: from seafaring to the catering trade

The first wave of immigration. The history of the Chinese in Britain is characterized by various different waves of immigration and the diverse entrepreneurial activities they have engaged in. The first Chinese workers to reach British shores were hired to replace British sailors sent to fight in the Napoleonic Wars. In the following decades, most of the Chinese who decided to stay behind were transient sailors working on British vessels. Shipping companies like Blue Funnel were achieving economies by employing Chinese crews in the Far Eastern trade, despite the fact that "a legitimate concern for jobs" resulted in "anti-alien" attitudes developing among the British.[38] The early sailors came from Siyi and other parts of China's Guandong province, and built strong Siyi immigration chains (the Siyi region's economy and society was substantially shaped and sustained by remittances from these early migrants). As from 1885, Limehouse in London's Tower Hamlets borough became a point of disembarkation for Chinese seamen, and became the city's first 'Chinatown'. Those that left seafaring went into the laundry and restaurant (or café) business, and interestingly they seem to have brought with them certain methods of management and laundering originally developed by Chinese immigrants in the United States, thus representing an early form of transnational exchange (Benton 2003). The occupations of Chinese men in England in 1911 can be broken down as follows: 49 per cent were employed in the merchant navy, 36 per cent in (348) laundries, and 10 per cent in the retail business (including cooks and waiters) (1911 Census).

The Chinese presence in London grew quickly. Ng Kwee Choo estimates that by 1913 Limehouse contained about 30 Chinese shops and restaurants which had sprung up to serve a floating Chinese population of between 300 and 400, depending on which ships were docked. Most immigrants at the time planned to return to China, although some married English women and brought up families. However, apparently Chinese/English couples had little in common, cultural barriers were enormous, and they had no rapport with each other's social groups, and consequently "mistrust divided them". Furthermore, English wives were "women with an emotionally and financially insecure background, or social outcasts who will only marry a Chinese with money" (Ng Kwee Choo 1968: 27–28). On the other hand, local police reports of the time underlined that "Chinamen treat women well, they are sober, they do not beat their wives ... they represent no threat to public order".[39] Many official reports were noticeably lacking in accounts of any manifestation of hostility to the Chinese from the communities in which they lived, Chinese were "mostly unobtrusive and respectable" although their presence was becoming a problem because the "suspicion lingered of an active Chinese underworld of crime associated with drugs-dealing and protection rackets".[40]

Business activities were fostered by the isolation of the Chinese in London: scant knowledge of English meant that once they had settled in Limehouse, the Chinese tended to work exclusively within their own immigrant community. "Shops selling Chinese ingredients served the Chinese restaurants which served overseas Chinese which in turn gave Chinese-specific employment to the Chinese community".[41] However, the laundry business soon expanded outside Limehouse and by the First World War there were Chinese laundries all over London; this led the journalists of the time to write of a Chinese "industrial invasion" (Seed 2006: 72). They started "springing up like mushrooms" as from 1891, and by 1911 "this expansion appeared especially injurious to the native poor since it displaced female labour of widows or the wives of labourers who customarily took in washing to supplement miserable incomes".[42]

The growth of a real Chinese community in Limehouse was accompanied by the establishment of certain facilities such as Chinese social clubs and schools, and (illicit) gambling dens. As in the case of Bologna, the associations founded here by pre-1930s immigrants were politically aligned with the Kuomintang, and similarly they represented important meeting places for the local ethnic community.[43] The privately-funded Chung Hwa Chinese School opened in Pennyfields in 1925 thanks to Irene Cheng's father who donated £500 for the purchase of the building located at 35 Pennyfields to be used as a clubhouse for the children of the Chinese Community in East London.[44] The Oi T'ung Association was founded within the East End Chinese Community in 1907, with the aim of organizing overseas Chinese so that they could help one another. The association (with a fee) sought to maintain harmony within the community by encouraging its members to refer any internal business disputes or violence to the Association for investigation at a specially convened meeting. The Chinese club also provided healthcare services to its members (including funeral arrangements), and provided meals as well as gambling facilities where Chinese immigrants played mah jong, p'ai-kau (dominoes) and also pak kap piu, a lottery game.[45]

Another business that the Chinese seamen introduced to London was the opium trade. However, in around the year 1900, police opinion on the Chinese bore a clear lack of concern about opium dealing and smoking. In 1906 police found that: "Opium smoking is no doubt common amongst them, but it amounts to no offence against the law and no crimes due to it have come to the knowledge of the police". In those days, the racial character and perceived racial characteristics of the Chinese were of little concern to the majority of Britons amongst whom they lived and worked, and their habits were of no significant concern for the authorities.[46] The "Chinese opium-dens and gambling hells" in the East End of London were a Chinese problem: they were chiefly frequented by members of the Asiatic crews of ships discharging cargo in the East and West India Docks.[47] However, two scandals shone the spotlight on Chinatown in the autumn of 1918, when a prosperous shipping merchant died of an opium overdose and an actress, Billie Carleton, was found dead of cocaine poisoning in her Savoy Hotel suite. Connections to Chinatown were made, and newspaper headlines spread the fear of a "Yellow peril in London" (Seed 2006: 70). The Chinese in London started attracting considerable, hostile press attention. Chinatown quickly became notorious for its opium dens and for the fact that the police

> are rarely successful in laying hands on the paraphernalia of the trade ... Most of the opium that comes into this country is smuggled thorough the bilges and engine-rooms of cargo ships. A piece of the size of a walnut will sell for £25 to 30 ... Amazing fortunes have been amassed by Chinamen in this illicit trade.[48]

Chinatown opium dens had become quite popular among the English population too, and the newspapers often reported deaths from opium and morphine injections not only in Limehouse, but also elsewhere. Letters of complaint to the local newspaper were common during and after the First World War: "Can our borough council do nothing against this evil? It seems we are drawing near to a time when these foreigners will take absolute command of this locality".[49]

This form of Chinese business was about to end. In 1926 Arnold Palmer wrote the following in the Sphere:

> Chinatown population in 18 months has dropped from 2,000 to less than half that number, it is a result of successful efforts by the police to make life there a little duller. The good old days of the (opium) business are over. Those who remain are excellent citizens, good husbands to their English wives.[50]

Two years later, another journalist was complaining that Chinatown was now "so unromantic"; not only opium, but also fireworks, had in fact been banned.[51] The ensuing 1929 crisis soon transformed Limehouse into an isolated and declining Chinese community: the slump in shipping entering the London Docks was "killing the Chinese population" according to a local café owner. Chinese people started to leave Limehouse, and the new immigrants arriving in London settled in other parts of London. In 1951 Peter Fryer of the *Daily Worker* found just a few cafés (8) and laundries, some Chinese seamen and a fairly impoverished population of 50 resident families (a quarter of what it had been before the 1940 Blitz, the German bombing raids on London). Data confirm the redistribution of the Chinese population away from Limehouse to other parts of London (See Table 6.3).

In general, the Chinese population was extremely small throughout the period in question: before the First World War it numbered 0.5 per cent of the entire foreign-born population of Britain, and by the 1930s this figure had only reached 1 per cent. Just to give an idea of the limited entity of Chinese immigration, in 1931 there were 1,194 Chinese, but 11,000 Italians, living in the UK.

The second wave of immigration and the role played by Britain's colonial ties. From the 1950s onwards a different kind of Chinatown began to develop in London, this time in the West End around Soho's Gerrard Street. A new generation of post-war Chinese immigrants typically from Hong Kong settled here (Seed 2006). This second wave of immigrants mostly went into the restaurant and catering business, and a few also into the importing of Chinese foods.[52] After the Second World War, a multitude of inexpensive Chinese restaurants were established in the area: English people began to eat out in Soho, while colonial officers had acquired a liking for Chinese food. At the beginning these restaurants mainly served the local community; however, the owners soon saw the opportunity of serving customers from beyond the local Chinese community, including members of the "white" community (Chaudhry and Crick 2004). By 1961 London had 150 Chinese

Table 6.3 Chinese in London, 1881–1931

	London	*Limehouse*
1881	109	70
1891	302	82
1901	120	55
1911	247	101
1921	711	337
1931	1,194	167
1951	1,350 (586 from HK)	
1961	2,784 (1866 from HK)	

Source: Census reports – HK: Hong Kong.

restaurants, and that same year the Association of Chinese Restaurateurs was founded (Ng Kwee Choo 1968).

In the words of Gomez and Cheung (2009: 136):

> The burgeoning food catering business, which led to a demand for labour in the industry, contributed to a rise in Chinese migration from Hong Kong to Britain. A number of other factors encouraged Chinese migration to the UK after the War, including the Sino-Japanese war, the internal strife that led the Communist Party to power, as well as the Cultural Revolution. The takeover of mainland China by the Communist Party in 1949 had led to a large influx of refugees into Hong Kong, then a British colony. While Hong Kong's population was 600,000 in 1945, it was well over two million by 1951, inevitably resulting in severe socio-economic problems. Since the Commonwealth Act facilitated the entry of members of the Commonwealth into Britain, this country became another venue for Chinese migrants from Hong Kong. Compared to the approximately 1,900 ethnic Chinese in the UK in 1931, this community's estimated population by the early 1970s was at least 96,000.

Hong Kong Commonwealth citizens were allowed to enter England freely until 1962. In November 1961 a worried telegram from the UK representative in Hong Kong to the Secretary of State for the colonies emphasized the fact that there was "a steady stream of indigenous New Territories[53] villagers who go to Britain principally to enter the Chinese restaurant business". These villagers had a "tradition of taking overseas employment" and their remittances had brought a modest degree of prosperity to many otherwise poor rural areas of China. The UK representative wanted clarification regarding the upcoming legislation which would make it necessary to obtain entry vouchers to access the British market, but which were to be granted freely "to any Hong Kong applicant who can show that employment awaits him in a Chinese restaurant".[54]

In 1962, the Commonwealth Immigration Act established a system of employment vouchers to be issued by the Ministry of Labour, which in effect conferred a right of settlement on the voucher holder. In 1965 the number of vouchers was reduced from over 30,000 to just 6,500 a year. Finally, as from 1973 Commonwealth citizens definitively lost their preferential treatment and were admitted to England subject to the same condition that had always applied to aliens (i.e. for a maximum initial period of 12 months only).[55] Indeed, the 1962 restrictions required each Commonwealth immigrant to have a job waiting for him/her upon arrival in the UK; however, this clause did not discourage immigration, and indeed had the opposing effect, precipitating "a beat-the-ban rush of immigrants from India, Pakistan and the West Indies and Hong Kong into Britain ... Between 1962 and 1966 the number of Chinese dependants and relatives arriving from Hong Kong – wives, children, elderly parents - rose almost tenfold".[56] They took advantage of opportunities to circumvent restrictions by bringing dependants of Chinese immigrants into the country. These dependants, usually the wives and children of the first Hong Kong migrants, were also a crucial source of labour for a number of Chinese who had left their employers to set up their own businesses (Gomez and Cheung 2009).

They were mostly involved in catering with the ensuing – worrying – characteristics underlined by a House of Common report: a geographical dispersal of the Chinese population (reinforcing isolation); lack of English and difficulties in acquiring it (meaning ignorance of British law and welfare services); a preference for self-help and mutual aid and a reluctance to complain: "The family (extended) is the basic unit and the focus of loyalty to a much greater extent in British society as a whole. Strengthening the preference for self-help is the traditional Chinese suspicion of authority" (House of Commons 1985).

Soon after, the 1986 Report of the Commission on Racial Equality portrayed a similar picture. The vast majority of the Chinese living in England had emigrated from the rural areas of Hong Kong, were (still) not literate in English, and formed a tight, isolated community whose fulcrum was the family. After the head of the family had migrated, the other members of the family joined him at a later stage when he had saved enough money to start his own business, usually in the catering trade: "The whole family was thus transformed into an economic unit and its members, especially women and children received an allowance from the income of the catering business as distinct from wages. To run a catering business successfully the entire family must be involved. The commitment to family business becomes so overwhelming that youths find little or no time for their studies".[57]

As a matter of fact, the wide dispersal of the Chinese is a reflection of their concentration in a single area of economic activity, namely the Chinese restaurant, take-away or catering business, which was virtually ubiquitous as early as the 1970s (Watson 1977). Figure 6.4 confirms the importance of the food and catering trade in the years thereafter as well, when a third wave of immigrants from Southeast China settled in the UK, and started working not only in the hotel and restaurant sector, but also in the wholesale and retail trade as well.

The third wave of immigration and the increase in the number of Chinese from Mainland China. The third wave of immigration to London from China commenced in the mid-1980s, and coincided with the Chinese government relaxing restrictions on emigration (as happened in the case of Italy). A sizeable proportion of Chinese immigrants came from Fujian province in southeast China, whereas the numbers of Hong Kong immigrants started to fall. Before entry visa applications (of all types) for 2011 show that China, with 283,008 applications (ranked second to India) while Hong Kong generated

Table 6.4 Chinese businesses in 2001

	Hotel and restaurants	*Wholesale and retail trade*	*Manufacturing*	*Transport and communication*
Outer London	4,356	2,707	33	16
Inner London	2,979	2,114	69	34

Source: Census reports – HK: Hong Kong.

only 8,574 applications. The 2011 census showed 98,724 people from Hong Kong were living in the UK, out of a total of 393,391 Chinese people (of whom 124,250 were living in London). Quite interestingly, despite a shift in their geographical origins from the mid-1980s on, and despite the growing numbers of well-educated Chinese from South East Asia and Hong Kong emigrating to the UK, a great many Chinese remained "trapped in the traditional catering trade despite their expressed aspirations for top professional jobs" (cit. Chen 1995; Eade 2000; Barrett and McEvoy 2005; Spaan 2005).

Recent studies based on empirical analyses of the business practices of Chinese restaurants operating in the UK, have indicated that almost all entrepreneurs think self-employment to be the obvious way forward given the discrimination in the labour market and the resulting high unemployment rates among minority communities in general (Chandhry and Crim 2004). A study of small-scale Chinese entrepreneurs in London has found evidence that Chinese EMSBs (ethnic minority small businesses) have remained within their ethnic networks rather than breaking out into the mainstream system and embedding themselves in the wider opportunity structure. These findings also reveal that Chinese-owned EMSBs are more entrepreneurially oriented and more likely to pursue growth through acquiring additional business premises (Wang and Altinay 2010).

Gomez argues that there is little or no indication of intra-ethnic or interlocking business ties among firms in the food chain. Major differences exist among ethnic Chinese, including sub-ethnic differences, period of migration to the UK, and divisions based on social class. Indeed, these firms compete ferociously with each other. They have purposefully distanced themselves from one another because of this competition, a reason for the community's highly dispersed nature. What emerges is that while there is a clear attempt to develop these firms as a family business

> there is little attempt by the owners to cooperate in terms of joint ownership or mergers … This review of the firms in the food distribution sector and the case studies reveal a heterogeneity of business styles among the owners of these firms, bringing into question a specific form of "ethnic enterprise" or "ethnic economy".
>
> (Gomez and Cheung 2009)

This study indicates that the most useful concepts when trying to understand Chinese enterprise include entrepreneurship and class resources, rather than ethnic enterprise (Wong 1985; Yang 1994; Yeung *et al.* 2000).

While the first Chinatown in Limehouse offered a good example of an enclave economy with a close-knit Chinese community developing mutual services, there is little evidence today that ethnic self-employment in the UK is the product of an enclave economy based on a shared language or culture, or the production of ethnic goods (Clark and Drinkwater 2002). The main aspiration is "to go it alone", which seems to apply to the case of the Chinese in Bologna as well.

Comparing the Chinese in Bologna and London: some final thoughts

Ethnic entrepreneurship has many facets, each revealing a partial truth, and is difficult to situate within a general theoretical framework, as it depends on too many human, geographical and historical factors. This is why the comparison between Chinese immigrant entrepreneurs in Bologna and London is enlightening, as it can help shed light on interesting differences and unexpected similarities between the two experiences.

How do migrants choose where to disembark?

Nowadays the standard neoclassical economic model of migration, according to which migration is predicted to occur when the expected net present value of earnings from migrating, weighted by the probability of employment in the destination country, is positive, has been supplanted by new economic theories of migration: these new theories perceive the probability of migrating to a country as positively dependent on the social networks linking the migrant to that country (Todaro, Moretti). Chinese migration to London and Bologna fits in with both visions. The high mobility of Chinese migrants throughout Europe seems to support the idea that in the end they settled where they expected to find better earning opportunities. Chinese migrants were attracted to London and Bologna not because of their particular inclinations or skills (Bonacich and Modell 1980; Wu and Zanin 2007), but because of the opening up of migration opportunities and the concrete possibilities of self-employment. This was true of the masses of Chinese arriving in London from Hong Kong and taking advantage of free entrance to the country as Commonwealth citizens, but it was also true of the Chinese migrating to Bologna.

The migration chain also plays a pivotal role, at least in determining the first place that third wave new migrants go to. There are two possible different interpretations of this role. According to some sociological studies, ethnic business development may evolve from racial disadvantages or denied opportunities that immigrants may turn to their advantage: e.g.

by transforming the difficulty in finding a good enough job into a propensity for self-employment. According to this cultural interpretation, migrants bring their cultural heritage, cluster in industries in which they can exploit the advantages connected with their ethnic group, and become successful entrepreneurs thanks to risk taking and opportunistic behaviour (Wah 2001; Santini, Rabino and Zanni 2011). In this way, the focus is on the benefits inherent to the migrant group. This pattern has been largely used to explain the entrepreneurial attitude of Chinese immigrants in a variety of countries including Italy and the UK. A second approach focuses on ethnicizing practices. In her book *City Making and Global Labour Regimes*, Antonella Ceccagno showed that the employment of workers from the same ethnic group is "a practice of employing co-nationals only in order to erase some factors that can hamper the inter-workshop organization of production and ultimately the swiftness of production and can therefore be conceptualized as compression of the workforce diversity in order to speed up production and guarantee increased profit" (Ceccagno 2017: 261).

The cultural explanation would seem to be pertinent in the case of London's first Chinatown, while the ethnicizing of the workforce describes the way Chinese business has developed since the 1930s in Bologna, and since the 1950s in London too. In the case of Bologna it is also clear that the first street vendors moved up the value chain during the 1930s, and started to produce ties and bags by chance. However, in doing so they accumulated skills that could be easily transmitted to newcomers after the Second World War, thus stimulating the emergence of a leatherette bag district in the city.

In both cases, the place where immigrants settled is characterized by the existence of ethnic or ethnicizing enterprises.

In which sectors do Chinese entrepreneurs focus their business operations?

Chinese entrepreneurs have interacted with the local economic fabric in different ways. Some studies suggest that Asian immigrant entrepreneurs have achieved success by operating in low growth or declining industrial sectors. They are clearly disadvantaged when it comes to starting up a business: they have little or no political power, and therefore limited access to resources, and they do not possess local linguistic skills or locally recognized qualifications (Pang and Lau 1998: 868). But rather than taking the low-paid jobs rejected by the local inhabitants and perhaps facing racism and discrimination in the wider labour market, they choose to become self-employed (Waldiger 1986; Aldricht 1975; Bates 1993), often engaging in a strategy of self-exploitation by working longer hours for lower prices (Ceccagno 2017; Battilani Fauri 2018).

As a matter of fact, Chinese entrepreneurs both in Bologna and London typically choose to set up business ventures in sectors with low barriers to entry, such as the restaurant, catering and laundry sectors in London, or the leather and leatherette manufacturing sector in Bologna in the 1950s.

However, in the case of Bologna, Chinese entrepreneurs were involved in the development of the leather district in a way that made it impossible to distinguish their enterprises from the Italian ones. They made a living from leather bag manufacturing, became part of a buoyant craft community and thrived during the years of the "economic miracle" as they took advantage of the increased demand for their goods. In England, on the other hand, Chinese immigrants specialized in a niche market at first – laundries and ethnic restaurants – which initially relied mainly on demand from sailors and fellow citizens embarked on ships. We would thus argue that the different levels/stages/characteristics of industrial development in Bologna and London had a different impact on the economic specialization of migrant entrepreneurs in the two cities.

Furthermore, the way they operated their businesses was strictly connected with the local traditions (and needs) of the destination country. So in Bologna they adopted the putting-out system, while in London they focused on small workshop operations linked to their ethnic enclave (Limehouse's Chinatown). In the case of the third wave of Chinese immigrants arriving after the opening up of the People's Republic of China, many went into the catering trade in London, whereas in Bologna the new incomers took up manufacturing spaces that were being vacated as a result of the crisis of the industrial sector, but also set up small businesses in the buoyant services sector (restaurants, bars, personal care services). In both cases, they tended to meet the needs of the destination area.

The role played by family and community

One important similarity between the two cases of London and Bologna concerns the role of the family, the importance of traditional Chinese cultural values, and the value given to personal connections and trust (Meyers 1989). In the words of Wong (1985), familism is the essence of Chinese economic organization: this equates to nepotism or preferential recruitment, the promotion of kin, a paternalistic idea of how superiors and subordinates should interact, and a strong emphasis on maintaining family ownership.[58]

Familism is a very important component of Chinese economic organization, and this clearly emerges in both the Bologna and London experiences of the Chinese community, where in the case of the first wave of immigrants the fulcrum of the community was the family, and the whole family was transformed into an economic unit in order to run a business successfully. However, the family was often the result of mixed marriages in both cases, while in the case of Bologna the first craft firms set up by Chinese immigrants also employed Italian workers (mainly women) in the production of leather goods. Consequently, more intercultural families initially characterized the presence of Chinese immigrants in Limehouse and Bologna. This first distinguishing feature was completely changed by the subsequent, much larger waves of immigration.

In addition to the key role played by the family, sociologists have also emphasized the role of the Chinese community. The ethnically cohesive Chinese community can provide the so-called 'ethnic advantage' in terms of ready access to start-up capital, a supply of cheap, dependable family or co-ethnic labour, assistance from immigrant institutions, and general respect for ethnic norms and values (Dana and Morris 2007; Chan 2012). However, the role of the ethnic community (or 'ethnic advantage') differs significantly between the two cases, in virtue of the historical periods in which Chinese immigrants arrived in these two cities, and of the type of business enterprises the immigrant entrepreneurs became involved in. While we can talk of a community in the case of Limehouse before the Second World War, and of Bologna in the 1950s and 1960s, nowadays this no longer seems to be the case.

In general, recent studies have confirmed that paternalistic family business structures still dominate overseas Chinese family undertakings, where the employment of co-ethnics and illegal immigrants is quite common (Jones et al. 2006). However, nowadays success is more a personal achievement based upon a relatively simple "personally managed" organization, often competing with similar businesses run by other Chinese (Chen 1995; Kao 1993; Carney 1998).There are also differences of course, but these can be better understood within a historical perspective.

In England, Chinese migration started earlier than it did in Italy, although in both countries prior to 1939 the small Chinese community came from mainland China, and was headed by male immigrants who had set up selected businesses: peddling wares and producing leather bags in the case of Bologna (and Milan); seafaring, laundries and restaurants in the city of London (and other UK ports). Typically, the first immigrants to both Italy and the UK were politically aligned with the Kuomintang; furthermore, they set up clubs where people could meet and play traditional Chinese gambling games, and they organized social gatherings and celebrated national festivities. In both countries, the Chinese constituted an authentic community, and Chinese men were interconnected with the local population through their (local) wives. In the beginning, intermarriage was quite a common phenomenon, as was the involvement of wives in the business, both in Bologna and London.

In conclusion, the question posed at the start of this chapter was whether immigrant communities from the same country share the same features wherever they may be, or whether they tend to be different depending on the destination country. Our answer to that question is that certain cultural and social features, such as the role of the family and the community, which are strictly linked to the culture of the country of origin, tend to be preserved regardless of the immigrants' place of destination. However, Chinese immigrant entrepreneurs have tended to adapt to the market features of the destination society, and this has proven an important factor accounting for their business success.

Notes

1 The structure of the Chinese family may account for the overall low numbers of Chinese women immigrating. As in many parts of southern and eastern Europe, the ideal family in China was a multigenerational patriarchal stem family. The preservation of this lineage over time, with property and land ownership kept intact, was often a higher priority than the co-residence of spouses and children. Young men were frequently sent to cities and abroad to make money that would ultimately be used for the benefit of maintaining the family, while women stayed at home to take care of the household, farm, children, and the elderly (McKeown 2010).

2 In the case of Prato, Ceccagno argues that the main opportunity for Chinese immigrants is not a vacant industry, but the crisis affecting the Italian fashion industry in recent years. Chinese immigrants have helped to contain the crisis and have also made it possible for there to be economic expansion in certain areas (Ceccagno 2017).

3 Other estimates taken from newspapers range from 136 to 300. "Cinesi di Milano e il loro lavoro" in *Il Corriere della Sera* 30 August 1938. Then there were the figures given by the Chinese community of that time. "Before the Second World War, there were 700–800 Chinese in Italy. After the war there were 60 in Milan, 25–28 in Bologna, 10 in Rome, 10 in Florence, 7–8 in Genoa. In Italy they were fewer than 300 in total. At the end of the war the majority of them returned to China", these are the words of Nino Tchen interviewed by Patrizia Battilani and Luigi Liao in Bologna on 8 June 2015. Nino Tchen, who was born in 1943, migrated to Italy in 1959, two years after his father and about 30 years after his grandfather.

4 All interviews are available. Please contact the authors.

5 Bologna Municipal Archive, Commercial licences, 1930s. Licence granted to Tzen Tri Shan, Wang Huan Yao, Wang Chon Ming Vincenzo, Tong Ling Sin Giovanni, Wang Iso Ping Giuseppe.

6 The first ten Chinese who arrived in Bologna during the 1930s left China when they were between 17 and 25 years old. See Bologna Municipal archives, Commercial licences.

7 Interview with S.Y. conducted by Patrizia Battilani, Francesca Fauri and Luigi Yen Liao, Bologna, 31 January 2015. Interview with Antonio Tong conducted by Patrizia Battilani and Luigi Yen Liao, Bologna, 31 June 2015.

8 Interview with Maria Grazia Sun conducted by P. Battilani, A. Ceccagno and F. Fauri, Bologna, 29 January 2015. Interview with Gianni Wang conducted by P. Battilani and L. Yen Liao, Bologna, 20 June 2015.

9 Interview with Giampiero W. conducted by Luigi Yen Liao, Bologna 22 November 2015; Interview with Tommasina Wang conducted by F. Fauri and L. Yen Liao, Bologna, 9 September 2015; Interview with Gianni Wang; Interview with Antonio Tong conducted by P. Battilani and L. Yen Liao, Bologna, 30 June 2015.

10 Our data are taken from the Bologna Chamber of Commerce Archives, the Municipal Archives, and the interviews conducted.

11 On 14 September 1940, Mussolini signed a Decree establishing 43 internment camps for the citizens of enemy states living in Italy: 147 Chinese were interned at the camp in Tossiccia (Abruzzo) in 1941, then from September 1942 to October 1943 at Isola del Gran Sasso (Capogreco and Ferramonti 1987; Capogreco 2004).
12 The Ghisiliere prison, located near Bologna (Colle Ameno-Sasso Marconi) also held a Chinese man who usually sold ties in Bologna (Giorgi 1976).
13 Interview with Antonio Yen conducted by Patrizia Battilani and Luigi Yen Liao, Bologna, 5 October 2015. A. Yen was born in China in 1949, his parents having returned to China from Italy prior to his birth. Interview with Giovanna Rilli conducted by P. Battilani, Bologna, 18 March 2016. Interview with Giovanna Rilli conducted by P. Battilani, Bologna, 18 March 2016. G. Rilli lived in China for five years.
14 Interview with Antonio Tong conducted by P. Battilani and L. Yen Liao, Bologna, 30 June 2015.
15 Chamber of Commerce Archives.
16 Catalogo Esportatori ed Importatori della Provincia di Bologna (Catalogue of Bologna's important-export companies) covering the period 1952–1978.
17 Vincenzo Wang Chong Ming registered the brand of his "Cravatta Tre Palme" ties. See the Italian Central Patent Office's on-line database. Other Chinese entrepreneurs designed their own brands without registering them.
18 Interview conducted by P. Battilani and L. Liao with Lo Heung Yuk, Bologna, 24 April 2016; Interview with Nino T. conducted by P. Battilani and L. Yen Liao, Bologna, 8 June 2015; Interview with Pietro Sun Pai Chang conducted by Luigi Yen Liao, Bologna, 16 April, 2015.
19 Chiang Kai-shek' son, Chiang Ching-kuo (1910–1988) became Minister of Defence in 1965, Vice-Premier in 1969 and finally premier of the Republic of China (Taiwan) in 1972. When he arrived in Taiwan he was appointed director of the secret police up until 1965.
20 Interview with Maria Grazia Sun conducted by P. Battilani, A. Ceccagno and F. Fauri, Bologna, 29 January 2015.
21 Interview with Cecilia Geslao, who married Wu Lung King Paolo in 1949, conducted by L. Liao Bologna, 7 July 2015.
22 Interview with Maria Grazia Sun conducted by P. Battilani, A. Ceccagno and F. Fauri, Bologna, 29 January 2015.
23 See the interview with the Bologna wholesaler of the time. Chamber of Commerce Archives and the Interview with V.N. conducted by L. Yen Liao, Bologna, 1 June 2015; Interview with Corrado Veronesi conducted by L. Yen Liao and P. Battilani, Bologna, 6 May 2015.
24 Interview by L. Yen Liao with Pietro Sun Pai Chang, Bologna, 16 April 2015.
25 Interview by L. Yen Liao with Silvia Huang, Bologna, 16 May 2015; Interview by L. Yen Liao with Zhang Min, Bologna 15 April 2015.
26 Interview by P. Battilani and L. Yen Liao with Sun Weng Long, Bologna 15 April 2016.
27 Interview with Mei Jin Fan conducted by L. Yen Liao, Bologna, 12 May 2015.
28 Interview with Silvia Huang conducted by L. Yen Liao, Bologna 16 May 2015.
29 Interview with Zhang Min conducted by L. Yen Liao, Bologna, 15 April 2015.
30 Umberto Sun opened the Chun Kuo Restaurant in 1970; Chan Sin Cheung opened the Fior di Ming in 1972; Hang Chu Kwang opened the Chung Fua

Restaurant. Each of them had run a bag workshop beforehand. Source: Bologna Chamber of Commerce Archives.

31 Interview with Marco Tung conducted by L. Yen Liao, Bologna, 11 April, 2014. Interview with Mach Angelo conducted by L. Yen Liao, Bologna, 14 April 2020. Interview with Tse Wei Wang Ugo conducted by Luigi Yen Liao, Bologna, 15 March 2015.

32 Interview with Marco Tung conducted by L. Yen Liao, Bologna, 11 April 2014.

33 Interview with Cecilia Geslao conducted by P. Battilani and L. Yen Liao, Bologna, 7 July 2015. Interview with Adriana Wu conducted by P. Battilani and L. Yen Liao, Bologna 25 June 2015. Interview with Maria Grazia Sun conducted by P. Battilani, A. Ceccagno and F. Fauri, Bologna, 29 January 2015. Interview with Dick Ting conducted by Luigi Liao, Bologna, 20 April 2015.

34 Interview with Nino T. conducted by P. Battilani and L. Yen Liao, Bologna, 8 June 2015. Nino T., born in 1943, emigrated to Italy in 1959, two years after his father and about 30 years after his grandfather had done likewise.

35 Interview with Nino T.'s son conducted by P. Battilani and L. Yen Liao, Bologna, 8 June 2015.

36 Interview with Nino Tchen conducted by P. Battilani and L. Yen Liao, Bologna, 8 June 2015.

37 On the relationship between craftsmen and suppliers, see the interview with V.N. conducted by Luigi Liao, Bologna, 1 June 2015. Interview with Corrado Veronesi conducted by L. Yen Liao and P. Battilani, Bologna, 6 May 2015.

38 Tower Hamlets Local History & Archives (THLH & Archives), 410 Pamphlets LP 5936, P.J. Walker, The Chinese (paper cutting of a newspaper article).

39 THLH & Archives, 410 Pamphlets, LP 4857, J.P. May, The Chinese in Britain 1860–1911.

40 THLH & Archives, 410 Pamphlets, LP 5936, P.J. Walker, The Chinese.

41 Chinese restaurants were generally avoided by local white people, except for some members of the lower working class who presumably had to overcome their racial and gastronomic prejudices in search of a cheap meal. THLH & Archives, 410 Pamphlets, G000273475, Sarah Cheang, The Dark Night of Chinatown, BA History of Design, Year 1997.

42 During the transport workers' strikes in July 1911, all 30 Chinese laundries in Cardiff were wrecked by rioters. THLH & Archives, 410 Pamphlets, LP 5936, P.J. Walker, The Chinese.

43 THLH & Archives, 410 Pamphlets, LC7282, J. Seed, The Limehouse Blues: Looking for Chinatown in the London Docks 1900–1940, History Workshop Journal, issue 62 Autumn 2006: 58–85.

44 However, it was short lived as the teacher was sent back to China in 1929 and thereafter children attended local English schools. THLH & Archives, File Chinatown/pictures/ paper cuttings.

45 THLH & Archives, 410 Pamphlets, G000273475, Sarah Cheang, The Dark Night of Chinatown.

46 THLH & Archives, 410 Pamphlets, LP 4857, J.P. May, The Chinese in Britain 1860–1911: 111–122.

47 THLH & Archives, 410 Pamphlets, LC7282 J. Seed, The Limehouse Blues: Looking for Chinatown in the London Docks 1900–40: 70.

48 THLH & Archives, File Chinatown/pictures/ paper cuttings, STAR 9 Jan. 1919 "The evil trade in opium" and *New Chronicle* 14 Dec. 1918 "In the heart of Chinatown" published in the *Times* 28 August 1918 "East-end opium dens".
49 Ibid.
50 THLH & Archives, File Chinatown/pictures/ paper cuttings, *The Sphere*, 8 May 1926 article by Arnold Palmer.
51 THLH & Archives, File Chinatown/pictures/ paper cuttings, *Westmininster Gazzette*, 24 January 1928 Trevor Allen.
52 Woon Wing Yip, who is 79, arrived in London by boat from Hong Kong in 1959 with just £10 in his pocket. After working in the catering business he decided to open a store selling Chinese culinary ingredients. Today, Wing Yip supplies more than 2,000 Chinese restaurants throughout the UK, and he is among the richest people in the UK. www.business-live.co.uk/economic-development/rich-list-2018-no46-woon-14163424.
53 As a result of the Opium War (1840), the island of Hong Kong was ceded to Britain on the basis of the Nanking Treaty of 1842. In 1860 the Convention of Peking was signed according to which Hong Kong including Kowloon, the New Territories and more than 200 islands, in all about 1,000 sq. km., was ceded (in perpetuity) to Britain; that is, until 1997 when the sovereignty over these territories was transferred to the PRC (Chan & Chan 1997: 123–131).
54 Public Record Office (PRO), CO 1032/330 Telegram from Hong Kong (Sir R. Black) to the Secretary of State for the Colonies, 1 November 1961.
55 PRO, PREM 16/1689 Draft government reply to the report on immigration of the Select Committee on Race Relations and Immigration.
56 Chinese people also arrived in Hong Kong as refugees from Kwangtung province: they were referred to as stateless aliens (Pan Lynn 1990).
57 THLH & Archives, 410 LP 8078, A. Chan, *Employment Prospects of Chinese Youth in Britain*, published by the Commission for Racial Equality in July 1986.
58 Sociologists have emphasized the role of strong and weak ties in helping the immigrant entrepreneur solve various different problems. Depending on what they want or need, they turn to different sources for help: "For example money is borrowed from extended family members while information on markets and how to run a business as well as advice on the hiring of labour is obtained through weaker ties such as acquaintances and colleagues" (Rath 2000: 152–153).

References

Aldrich H. (1975). Ecological Succession in Racially Changing Neighbourhoods: A Review of the Literature. *Urban Affairs Quarterly*. 10 (3): 327–348.

Barrett G.A. and McEvoy D. (2005). Not all Can Win Prizes: Asians in the British Labour Market. In Spaan E., Hillmann F. and van Naerssen T. (2012). *Asian Migrants and European Labour Markets*. London and New York: Routledge, 21–41.

Bates T. (1993). *Determinants of Survival and Profitability among Asian Immigrant-Owned Small Businesses*. Center for Economic Studies U.S.-Census Bureau: Working Papers, 93–11.

Battilani P. and Fauri F. (2018). Chinese Migration to Italy: Features and Issues. In Fauri F. and Tedeschi P. (eds.). *Labour Migration in Europe. Volume I: Integration and Entrepreneurship among Migrant Workers – A Long-Term View*. Basingstoke: Palgrave Macmillan, 11–42.

Battilani P. (2020). The Shaping of Historic Cities between Creative Industries and Manufacturing: A Case Study of Bologna in Italy. In Inoue N. and Orioli V. (eds.). *Bologna and Kanazawa: Protection and Valorisation of Two Historic Cities*. Bologna: Bonomia University, 89–104.

Benton G. (2003). Chinese Transnationalism in Britain: A Longer History. *Identities-global Studies in Culture and Power.* 10(3): 347–375.

Bonacich E. and Modell J. (1980). *The Economic Basis of Ethnic Solidarity*. University of Illinois at Urbana-Champaign's Academy for Entrepreneurial Leadership Historical Research Reference in Entrepreneurship: https://ssrn.com/abstract=1496171.

Bun C.K. and Hui O.J. (1995). The Many Faces of Chinese Entrepreneurship. In Cohen R. (ed.). *The Cambridge Survey of World Migration*. New York: Cambridge University Press.

Brini G. (1978). *Artigiani a Bologna: cenni di storia e attualità*. Bologna: CNA-APB.

Capogreco C.S. (2004). *I campi del duce: l'internamento civile nell'Italia fascista, 1940-1943*. Torino: Einaudi.

Capogreco C.S. and Ferramonti C.S. (1987). *La vita e gli uomini del più grande campo d'internamento fascista, 1940-1945*. Firenze: Giuntina.

Carney M.S. (1998). A Management Capacity Constraint? Obstacles to the Development of the Overseas Chinese Family Business. *Asia Pacific Journal of Management*. 15(2): 137–162.

Catalogo esportatori ed Importatori della Provincia di Bologna (Catalogue of exporting and importing companies in Bologna) years 1952-1978.

Ceccagno A. (2017). *City Making and Global Labour Regimes*. London: Palgrave Macmillan.

Chan A. (1986). *Employment Prospects of Chinese Youth in Britain: A Report*. Commission for Racial Equality.

Chan K.B. (2012). *Migration Ethnic Relations and Chinese Business*. London: Routledge.

Chan Y.M. and Chan C. (1997). The Chinese in Britain. *Journal of Ethnic and Migration Studies*. 23(1): 123–131.

Chaudhry S. and Crick D. (2004). The Business Practices of Small Chinese Restaurants in the UK: An Exploratory Investigation. *Strategic Change*. 13(1): 37–49.

Chen M. (1995). *Asian Management System*. London: Routledge.

Clark K. and Drinkwater S. (2002). Enclaves, Neighbourhood Effects and Economic Activity: Ethnic Minorities in England and Wales. *Journal of Population Economics*. 15(1): 5–29.

Cologna D. (1997). Dal Zeijian a Milano. Profilo di una comunità in transizione. In Ceccagno A. (ed.). *Il caso delle comunità cinesi: comunicazione interculturale ed istituzioni*. Milano: Armando Editore, 23–35.

Cologna D. (2005). Differential Impact of Transnational Ties on the Socio-Economic Development of Origin Communities: The Case of Chinese Migrants from Zhejiang Province in Italy. *Asian and Pacific Migration Journal*. 14(1–2): 121–147.

Cologna D. (2014). Chinese Descendants in Italy: Emergence, Role and Uncertain Identity. *Ethnic and Racial Studies*. 37(7): 1239–1252.

Corriere della Sera (1926). *Biglietti falsi appioppati ai cinesi venditori di perle*. May 7th.

Dana L.P. and Morris M. (2007). Towards a Synthesis: a Model of Immigrant and Ethnic Entrepreneurship. In Dana L.P. (ed.) *Handbook of Research on Ethnic*

Minority Entrepreneurship. A Co-evolutionary View on Resource Management. Cheltenham: Edward Elgar, 803–810.

Eade J. (2000). *Placing London: From Imperial Capital to Global City.* New York: Berghahn Books.

Giorgi R. (1976). *Sasso Marconi: cronache di allora e di dopo.* Sasso Marconi: APE.

Gomez E. and Cheung G. (2009). Family Firms, Networks and "Ethnic Enterprise": Chinese Food Industry in Britain. *East Asia.* 26(2): 133–157.

House of Commons (1985). *Second Report from the Home Affairs Committee.* Session 1984-5, Chinese Community in Britain, Vol. 1, London: HMSO.

Jones T., Ram M. and Edwards P. (2006). Ethnic Minority Business and the Employment of Illegal Immigrants. *Entrepreneurship and Regional Development: An International Journal.* 18(2): 133–150.

Kao J. (1993). The World Wide Web of Chinese Business. *Harvard Business Review.* 71(2): 24–36.

Macke J.A.C. (1992). Overseas Chinese Entrepreneurship. *Asian-Pacific Economic Literature.* 6(1): 41–64.

McKeown A. (2010). Chinese Emigration in Global Context, 1850-1940. *Journal of Global History.* 5(1): 95–124.

Myers R. (1989). Confucianism and Economic Development: Mainland China, Hong Kong and Taiwan. In *Chung-hua Institute for Economic Research.* Taipei: Conference Series. 13, 281–302.

Ng Kwee Choo (1968). *The Chinese in London.* Oxford: Oxford University Press.

Pan Lynn M.Y.N. (1990). *Sons of the Yellow Emperor The Story of the Overseas Chinese.* London: Secker & Warburg.

Pang M.Y.N. (1996). Barriers Perceived by Young Chinese Adults to their Employment in Companies in the UK. *International Journal of Human Resource Management.* 7(4): 891–904.

Pang M.Y.N. and Lau A. (1998). The Chinese in Britain: Working Towards Success? *The International Journal of Human Resource Management.* 9(5): 862–874.

Portes A. (1981). Modes of Structural Incorporation and Present Theories of Labor Migration. In Kritz M., Keely C.B. and Tomasi S.M. (eds.). *Global Trends in Migration: Theory and Research on International Population Movements.* New York: The Center for Migration Studies, 279–297.

Rath J. (ed.) (2000). *Immigrant Businesses: The Economic, Political and Social Environment.* London: Palgrave Macmillan.

Santini C., Rabino S. and Zanni L. (2011). Chinese Immigrants Socio-Economic Enclave in an Italian Industrial District: The Case of Prato. *World Review of Entrepreneurship, Management and Sustainable Development.* 7(1): 30–51.

Seed J. (2006). Limehouse Blues: Looking for Chinatown in the London Docks, 1900-40. *History Workshop Journal.* 62(1): 58–85.

Spaan E., Hillman F. and van Naerssen T. (2005). *Asian Migrants and European Labour Markets.* London: Routledge.

Strangio D. (2020). *Italy-China Trade Relations: A Historical Perspective.* New York: Springer.

Wah S.S. (2001). Chinese Cultural Values and Their Implication to Chinese Management. *Singapore Management Review.* 23(2): 75–83.

Wang C.L. and Altinay L. (2010). Social Embeddedness, Entrepreneurial Orientation and Firm Growth in Ethnic Minority Small Business in the UK. *International Small Business Journal.* 30(1): 3–23.

Watson J.L. (1977). The Chinese: Hong Kong Villagers in the British Catering Trade. In Watson J.L. (ed.). *Between Two Cultures: Migrants and Minorities in Britain*. Oxford: Blackwell, 181–213.

Wong S.-L. (1985). The Chinese Family Firm: A Model. *The British Journal of Sociology*. 36(1): 58–72.

Wu B. and Zanin V. (2007) *Exploring Links between International Migration and Wenzhou's Development*. Nottingham: University of Nottingham.

Yang M.M. (1994). *Gifts, Favors, and Banquets: The Art of Social Relationships in China*. Ithaca and London: Cornell University Press.

Yeung H.W. and Kris, O. (2000). Globalizing Chinese Business Firms: Where are They Coming From, Where are They Heading? In Yeung H.K. and Olds K. (eds.). *The Globalization of the Chinese Firm*. London: Palgrave, 1–128.

Archives

CCA-Chamber of Commerce Archives (Bologna)
Bologna Municipal Archive (Bologna)
PRO-Public Record Office (Kew)
THLH Archives-Tower Hamlets Local History & Archives (London)

7 Immigration and sustainability of the pay-as-you-go social security system in Italy

Anna Attias and Donatella Strangio

Introduction

The labour market is a privileged sector for analysis and represents the place of confrontation between immigrants and Italian society; it is also the area in which the contradictory nature of migration policies (Italian and European) emerges.

In Italy, the working dimension plays an important role in the formation of social inequalities. To tackle the relationship between immigrants and the labour market, it is first of all necessary to identify the social dynamics that regulate the management of foreign labour on Italian territory (Bonifazi 2007; 2013; Colucci 2018). This is because, over the years, some factors linked to the labour market have had a marked influence on the formation of inequalities: this is the case of the dynamics of access to employment, classification, mobility and salary remuneration. Most of the foreign workers are employed in the lower segments of the labour market, in sectors at high risk of accident and low pay. Foreigners are over-represented in jobs such as agricultural labourers, cleaners, domestic workers, general workers and construction workers (Fullin and Reyneri 2011; Gesano and Strozza 2011; Triandafyllidou and Marchetti 2013; Fondazione Leone Moressa 2018). Their concentration in these areas is the result of a typical segmentation of the contemporary labour market. In particular with regard to the female foreign population, labour inequality involving immigrants is a systematic inequality and permeates the entire work experience of this segment of the population. Demographic changes therefore have important implications especially for economic and social issues, and also for the pension systems. The role of demographic equilibrium is crucial for the sustainability of a pay-as-you-go pension system, where the pensions are mostly paid from the current contributions by the active age groups. Immigrants must/should? be thought of as a resource for stabilizing the population distribution in order to achieve sustainability of the pay-as-you-go pension system. We extended the classical Leslie population growth model (built for insects) to a control model, appropriate for a dynamic simulation of the demographic background of a human population with reference to the pension system, in order to consider different scenarios with the presence of immigrants. The present work, also based on the modified Leslie model, aims to contribute to the national and international debate on sustainability by combining socio-economic and actuarial issues with the logic of immigration policy in Italy and in Europe in a historical context full of changes.

Labour market

As is known, shortcomings have already been found in key sectors: science, technology, engineering and health. Other and more serious shortcomings are foreseen in the immediate future: by 2020, the European Commission estimates a deficit of 756,000 highly qualified professionals in telecommunications and about one million in the health sector among doctors, nurses, dentists, midwives and pharmacists. Unfortunately, these deficits cannot be filled by the 12 million long-term unemployed present in the EU employment market because, in more than half of these cases, they have a low level of skills (this is the reason for their difficulties in job placement). This being the case, the lack of skills and the consequent imbalances between the demand for and supply of skilled labour are considerable: the European Commission estimates that 40 per cent of European employers are currently already finding it difficult to find the qualified personnel they need to support competitive production. In this context, the European Skills Agenda (European Commission 2016), together with the objectives of increasing the quality and relevance of training, enhancing the analysis of needs and improving professional choices, has included among its pillars of intervention "the improvement of transparency and comparability of qualifications" and "the timely recognition of immigrants' skills and qualifications". Currently, in fact, due to the delays involved in this recognition, both EU and non-EU workers who have moved to a Member State encounter difficulties in obtaining a placement corresponding to their profile, receive lower wages than the natives and, as a result, struggle to become more integrated into the host societies. From this point of view there is no lack of support: the 2005/36/CE directive concerning the mutual recognition of qualifications and access to regulated professions, the establishment of a "European qualifications framework for lifelong learning" (EQF) and the "Skills Determination Tool for Third Country Nationals". These decisions were important steps forward to enable employers to overcome the differences between national education and training systems and to achieve an effective assessment of the skills of people with qualifications issued in countries other than their own. Europe must therefore consolidate its skills base and, in order to satisfy the unmet needs of qualified contributions, it must also prepare for the inclusion of immigrant workers in the current labour market. This is the way to sustain competition with globally more dynamic economies (from China to the United States) and to attract workers with the professional skills that are lacking. Thus, for example, Japan, one of the countries traditionally most closed to immigration, has recently changed its approach and approved a package of reforms, including facilities and incentives for highly qualified workers from abroad. It is also appropriate to recall the exemplary experience of Canada, which, starting with the Immigration Act of 1967, introduced a points system that favours the entry of qualified immigrants that are young and familiar with the languages of the place. However, there are a number of peculiar factors that characterize this type of migration: the inability or impossibility of the economic or productive system of one's own country to exploit highly qualified people, better salaries or professional opportunities in other countries, better chances to perfect one's studies abroad or the impossibility of remaining in one's own country for religious or political reasons. In the course of history, there have been many cases of forced or voluntary, collective or individual migrations, which have seen intellectuals, technicians, professionals and highly specialized workers leave their land to seek their fortune elsewhere, such as the forced migration resulting from the religious wars that had tormented Europe since the beginning of the sixteenth century. The religious controversies that had marked the first half of the sixteenth century, politically as well as religiously, came to an end, at least formally, with the Peace of Augusta (1555). The last formal act of the Emperor Charles V before his abdication, intended to give stability and peace to the principalities of the Empire on the basis of the Cuius regio eius religio principle, according to which the population had to adhere to the confession, Catholic or Reformed, professed by the Prince. Those who did not conform to this principle were forced to migrate to another territory. We then recall the expulsion of the moriscos at the beginning of the seventeenth century, when over 300,000 Muslims were forcibly converted to Christianity, but suspected of having remained secretly faithful to the original religion, were then expelled between 1609 and 1614 from the Iberian peninsula by order of Philip III. The moriscos, although expelled from the Christian corporations, were skilled craftsmen, who excelled in construction, agriculture and commerce and were esteemed doctors. Not being able to access the aristocracy or military careers, the moriscos were engaged in the productive system and, given the rigidly noble social structure, manufacturing, craftsmanship and commercial entrepreneurship were certainly the most significant elements of economic development of the firm of the time. The economic and social consequences of this expulsion lasted for years, in particular in the Kingdoms of Valencia and Aragon, from which one third and one sixth respectively of the population was expelled and then experienced a long recessive period due to this forced removal of energies more technically qualified and productive of the firm. We have reported these two macroscopic examples, but there are many others because, as already mentioned, highly qualified migrations often represented a part of larger migration flows. Things began to change between the late eighteenth and early nineteenth centuries when some technological discoveries were applied to production systems and began to rapidly transform production systems.

Italian welfare state

The Italian social security system and access to healthcare are fundamental tools of inclusion, as they provide effective protection against unemployment, accidents at work, sickness and invalidity. Individual Member States, on the basis of their own history and national peculiarities, have elaborated a specific social security system.

In countries where immigration is a recent phenomenon, only a few aspects of the relationship between third-country nationals and social security are known, namely the fact that third-country workers' pay very high social security contributions every year, while having limited access to retirement. We should not limit ourselves to considering the most reassuring aspects of this phenomenon, because in the future the number of third-country national retirees will increase. Moreover, we should take into consideration the issuing of new restrictive laws, from the point of view of third-country nationals; for example, the increase in the age required to receive the old age pension which, together with the decision to practically suspend any new bilateral agreement with countries of origin, will have a strong negative impact on third-country national workers. Concretely, this may result in the impossibility for many to obtain, by summing up insurance accrued in Italy and the country of origin, the minimum contribution requirement necessary to be able to receive pensions.

The IDOS's report (2017) has been able to build upon its experience in preparing and editing, in the recent past, four Reports on Immigrant Workers in the Social Security Archives on behalf of and with the collaboration of the Italian Social Security Institute (INPS).[1] The pre-existing, fruitful collaboration between IDOS and the National Insurance Institute for Accidents at Work (INAIL)[2] was also very valuable.

Labour force survey data: employment, unemployment and inactivity social security benefits largely depend on the contributions paid during an employee's working life; for this reason, it is appropriate to analyse the relevant data on the inclusion of immigrants in the labour market in 2012, as recorded by the Labour Force Survey. Due to the economic crisis, the employment rate of third-country workers decreased to 58.5 per cent – a higher rate compared with Italian workers (56.4%) but lower than EU workers (65.3%) who usually enjoy greater protection in times of crisis. In 2008, the employment rate was two points higher for Italian and third-country workers and four points higher for EU workers. In contrast, the unemployment rate increased (10.0% for Italians, 12.6% for EU workers and 21.3% for third-country workers, a rate that is more than twice that of Italian workers). The inactivity rate affects four out of ten Italian people of working age (43%), and more than three out of ten for EU workers (31.0%) and of third-country workers (36.0%). In all three cases, the highest unemployment rates are found among women. Immigrants under the age of 14 total 826,579 and account for 10.1 per cent of all residents of this age group (8,513,222) of whom 7,650,643 are Italians. Third-country national immigrants alone account for 7.9 per cent. In contrast, there are only 106,850 immigrants over the age of 65 (of whom 75,379 are third-country nationals) and account for 0.9 per cent of all residents in this age group (12,300,934) of whom 12,194,084 are Italians (Istat 2015).

The main statistics begin to record a significant number of foreigners registering from abroad only starting from the two-year period 1987–1988, following the first important regularization, that established by Law no. 943/1986 (Strozza 2018). From that moment on, the personal data flow of foreign immigrants increased progressively up to 2008, with clear peaks depending on the periodic regularization and the programming of the flows (Blangiardo 2018a; 2018b; Strozza 2018). In fact, the peak of 1990 is due to the amnesty introduced by the Martelli law, that of 1996 to the effects of the Dini decree, while the subsequent one of 2000 is attributable to the introduction of the quota policy inaugurated with the Turco-Napolitano law. The highest point recorded in 2003–2004 is the effect of the Bossi-Fini law of 2002 (and subsequent provisions) which led to the emergence of over 700,000 irregular positions and enabled slightly less than 650,000 regularizations, translated in the two years following in registrations from abroad.

The increase in the foreign population residing in the country in the period 2002–2017 (from 1.5 to 5.1 million) depends in part on the natural dynamics (positive natural balance of over 950 thousand units) but above all on net migrations from abroad (almost 2.7 million). If we consider that in the last 16 years more than 1.2 million people have acquired Italian citizenship, we can see that in the period considered, the growth of the total resident population is due exclusively to the foreign component, since the Italian population has registered both a negative migratory balance (908,000–1,215,000 = –307,000), mainly due to the net emigration of the last three to four years, and a largely negative natural balance (–1.9 million people). In the absence of migration (and due to the accuracy of foreign immigration figures), the population expected at the beginning of 2018 would have been just over 56 million people, 1.75 million less than that recorded at the beginning of 2002.

The slight increase in the number of employees over the entire period is the result of a decrease of about 1 million jobs among Italians and an increase of around 1.2 million jobs among foreigners. The decrease in the number of employees with low educational qualifications was close to 2.2 million, a figure limited by the net entry into the production system of over 600,000 foreigners with low education. In fact, among the Italians, leaving the world of work above all due to quiescence has in recent years concerned generations with low levels of education being replaced by more educated younger generations. The number of Italian employees in possession of a secondary school diploma remains substantially unchanged, while the number of graduates (1.6 million more) has increased. The number of graduates and graduates has also grown among the foreign employed, but far less so compared with the increase in the number of those without or with low educational qualifications.

The greater difficulties for foreigners entering the labour market compared with Italians are clearly shown by the ever higher unemployment rates, which recorded a greater growth in the period of the economic crisis than that observed among Italians. During the period of the crisis, their employment rate also decreased, which remained higher than that of the Italians but with a differential that was significantly reduced. The significant role of education is evident in guaranteeing greater possibilities for finding a job for both Italians and foreigners.

The comparison between profiles by sector of activity and professions of the two groups highlights their complementarity, at least by sector of employment (the dissimilarity in the percentage distribution by sector of activity is equal to 40%), and the disadvantage of foreign workers compared with Italians is not very present in the qualified professions (7.1% against 37.8%) and are concentrated in non-qualified activities (34.5% against 8.3%). Foreigners, who represent 10.6 per cent of the employed, are in agriculture (18%), construction (17%), hotels and restaurants (almost 19%), but above all in services to families (51%), a larger employee share than the overall average. The change in employment in the period 2005–2017 by sector of activity shows how the reduction of Italian employees in the primary and secondary sectors, as well as in the tertiary sectors related to trade and other social services and to people, was partially offset by foreign employment. The variation in the number of employees by profession confirms that the jobs lost by the Italians mainly concern artisanal or in any case specialized activities, while the growth of jobs held by foreigners mainly concerns those in charge of trade and services and general workers.

An actuarial reflection for sustainability

The pay-as-you-go pension systems, as found in Italy and in many European countries, need demographic stability to be sustainable. The system pays pension benefits with contributions paid in, and therefore the active population has to be numerically greater than that of the third age population. Looking at the following Italian age pyramids for 2019 and those projected for 2049 it is easy to see what the problem is (Figure 7.1).

Today we have an "urn" shape, where each new vintage is weaker than the previous one, while in the forecast the shape tends to look like a "drop". It is possible to see that below the baby boom phenomenon, which is the numerous demographic cohort born between 1946 and 1966, there is a

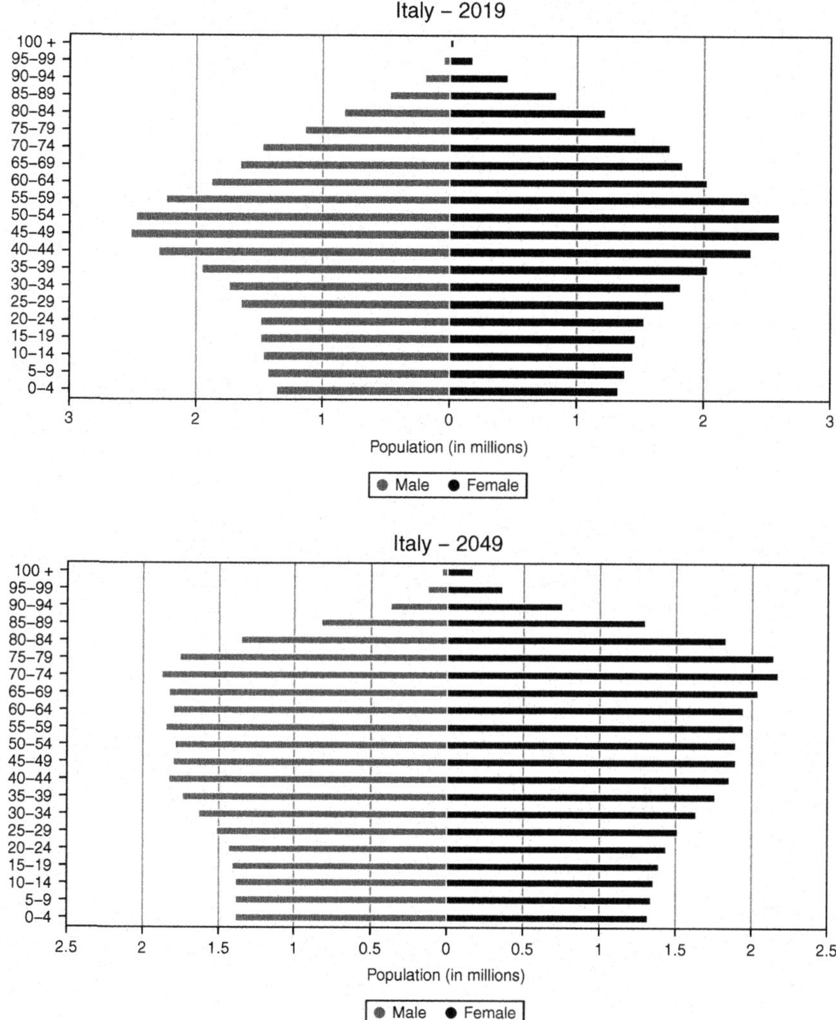

Figure 7.1 Age Pyramids 2019 and 2049

"hole" due to a lower number of births from the 1970s onwards. It is impossible to think of filling the chasm because for too many years the population replacement rate was out of "social security check". That is to say, the fertility rate necessary to keep the population volume constant was and is too far below 2.1, which is the ideal value for guaranteeing equilibrium. Hence, in a pay-as-you go pension system, demographic factors (Varga 1984; Myers 1994; Varga et al. 2011) such as fertility and life expectancy are crucial. Italy recorded a birth rate of 1.44 per cent in 2019, of 1.2 per cent in 2007 and a historical low of 1.19 per cent in 1995. This increase is attributable to women immigrants who, at least in the first generation, have a much higher number of children on average than Italian women, but also to older first-time mothers (Società Italiana di Statistica 2011), namely women over the age of forty deciding to have children. Life expectancy at birth is higher on average for both sexes at up to 80 years of age (80.8 years for men and 85.2 for women) and life expectancy upon retirement has also increased considerably, to about 21 years on average (Both 2006; European Commission 2009). Thus the correct estimation of the systematic risk stemming from the uncertainty of the future mortality trends becomes very important, known in the literature as the longevity risk.[3] This problem, which is huge for Italy as the second most long-lived country after Japan, can be extended to much of Europe, which has very similar characteristics. Thus the population declines as there are not enough births to replace those who die, leading to the creation of "gaps", which will become explosive from a social security point of view when the baby boomers, i.e. the current "belly" of the workforce in Italy, retire.

A buffering hypothesis could be attempted for this problem over time, albeit a partial one, in the sense that a migration policy could be implemented that assesses the entry of immigrants in a "scientific" way.

In order to reflect on the logic of immigration in relation to the sustainability problems of pay-as-you-go pension systems, we can begin with the classic demographic models.

Among these, we considered the Bernadelli model (1941) that describes the dynamics of a population of insects with three development stages, each one corresponding to a period of time correlated with the age of the insect. The author assumes that the insect is not reproductive in the first two stages, as it has no gender, but it is in the third stage. The large numbers in the various age groups $x_i(t)$, in time t, with an index i=1,2,3, corresponding to the development stage can be shown as follows:

- first phase from 0 to 1, $x_1(0)$;
- second phase from 1 to 2, $x_2(0)$;
- third phase from 2 to 3, $x_3(0)$.

With the vector $\mathbf{x}(0) = \begin{bmatrix} x_1(0) \\ x_2(0) \\ x_3(0) \end{bmatrix}$ that allows us to measure the numbers in the various groups for each year to obtain the vectors referring to the different years. Since the purpose is to describe the dynamics of the insect population and to be able to make forecasts about its future state, Bernadelli assumes, as we have said, that only the third group is reproductive, with a given reproduction rate and a given survival rate.

Leslie (1945; 1948) generalizes Bernadelli's model by assuming that all age groups are reproductive, that is to say that he divides the insect population into age groups with different reproduction rates $\alpha_i \geq 0$ and survival rates ω_i $(0 < \omega_i < 1)$, irrespective of gender.

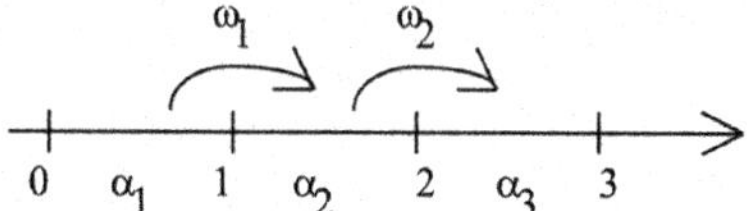

Leslie therefore defines the matrix $L := \begin{bmatrix} \alpha_1 & \alpha_2 & \alpha_3 \\ \omega_1 & 0 & 0 \\ 0 & \omega_2 & 0 \end{bmatrix}$ which makes it possible to express the general dynamics of the insect population by using the relation $x(t+1) = L\,x(t)$.

On the basis of the Leslie model and the Perron-Frobenius theory (Berman and Plemmons 1994), it has been proved (Angrisani et al. 2004) that it is possible to evaluate the human population, and in particular that a population having a pension system converges on a situation of balance from the point of view of age distribution if the reproduction and survival rates remain constant and in the absence of migratory flows (Alho and Spencer 2005). Instead, there are a number of studies on immigration (Nannestad 2007; Wenko 2008), but none of them reach a definition of an optimal immigration strategy such that the population converges on a balance from the point of view of age distribution. A first step towards an algorithm for an immigration control model was taken by Angrisani and colleagues (2010; 2012).

Many European countries have faced this problem: Fehr and Haberman (2006) for Germany, Blake and Mayhew (2006) for the United Kingdom, and Sànchez and Alfonso (2010) for Spain, to name but a few. It was actually Europe that had already pointed out, first in the 2010 Green Paper and then in its reports (European Economic and Social Committee 2010; European Commission 2010; 2018a; 2018b), that "an adequate and sustainable retirement income for EU citizens now and in the future is a priority for the European Union". There are also countless works that deal with the problem of sustainability, such as that of Alonso and colleagues (2018) who adopt a dynamic actuarial model to analyse the sustainability of pension systems in the short and long term but, as we said before, the first papers that consider the "logical exploitation" of the immigrant population with a view to sustainability are those of Angrisani and colleagues (2010; 2012) and also Pianese and colleagues (2014; 2017; 2020). Among other things, these papers formalize a mathematical/actuarial implant in order to evaluate an optimal immigration control for the purpose of scientifically exploiting actual and potential substantial migratory flows for the sustainability of pay-as-you-go pension systems.

Starting from Leslie's classic model and using analogous parameters, the human population is considered and divided into N age groups, the extended matrix and the population trend $x(t + 1) = L\,x(t)$ are constructed. The fertility rate per thousand is indicated by f_i, q_i^F and q_i^M are the male and female mortality rates and ϕ is the share of females at birth: hence the Leslie matrices are constructed for females and males that make it possible to identify the dynamics of the male and female subpopulations

$x^F(t+1)=L^F x^F(t)$ and $x^M(t+1) = L^M x^M(t) + \dfrac{(1-\phi)}{\phi} e_1 \circ L^F x^F(t)$ [4]

$$L^F = \begin{bmatrix} 0 & 0 & \dots & \alpha^F{}_{15} & \dots & \alpha^F{}_{50} & 0 & \dots & 0 & 0 \\ \omega_0^F & 0 & \dots & 0 & \dots & 0 & 0 & \dots & 0 & 0 \\ 0 & \omega_1^F & \dots & 0 & \dots & 0 & 0 & \dots & 0 & 0 \\ . & . & \dots & . & \dots & . & . & \dots & . & . \\ 0 & 0 & \dots & 0 & \dots & 0 & 0 & 0 & \omega_{108}^F & 0 \end{bmatrix}$$

$$L^M = \begin{bmatrix} 0 & 0 & \dots & 0 & \dots & 0 & 0 & \dots & 0 & 0 \\ \omega_0^M & 0 & \dots & 0 & \dots & 0 & 0 & \dots & 0 & 0 \\ 0 & \omega_1^M & \dots & 0 & \dots & 0 & 0 & \dots & 0 & 0 \\ . & . & \dots & . & \dots & . & . & \dots & . & . \\ 0 & 0 & \dots & 0 & \dots & 0 & 0 & 0 & \omega_{108}^M & 0 \end{bmatrix}$$

By indicating the state vector with $x = \begin{bmatrix} x^F \\ x^M \end{bmatrix}$, d the 109 dimension row vector with reference to the assumption of the maximum attainable age, $d = [0 \;\; \dots \;\; 0 \;\; (1-\phi)\alpha_{15} \;\; \dots \;\; (1-\phi)\alpha_{50} \;\; 0 \;\; \dots \;\; 0]$, cutting the Leslie males matrix from the first line and indicating it with L_1^M, we build the block matrix $\Lambda = \begin{bmatrix} L^F & 0 \\ d & 0 \\ 0 & L_1^M \end{bmatrix}$ and the population trend $x(t+1) = \Lambda x(t)$.

The matrix referring to the entire population does not satisfy the Perron Frobenius conditions (Berman and Plemmons1994) for the non-negative primitive and irreducible matrices, but these conditions are satisfied by the submatrix of the female population. The existence of an asymptotic demographic equilibrium is verified for this matrix, a result that can be extended to the entire population through the following theorem, demonstrated by Angrisani, Attias and Varga in 2004.

Theorem 1. A demographic equilibrium exists, a state x^0 of the population such that x^0 is a non-negative eigenvector of matrix Λ associated with a positive eigenvalue λ_0. Therefore the age distribution of the population converges to a demographic equilibrium, meaning that for each initial state $x(0)$ there is a number *s>0*, dependent on $x(0)$, such that:

$$\lim_{t\to\infty}\frac{x(t)}{\lambda_0^t} = sx^0$$

By maintaining this logic and this notation, the impact of the immigrant component on the population dynamics is verified.

This is above all in light of the fact that the foreign population, especially the non-EU population, has a considerably higher "propensity for reproduction" than the Italian or European populations.

The aim is to try and quantify how to "exploit" the wealth that comes from the immigrant population from the point of view of long-term demographic stabilization for the sustainability of pay-as-you-go pension systems, i.e. to analyse the effect of controlled immigration on the demographic equilibrium.

Applying the theorem showed that it will take about 150 years for the population to stabilize at levels that are acceptable for our pension-related purposes, and so as Baudelaire would put it, it will be a long time before the demographic/social security spleen declines, i.e. the system's inability to react to the state of "demographic/social security depression".

Inserting the immigrant component with its particular fertility and life expectancy characteristics means that the time frame is necessarily reduced. If we want to be pessimistic, however, we must underline the two demographic phenomena mentioned previously, which must be taken account of and which refer to the adaptation theory and thus to the assumption that, in the short term, perhaps even within a generation of those born in the host country, life expectancy will align with that of the native population and that in the long term there will be significant changes in the fertility rates of immigrants, which could tend to approach those of women in the host country, moving away from those of the country of origin, within the second/third generation and quite often with in the first generation. Bearing all of this in mind, it is predicted that by 2050, immigrants will account for between 16.1 and 18.4 per cent of Italy's population.

Maintaining the previous notation, set $\bar{\alpha}_i(0) := \alpha_i^F$, let us suppose that immigration is controlled in order to "steer" the current population into a demographic equilibrium. Suppose that the reproduction rate of immigrant females of age class i is α_i' (positive for $i = 15, \ldots, 50$), with $\alpha_i' \geq \bar{\alpha}_i(0)$ for all $i = 15, \ldots, 50$. The survival rates for both sexes are supposed to be the same for immigrants as for the whole population, because of what has been said before.

Let $y^F(t)$ be the immigrant female population vector in year t. For $i = 15,...50$ the average female reproduction rate dynamic is

$$\bar{\alpha}_i(t+1) := \frac{\omega_i^F x_i^F(t)}{\omega_i^F x_i^F(t) + y_i^F(t)} \bar{\alpha}_i(t) + \frac{y_i^F(t)}{\omega_i^F x_i^F(t) + y_i^F(t)} \alpha_i'.$$

Now, for year t, in terms of these updated reproduction rates, we redefine the female Leslie matrix and the vector, connecting female and male populations as before:

$$\bar{L}^F(t) := \begin{bmatrix} 0 & 0 & \dots & \bar{\alpha}_{15}(t) & \dots & \bar{\alpha}_{50}(t) & 0 & \dots & 0 & 0 \\ \omega_0^F & 0 & \dots & 0 & \dots & 0 & 0 & \dots & 0 & 0 \\ 0 & \omega_1^F & \dots & 0 & \dots & 0 & 0 & \dots & 0 & 0 \\ \cdot & \cdot & \dots & \cdot & \dots & \cdot & \cdot & \dots & \cdot & \cdot \\ 0 & 0 & \dots & 0 & \dots & 0 & 0 & 0 & \omega_{\Omega-2}^F & 0 \end{bmatrix},$$

$$\bar{d}(t) = \begin{bmatrix} 0 & \dots & 0 & (1-\phi)\bar{\alpha}_{15}(t) & \dots & (1-\phi)\bar{\alpha}_{50}(t) & 0 & \dots & 0 \end{bmatrix},$$

and for the new system matrix we get $\bar{\Lambda}(t) := \begin{bmatrix} \bar{L}^F(t) & O \\ \bar{d}(t) & 0 \\ O & L_1^M \end{bmatrix}$

Now let $y^M(t)$ be the male population vector for the immigrants in year t, age classified in the same way as the domestic population. Then for the dynamics of the population with immigration it reads as follows:

$$x^F(t+1) = \bar{L}^F(t) x^F(t) + y^F(t)$$

$$x^M(t+1) = \bar{L}^F(t) x^M(t) + \frac{(1-\phi)}{\phi} e_1 \circ \bar{L}^F x^F(t) + y^M(t),$$

so we have $x(t+1) = \bar{\Lambda}(t)x(t) + y(t)$.

Obviously the analysis of the demography for the pension system is the first step towards a more general situation also including the economic and social components, such as the employment rate, economic increase, social costs of immigrant integration and so on.

In Angrisani and colleagues (2012), the dynamic immigration control, built with an algorithm by iteration, defined the immigration vector $y(t)$ in order to asymptotically arrive at a demographic equilibrium for each year t, defining a per year immigration quota for each age class, and minimizing the yearly total of immigrants. Mathematically speaking, it is a conditional minimum problem, with a vector inequality with a single control variable.

The sustainability indicator of the pension systems in the paper mentioned is the ratio between active workers and pensioners:

$$\text{inverse old-age dependency ratio:} = \frac{\text{Number of people aged 16-64}}{\text{Number of people aged 65 and over}}$$

It must be said that when considering a closed Italian population the result is tragic: in 30 years the population becomes half of the present one. The result is that we absolutely need immigrants.

For this indicator, it is not trivial to express what the ideal value is because it also depends on the desired substitution rate. This rate, defined by Angrisani (2000; 2002), is understood as the ratio between the first pension payment and the last salary received, and is thus an indicator of the adequacy of pension benefits. In light of this, we should remember what the European Union indicated in its reports, namely that "a pension can be considered adequate if, as well as preventing social exclusion, it allows people to maintain their standard of living during retirement".

To return to our problem, which wants to use a kind of ideal indicator that also depends on the substitution rate, we can say, without going into too much technical and actuarial detail, that if we expect an average substitution rate of 60 per cent, given a workers' contribution rate of around 30 per cent, the worker/pensioner ratio must be around 2. It is obvious that if higher substitution rates are wanted (as in Italy for today's pensioners who receive a pension that is more than 88 per cent of their final salary), given an unchanged contribution rate, the number of workers compared with pensioners must necessarily increase.

That said, we want to measure the sustainability of the Italian pension system by using the inverse old-age dependency ratio. In this optimal control model, the index grows along a prescribed trajectory, minimizing the annual immigration flow over a given time horizon. The simulation analysis of the model may help the policy makers to decide how to address the sustainability issue.

The control model is equipped with a convergence parameter of between 0 and 1. This regulates the speed of convergence and the total immigration at the same time. A value near 1 slows down the convergence but limits the yearly admission of immigrants, that is to say achieving an equilibrium faster has the cost of a greater flow. It is possible to consider the limitation to admit only immigrants under 35, to have real and potential active workers, and this supposition does not change the convergence of the algorithm.

In the control model, the yearly immigration can be determined for each age class and it means that the age distribution of the population moves towards a demographic equilibrium and that in each year the total immigration is minimized. At the same time, as we said before, in order to be rigorous, a parameter can be set to regulate the speed of convergence and the total immigration at the same time.

A simulation

To do a simulation with Italian data it is possible to compare the demographic dynamics corresponding to different decision scenarios: a strongly limited constant yearly immigration (for example 180,000 as it was with Bossi-Fini Law No. 189/2002), a constant yearly immigration (based on real values), a controlled immigration based on the algorithm moving the age distribution of the population towards a demographic equilibrium (Rother, Catenaro and Schwab 2003; Pitacco 2004).

It is clear that once a demographic equilibrium is approximately attained, it is possible to have the amount of contributions that would guarantee the financial sustainability of a pay-as-you-go pension system with a stable demographic basis, and in this case, the inverse old-age dependency ratio is satisfactory.

If we consider a constant yearly immigration with a quota of 180,000 as before, the inverse old-age dependency ratio declines from 3.2 to 1.6 in 43 years (2.15 in 100 years), as shown in Figure 7.2.

In this case, the Italian population decreases to 52 million in about 40 years and reaches 40 million in 100 years.

If we consider the real immigration figure, not the quota, with about 500,000 migrants (494,289 to be precise), the inverse old-age dependency

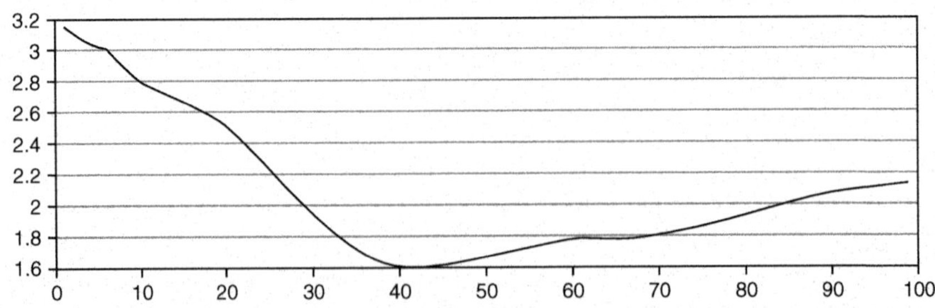

Figure 7.2 Inverse old-age dependency ratio, plotted against time in years. Scenario 1

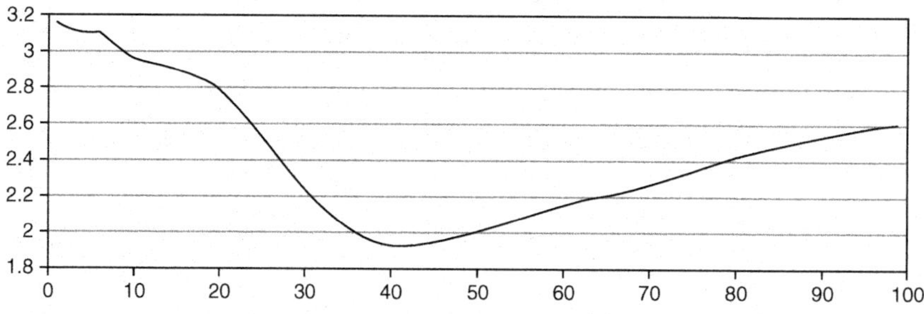

Figure 7.3 Inverse old-age dependency ratio, plotted against time in years. Scenario 2

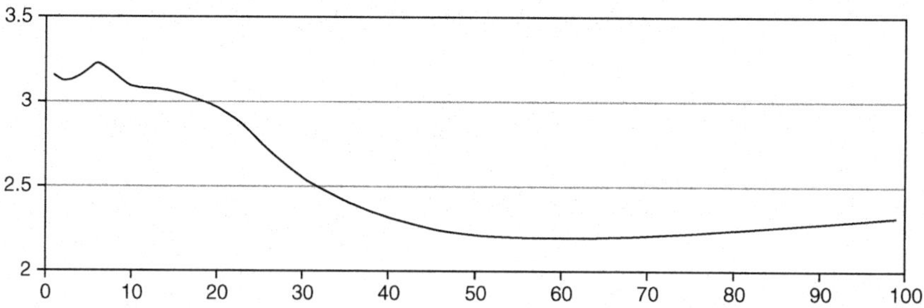

Figure 7.4 Inverse old-age dependency ratio, plotted against time in years. Scenario 3

ratio declines from 3.2 to 1.92 in 40 years (2.6 in 100 years) as shown in Figure 7.3.

In this case, the Italian population increases to 69 million in about 40 years and reaches 87 million in 100 years.

If we consider our control model, with an initial immigration rate of about 450,500 migrants (450,461 to be precise), the inverse old-age dependency ratio declines from 3.2 to 2.2 in 60 years (2.3 in 100 years) as shown in Figure 7.4.

In this case, the Italian population increases to 68.5 million in about 30 years and decreases to 58 million in 100 years. The idea is that when the population reaches a demographic equilibrium, as a consequence, the worker/pensioner ratio stabilizes as well.

In this way, there is a kind of guarantee of the worker/pensioner ratio that manages to remain stable over time, within the logic of a substitution rate that should not go below 60 per cent. With reference to this percentage, there is a draft law, the objective of which is not to go below this threshold and for which an actuarial mathematical model was created (Attias 2012), which was later compared with the Fornero Law currently in force (Attias et al. 2016).

The reality is that the forecasts, in terms of the substitution rate in Italy are not particularly rosy in the medium and long term. According to the Ministerial Committee for assessing and verifying the effects of the Dini Law No. 335/1995 (Commissione Ministeriale per la valutazione degli effetti della legge n. 335/95 e successivi provvedimenti 2001), which introduced the contributions-based calculation method, the substitution rate for those retiring to whom the exclusively contributions-based calculation method is applied will be between 31 and 40 per cent. The situation is slightly better for those retiring to whom the mixed calculation method is applied, partly earnings-based and partly contributions-based, the "pro-rata", who will receive a pension of between 47 and 72 per cent of their final salary.

It should be pointed out that the loss of continuity in income on retirement has in no way been remedied by Law No. 214/2011, known as the Fornero Law, which in Article 24, paragraph 28, merely recalls the principle of the adequacy of pension benefits, without introducing any indications or rules to follow.

To conclude with the logic of our model, it is possible to have a long-term stabilization in immigration policy, and it is possible to say that the algorithm allows for immigration oscillating at around a relatively low level.

Conclusions

To summarize, we can say that starting from the classical Leslie model, which allows an anticipated estimate of the social costs of sustainability in terms of immigration, an optimal control problem has been set that is appropriate for determining a controlled immigration process. Indeed the population can be controlled along a determined trajectory of the sustainability index, as it is possible to see by comparing the value of the ratio of active workers and pensioners in the above hypothesis.

It is necessary to say that immigration is important and unavoidably comes into play to support the Italian social security system.

These models could be useful tools for those interested in the evolution of employment, budget constraints, expected economic growth and other important socio-economic indicators.

In contrast to the former INPS president Boeri, the ex-Minister of the Interior in the first Conte government, Matteo Salvini, supports a strong reduction in migration flows, probably ignoring the effects on pension expenditure. The Security Decree (Law No. 132/2018 in GU 03/12/2018, No. 281) makes the conditions of some of the forced migrants precarious by limiting the granting of residence permits for humanitarian reasons to extremely specific situations. The entry into force of the decree, as it has been underlined by important Catholic associations, is causing a sharp increase in irregularities by blocking integration paths already in place (Dandolo, Strangio and Strozza 2019). It is currently risky to predict what the specific effects will be (and Parliament is looking for solutions). However, it can be deduced that the further and significant obstacles posed to legal entry into Italy, already evident before the measure – just consider that in 2018, only 12,850 arrivals of non-EU citizens were expected for non-seasonal work or of an autonomous type out of a total of 30,850 admissions – it will greatly increase the difficulty for non-EU employees in achieving a legal status.

Controlled immigration can be a possible solution for managing a difficult demographic transition characterized by a drop in the numbers of those born in Italy. Having a flow of legal immigrants would allow Italy to counteract the fall in the native population by having significant contribution flows for the sustainability of the social security system (Allievi 2018).

Notes

1 The National Social Security Institute (in Italian INPS-Istituto Nazionale della Previdenza Sociale) is the main social security institution of the Italian public pension system, with which all public or private employees and most self-employed workers, who do not have their own autonomous social security fund, must be registered. The INPS is subject to surveillance by the Ministry of Labour and Social Policies. In 1943, with Article 3 of Royal Decree 704/1943 it was named the National Social Security Institute, a body governed by public law with a legal personality and autonomous management with the aim of guaranteeing social security.

2 The National Institute for Insurance against Accidents at Work (INAIL in Italian) is a non-economic Italian public body, subject to the supervision of the Italian Ministry of Labour and Social Policies. Born on a voluntary basis in 1883, it was the first body in Italy to protect against accidents at work. In 1965, the fundamental principles of accident insurance were all collected in Decree No. 1124/1965 of the President of the Republic and over the years, subsequent modifications have extended its scope.

3 The risk of paying out pensions for a longer period than that expected owing to an underestimation of the probabilities of survival.

4 $\circ$ indicates the Hadamard product $a \circ b := (a_1 b_1, a_2 b_2, \ldots, a_n b_n)$.

References

Alho J.M. and Spencer B.D. (2005). *Statistical Demography and Forecasting*. Berlin: Sprinter.

Allievi S. (2018). *Immigrazione. Cambiare tutto*. Bari-Roma: Laterza.

Alonso-García J., Boado-Penas M. and Devolder P. (2018). Adequacy, Fairness and Sustainability of Pay-As-You-Go-Pension-Systems: Defined Benefit versus Defined Contribution. *The European Journal of Finance*. 24(13): 1100–1122.

Angrisani M. (2000). *Il tasso di sostituzione nella previdenza*. Seminario Università degli Studi di Sassari, Facoltà di Economia.

Angrisani M. (2002). La pensione integrata a punti. *Rivista della previdenza pubblica e privata*. 1(4): 47–65.

Angrisani M., Attias A., Bianchi S. and Varga Z. (2004). Demographic Dynamic for the Pay-as-You-Go Pension System. *PU.M.A. Pure Mathematics and Applications*. 15(4): 357–374.

Angrisani M., Attias A., Bianchi S. and Varga Z. (2010). *Dynamic Analysis of the Effect of Immigration on the Demographic Background of the Pay-as-You-Go Pension System*. Maf-Mathematical and Statistical Methods for Actuarial Sciences and Finance.

Angrisani M., Attias A., Bianchi S. and Varga Z. (2012). Sustainability of a Pay-As-You-Go Pension System by Dynamic Immigration Control. *Applied Mathematics and Computation*. 219(5): 2442–2452.

Attias A. (2012). A Two-Component Public Pension System under Demographic Equilibrium: A Substitution Rate for Benefit Adequacy. In Università degli Studi del Molise (ed.). *Proceedings XVIII Conference on Actuarial Risk Theory*. Bari: Libellula Edition, 37–74.

Attias A., Arezzo M.F., Pianese A. and Varga Z. (2016). A Comparison of Two Legislative Approaches to the Pay-as-You-Go Pension system in Terms of Adequacy: The Italian Case. *Insurance: Mathematics and Economics*. 68(C): 203–211.

Berman A. and Plemmons R.J. (1994). *Nonnegaive Matrices in the Mathematical Sciences*. Philadelphia: SIAM.

Bernadelli H. (1941). Population Waves. *Journal of the Burma Research Society*. 31(1): 1–18.

Blake D. and Mayhew L. (2006). On the Sustainability of the UK State Pension System in the Light of Population Ageing and Declining Fertility. *The Economic Journal*. 116(512): 286–305.

Blangiardo G.C. (2018a). L'aiuto al welfare e il peso del nero. *il Sole 24 Ore*, 16 luglio.

Blangiardo G.C. (2018b). Gli aspetti statistici. In Fondazione ISMU (ed.). *Ventiquattresimo Rapporto sulle migrazioni 2018*. Milano: Franco Angeli, 65–82.

Bonifazi C. (2007). *L'immigrazione straniera in Italia*. Bologna: Il Mulino.

Bonifazi C. (2013). *L'Italia delle migrazioni*. Bologna: Il Mulino.

Booth H. (2006). Demographic Forecasting: 1980 to 2005. *International Journal of Forecasting*. 22(3): 547–581.

Colucci M. (2018). *Storia dell'immigrazione straniera in Italia. Dal 1945 ai nostri giorni*. Roma: Carocci.

Commissione Ministeriale per la valutazione degli effetti della legge n. 335/95 e successivi provvedimenti (2001). *Verifica del sistema previdenziale ai sensi della legge 335/95 e successive provvedimenti, nell'ottica della competitività dello sviluppo e dell'equità*. Roma: Commissione Ministeriale.

Dandolo, S.D. and Strozza S. (2019). Immigrazione straniera ed esigenze economico produttive del mercato del lavoro: il caso del lavoro di cura. In Pizzuti R. (ed.). *Rapporto sullo Stato Sociale 2019. Welfare pubblico, welfare occupazionale*. Roma: Sapienza Editrice, 302–322.

European Commission (2010). *Green Paper, Towards Adequate, Sustainable and Safe European Pension Systems*. Brussels: COM(2010) 365 final.

European Commission (2018a). *The 2018 Ageing Report: Economic and budgetary projections for the 28 EU Member States (2016-2070)*. European Economy: Institutional Paper No. 079.

European Commission (2018b). *Pension Adequacy Report 2018. Current and Future Income Adequacy in Old Age in the EU. Vol. 2 - Country Profiles.* Luxembourg: Publications Office of the European Union.

European Economic and Social Committee (2010). *Proposal for a Council Decision on Guidelines for the Employment Policies of the Member States – Part II of the Europe 2020 Integrated Guidelines.* COM(2010) 193 final. Bruxelles: Reporteur-general: Wolfgang Greif.

Fehr H. and Habermann C. (2006). Pension Reform and Demographic Uncertainty: The Case of Germany. *Journal of Pension Economics and Finance.* 5(1): 69–90.

Fondazione Leone Moressa (2018). *Rapporto annuale sull'economia dell'immigrazione. Edizione 2018. Prospettive di integrazione in un'Italia che invecchia.* Bologna: Il Mulino.

Fullin G. and Reyneri E. (2011). Low Unemployment and Bad Jobs for New Immigrants in Italy. *International Migration.* 49(1): 118–147.

Gesano G. and Strozza S. (2011). Foreign Migrations and Population Aging in Italy. *Genus.* LXVII(3): 83–104.

IDOS (2017). *Rapporto immigrazione e imprenditoria.* Roma: IDOS.

Istat (2015). *Migrazioni internazionali e interne della popolazione residente. Anno 2013, Statistiche report.* Roma: Istat.

Leslie P.H. (1945). On the Use of Matrices in Certain Population Mathematics. *Biometrika*: 33(3): 183–212.

Leslie P.H. (1948). Some Further Notes on the Use of Matrices in Certain Population Mathematics. *Biometrika*: 35(3-4): 213–245.

Masi A.C. (2019). *Canadian Immigration Policies Patterns over Time: Similitarities and Differences with Those of the United States.* In Fauri F., Masi A.C., Strangio D., Strozza S., Withol De Wenden C. (eds.). *Migrations: Countries of Immigrants, Countries of Migrants. Canada, Italy.* Roma: Nuova Cultura, 85–177.

Myers R.J. (1994). Components of Population Aging and Their Effect on Social Security Programs: Transactions of International Congress of Actuaries. *Insurance: Mathematics and Economics.* 4(1): 209–218.

Nannestad P. (2007). Immigration and Welfare States: A Survey of 15 Years of Research. *European Journal of Political Economy.* 23(2): 512–532.

Pianese A., Attias A., Bianchi S. and Varga Z. (2020). On the Asymptotic Equilibrium of a Population System with Migration. *Insurance: Mathematics and Economics.* 92(C): 115–127.

Pianese A., Attias A. and Varga Z. (2014). Dynamic Immigration Control Improving Inverse Old-Age Dependency Ratio in a Pay-as-You-Go Pension System. *Decision Support Systems.* 64(C): 109–117.

Pianese A., Attias A., Bianchi S. and Varga Z. (2017). *A Demographic Model with Migration for a Payg Pension System.* Facoltà di Economia-Sapienza Università di Roma: Working Papers MEMOTEF No. 151.

Pitacco E. (2004). Survival Models in a Dynamic Context: A Survey. *Insurance: Mathematics and Economics.* 35(2): 279–298.

Rother P.C., Catenaro M. and Schwab G. (2003). *Ageing and Pensions in the Euro Area Survey and Projection Results.* Social Protection Discussion Papers 25986, The World Bank.

Sanchez M. and Alfonso R. (2010). Endogenous Retirement and Public Pension System Reform in Spain. *Economics Modelling.* 27(1): 336–349.

Società Italiana di Statistica (2011). *Rapporto sulla popolazione. L'Italia a 150 anni dall'Unità*. Bologna: Il Mulino.

Strozza S. (2018). Immigrazione e presenza straniera in Italia: evoluzione, caratteristiche e sfide attuali e future. In Frigeri D. and Zupi M. (eds.). *Dall'Africa all'Europa. La sfida politica delle migrazioni*. Roma: Donzelli, 297–330.

Triandafyllidou A. and Marchetti S. (2013). Migrant Domestic and Care Workers in Europe: New Patterns of Circulation? *Journal of Immigrant and Refugee Studies*. 11(4): 339–346.

Varga Z. (1984). *Un modelo en la dinámica de poblaciones*. Notas de Matemàticas de la Universidad Central de Venezuela, 84-ED-03 1-40.

Varga Z., Sebestyen Z., Gamez M., Cabello T. and Attias A. (2011). *Models of Applied Population Dynamics*. Mechanical Engineering Letters-Annual Technical-Scientific journal, Szent Istvan University. 4: 22–36.

Wenko B. (2008). *Immigration and the Pay-as-You-Go Pension System: The Impact of Immigration on Different Groups of Society*. Berlin: Vdm Verlag.

Part III

Immigrant networks, well-being and education

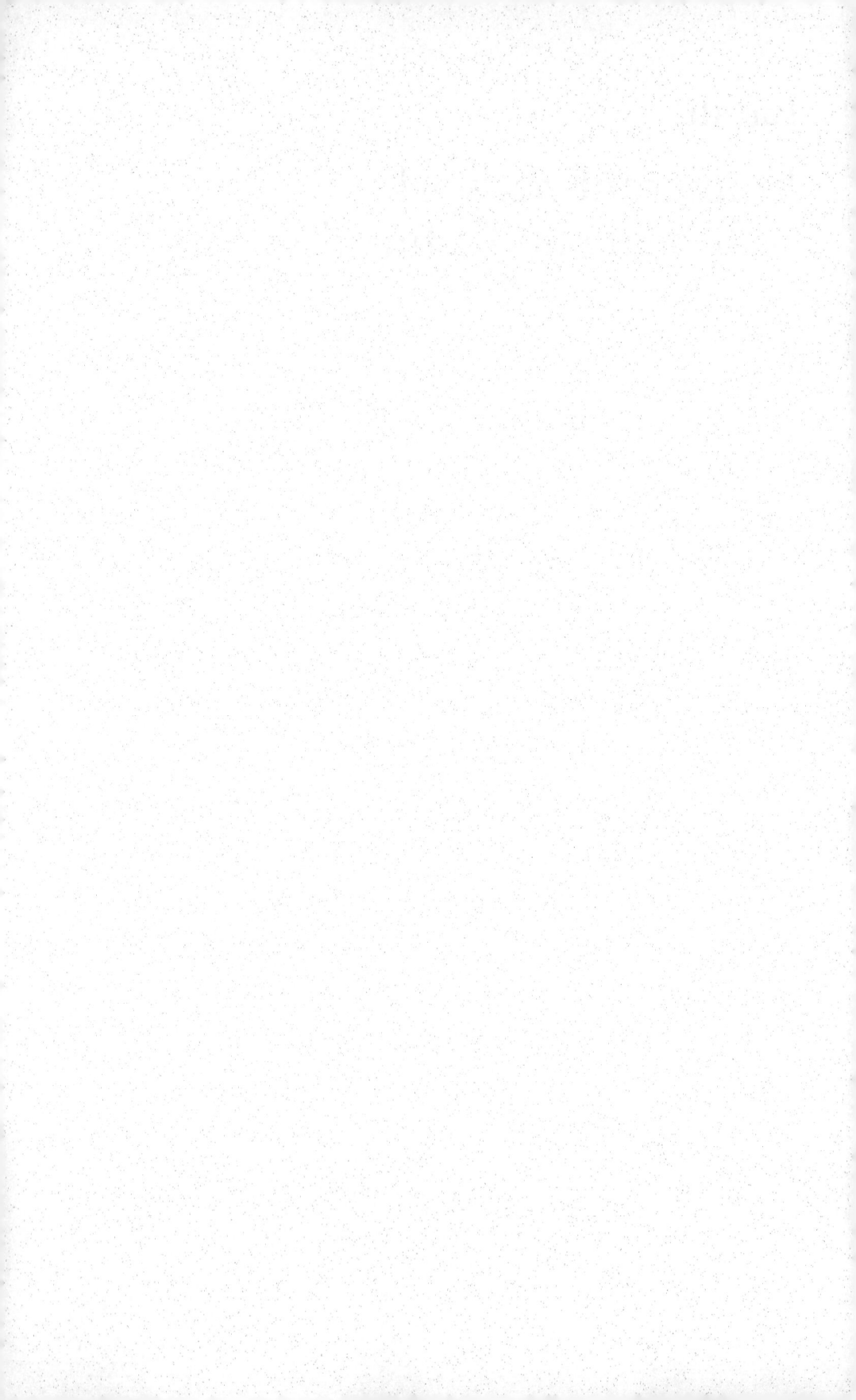

8 Blood, buddies, banks

Potential funding sources for starting a new business as perceived by Maghrebi, Filipino and Chinese immigrants in Italy

Giancarlo Gasperoni and Debora Mantovani

Introduction

Migration towards Western societies generates major socio-economic consequences. As regards the labour market, immigrants' self-employment rates have increased significantly and often exceed those of natives in many countries (Fairlie and Lofstrom 2015; OECD/European Union 2019). Several reasons may lead immigrants to enter self-employment. Starting up a new business may be either a *necessity* (discrimination, insufficient language skills, inadequate education, and lack of professional skills may hinder immigrants' access to wage employment) or an *opportunity* (desire for freedom, independence, ethnic enclaves, and upward social mobility aspirations encourage entrepreneurship) (Williams 2008). In the first case, immigrants are compelled (*pushed*) to become entrepreneurs in order to avoid the risk of unemployment; in the second, immigrants decide (*choose*) to invest in a business to exploit market opportunities and improve their socio-economic status.

Numerous factors – including structural economic and political opportunities (such as labour market and immigration legislation: Kloosterman and Rath 2001) – may lead immigrants towards (or away from) entrepreneurship and impact differently on individuals according to their ethnic background. Empirical research has stressed that not all ethnic groups display the same inclination towards self-employment, and cultural factors – such as values, internal solidarity and loyalty, work ethic, informal network relationships with co-ethnic members, personal motivation – play a crucial role in promoting entrepreneurship. Regardless of these cultural and ethnic differences, would-be entrepreneurs are accustomed to a recurring challenge: gathering enough capital to start up a business (Marlow and Patton 2005; Cetindamar et al. 2012).

This chapter explores the potential sources of financial assistance used by immigrants when they seek to establish a new business in their host country – an endeavour that typically needs to overcome many obstacles.

In particular, the findings reported here focus on the perception, among immigrants living in an Italian city, of the appropriate means for procuring start-up capital. Do different cultural backgrounds and experiences lead to different perceptions of apposite funding sources? What are the rationales underlying the identification of said sources?

The next section offers an overview of theories and research concerning entrepreneurship among immigrants and the modes of financing their business ventures. The following three sections examine, in more detail, entrepreneurship among the three immigrant groups involved in the empirical study: Maghrebis, Filipinos and Chinese. The next two sections focus on the method adopted in the study: the first describes field work activities and the three immigrant groups, as well as the native group used as a sort of benchmark; the second explains the non-directive, narrative-oriented research technique used, based on the administration of a "vignette".

Subsequent sections report and discuss the study's findings. Respondents' reactions pertaining to family members as potential lenders will be examined first, then those involving friendship and community networks, followed by banks and other market actors, and finally other (generally more marginal) potential sources of finance. Within each of these sections, the analysis will focus on both the relative (quantitative) incidence of each means and examples of comments highlighting respondents' attitudes and values. The final two sections provide an overview of the research findings and a discussion of their scientific relevance.

Migrant entrepreneurship and financing business activities

Financial capital, along with human and social capital, is a crucial resource for starting up a new business (Marlow and Patton 2005; Cetindamar et al. 2012). Empirical findings suggest that the amount of personal financial capital is often a precondition for a new entrepreneurial activity's success, especially if entrepreneurs have no (or limited) access to external financial capital supplied by banks or other financial institutions (Cetindamar et al. 2012). In other words, inadequate availability of personal savings and/or limited access to credit may nip entrepreneurial activities in the bud (Evans and Jovanovic 1989).

Since immigrants typically possess insufficient personal savings and/or are not very likely to obtain bank loans at good terms (Haynes et al. 2000; Oliveira 2003; Basa, De Guzman and Marchetti 2012), one might expect immigrants have restricted chances to launch a new business. These capital constraints also help explain why immigrant entrepreneurs are more likely to invest in small retail businesses: entry costs are low and less start-up capital is required (Zhou 2004; Edwards et al. 2016). Banks are indeed reluctant to lend money to first-time entrepreneurs lacking liquidity and/or personal assets that could be posted as collateral (home ownership, dividends, interests, rental income), and such circumstances are common among immigrants, who are often labelled as "unbankable" (Basa, De Guzman and Marchetti 2012). Furthermore, immigrants may experience episodes of prejudice: banks are less likely to grant a loan to non-natives, since they are perceived as unskilled, inexperienced and insolvent (Deakins, Majmudar and Paddison 1997; Haynes et al. 2000; Cavalluzzo and Wolken 2005; Fairlie 2005; Marlow and Patton 2005; Aldén and Hammarstedt 2016). Immigrants' low education levels, poor skills in speaking the local language and lack of knowledge of the credit system also hinder their ability to interact with banks (i.e., face the paperwork required to file a loan application: Servon et al. 2010; Bates, Lofstrom and Servon 2011).

Despite these substantial drawbacks and disadvantages, immigrants' propensity towards self-employment is hardly negligible. The number of immigrant entrepreneurs has increased in Western societies (especially in Europe) over recent decades, and immigrants' self-employment rates are higher than natives' in many countries (Fairlie 2005; Baycan-Levent and Nijkamp 2009; OECD/European 2019).

Sociological literature offers theoretical explanations about flourishing immigrant entrepreneurship. According to the *resource disadvantage theory* (or the *block mobility hypothesis*), self-employment is not an actual choice, but rather a "survival" strategy pursued by socially marginalized minorities in order to achieve economic integration. Immigrants are more likely than natives to be employed in low-paid, unskilled and demanding jobs and to suffer from unemployment and discrimination. Starting up a new business is perceived as a means to overcome exclusion in the core labour market (Glazer and Moynihan 1970; Waldinger, Aldrich and Ward 1990; Light and Gold 2000; Rath and Kloosterman 2000; Allasino et al. 2004; Reyneri and Fullin 2008; Edwards et al. 2016).

Other studies identify ethnicity as a crucial factor in explaining immigrants' entrepreneurship: not all ethnic groups display the same tendency to be self-employed. The *middleman minority theory* stresses that certain ethnic groups occupy an intermediate position between dominant and other subordinate groups. Although members of middleman minorities suffer from severe social and/or labour discrimination, they manage to succeed in labour-intensive, small-scale ethnic enterprises. Middleman minorities share distinctive cultural and societal traits, which favour strong in-group ties and reliance on family/co-ethnic members. They usually run small retail businesses, and their customers are typically non-co-ethnic members of other marginalized groups[1] (Bonacich 1973; O'Brien and Fugita 1982).

Ethnic enclave theory, conversely, refers to entrepreneurs who share ethnicity and a residential area with their clientele. Ethnicity, with its associated cultural norms and values, is crucial in accounting for why some ethnic groups are more likely than others to start a business: some cultures promote mutual help and rely on strong social ties, solidarity, trust and reciprocity. Such features nurture social capital and, in turn, an ethnic enclave economy: entrepreneurs establish their businesses in their own community and provide employment and services to their co-ethnic members. This entails opportunities for rapid upward social mobility, involving both ethnic entrepreneurs and the rest of the co-ethnic community (Light 1972; Portes and Zhou 1992; Zhou 1992; 2004; Portes and Sensenbrenner 1993; Light and Gold 2000; Rath and Schutjens 2015; Wingfield and Taylor 2016).

Ethnicity and cultural values help understand not only immigrants' attitudes towards entrepreneurship, but also their access to credit. Personal savings and commercial banks are only two potential finance sources, albeit the most commonly used by self-employers globally (OECD/European Union 2019). Family members and friends are an additional ethnic-based funding resource and may provide resources as either loans or gifts (Jarvis 2000; OECD/European Union 2019). Many immigrants rely on community networks for finance, insofar as they often offer a major advantage: interest-free loans (Kloosterman 2010; Fielden and Davidson 2012; van Delf, Gorter and Nijkamp 2000). Empirical studies emphasize that ethnic groups characterized by cultural values rooted in collectivist and familistic ideologies are more likely to be "entrepreneurial".[2] In these social contexts, the economic interest of the entire household – and the surrounding co-ethnic community – is prioritized over individual interest; family and collective needs are privileged; and resources are exploited for the benefit of the entire group. Strong kinship ties reinforce social capital, and availability of common financial and social resources supports business activities (Portes and Sensenbrenner 1993; Kibria 1994; Sanders and Nee 1996; Valdez 2008). As a consequence, ethnic entrepreneurs can start a new business with relative ease by using family labour (most ethnic businesses are "family-owned with no employees": labour is provided primarily by family members, and non-family wage workers needn't be hired: Light 1972; Tienda and Raijman 2004; Zhou 2006). As already mentioned, access to credit may be obtained by pooling immediate family members' resources, and perhaps extended family members' and friends' savings as well.

If family savings are insufficient, an alternative strategy commonly adopted to collect financial capital is given by rotating credit associations. Such associations are community-based and commonly used by immigrant entrepreneurs from Asia and West Africa to sponsor small businesses (Bates 1997; Collins 2000). Their underlying principle is that members can access credit in time of need by resorting to a common money pool fed by regular contributions deposited by association members (Light 1972; Light and Bonacich 1988; Dallalfar 1994; Fairlie 2005; Wong 2013).

Immigrant entrepreneurship may be encouraged by contextual-external opportunities, such as governmental programmes aimed at providing financial assistance to aspiring businesspeople.[3] Although the amount of capital provided by such initiatives is often insufficient to start up a business from scratch, such support can be effectively combined with other funding strategies (Piperopoulos 2010; OECD/European Union 2019). Unfortunately, few immigrant entrepreneurs are adequately informed about the existence and operational procedures of such schemes (Kushnirovich and Heilbrunn 2008). In other cases, pro-self-employment policies may be especially deleterious, since migrants are either formally denied access to them or passed over, in practice, due to prejudice and stereotypes affecting policy implementation (Kontos 2003).

Aspiring entrepreneurs finance their new enterprises by resorting to different (formal and informal) financial sources, which can be either used in an exclusive form or, more commonly, combined in different ways. Although immigrant entrepreneurs resort more frequently to co-ethnic resources than to formal commercial banks, a common pattern of financing is not easily detectable and may vary according to the ethnic group and/or the structural opportunities offered by the receiving country.[4] For example, Japanese and Korean immigrants are more likely to use personal savings, whereas Chinese, Hispanic and Taiwanese primarily tend to resort to loans from kin. Rotating credit associations are commonly used by Chinese, Filipinos and Koreans, but in general this is not their main source of financial support (Light and Bonacich 1988; Yoon 1995; Tseng 1997; Hosler 1998; Zhou 2004; Fairlie 2005; Kidwell, Hoy and Ibarreche 2012; Wong 2013). A focus on ethnic groups explored in this study is therefore auspicious.

Maghrebi migrant entrepreneurship

Sociological literature has paid little attention to entrepreneurial experiences of immigrants hailing specifically from Maghreb countries; empirical research tends to focus either on a specific national group – in particular Moroccans (Masurel et al. 2002; Semi 2006; Solano 2016) – or, more frequently, on Muslims,[5] analysing the effect of Islam on believers' penchant for business (Cooney et al. 2011; Zubairu et al. 2015; Alaslani and Collins 2017).

Moroccan immigrants' propensity towards entrepreneurship tends to be quite low, and repeated episodes of unemployment and discrimination experienced in the mainstream labour market might be responsible for their limited self-employment (Alaslani and Collins 2017). Their businesses typically involve retail trade and food services and are commonly ethnic-based (Masurel et al. 2002; Mizrachi 2005; Semi 2006; Avola and Cortese 2012). Moroccan entrepreneurs take advantage of their co-ethnic members' concentration in specific geographic areas and establish enterprises aimed at supplying goods which satisfy customers' specific ethnic-based needs. A few typical examples are clothing stores selling ethnic clothes for special occasions (i.e., weddings or baby showers) and *halal* butcher shops (Solano 2016). These activities service a vast clientele, which may include Maghrebi co-nationals as well as immigrants from other Islamic countries.

Religion is deemed a major element of Maghrebi culture and shapes observant Muslims' lives. Although Islam encourages entrepreneurship, rather than limit it, "moral" entrepreneurs must conduct their business activities in accordance with Islamic law (Chong and Liu 2009; Zubairu et al.

2015). According to the Quran, economic life – including finance – must be inspired by principles of justice and equity, and this is why any (exploitative) "increase" – *riba* (any form of interest on loans) – is unambiguously prohibited (Siddiqui 2004; Iqbal and Molyneux 2005). A saying (*hadit*) states: "Every loan that begets an interest or benefit/profit is *riba*" (Ilahiane 2014: 320), and interest charged by banks is also considered *riba* (Ariff 1988). Banks are not allowed to charge interest on loans (Khan 2010), and borrowers are not allowed to pay interest. This precept explains Islamic banks' profit-and-loss sharing paradigm, which pursues economic equity and justice through the reciprocal sharing of profits and losses between borrowers and banks (Ariff 1988; Ayub 2002; Iqbal and Molyneux 2005; Khan 2010). Islamic banking systems offer a unique mechanism to protect entrepreneurs from unfavourable business outcomes; for example, under the *mudarabah* system, "every risk of loss will be endured by the loaner while the entrepreneur will not receive any gains" (Hamid and Sa'ari 2011: 112).

Riba is a key topic in current debate among immigration researchers, since Western finance is interest-based. Some Islamic scholars are more tolerant towards Muslims' use of interest in non-Muslim countries, and some studies suggest that Muslim immigrants tend to reject *riba*. The greatest challenge faced by Muslim entrepreneurs starting a new business in Ireland is access to capital according to Islamic principles (Cooney et al. 2011). Fielden and Davidson (2012) stress that Muslim entrepreneurs – especially women[6] – are more likely to seek financial assistance from their extended family in order to heed the moral obligations of the Islamic way of life. Alternatively, in absence of Islamic loan products, most Muslims postpone the launch of their businesses until they can save up enough money. Resorting to personal savings is preferred over the informal financial practices of mutual help. Rotating credit associations are an infrequent strategy among Muslim immigrants (El-Massidi 2008; Cooney et al. 2011).

In the start-up stage of Moroccan entrepreneurship in the Netherlands, weak ties – involving co-ethnics rather than family and friends – are more relevant than strong ones in providing financial support, since Moroccan families – especially parents (in-law) – typically do not have enough money to provide loans (el Bouk, Vedder and te Poel 2013). Furthermore, Moroccans are less likely than natives to stipulate *written* agreements with informal money-lenders (parents, siblings, other relatives or friends), since money-lending presupposes a trustworthy relationship not requiring formal arrangements. Trust and solidarity characterize this ethnic community, which is founded on collectivistic values (Merz et al. 2009).

On the whole, the absence of Islamic finance, the lack of community pooling resources and the limited financial help obtained from family members tend to authorize Muslim immigrants to borrow money from commercial banks.

Filipino migrant entrepreneurship

By and large, Filipino migrants are less likely to start up an enterprise than other ethnic groups (Fairlie and Meyer 1996; Fairlie 2005; Johnson, Muñoz and Alon 2007; Maas 2011). Some scholars ascribe Filipino immigrants' high risk aversion and avoidance of leadership positions to their cultural traits. On the whole, Filipino culture is indeed collectivistic and strongly family-centred, which encourages family members to prioritize the household's economic interests over individuals'. Loyalty, solidarity, cooperation, interdependency and mutual support – in terms of emotional, practical, psychological and financial help – are key cultural values, which promote a solid sense of belonging to the family (Espiritu and Wolfe 2001) and hinder entrepreneurship for "the good of the family" (Agbayani-Siewert 1994: 430). Mangiafico (1988) stresses Filipinos' low degree of ambition and weak forward-looking vision; Hofstede (1991) detects a widespread low level of individualism in Filipino communities, which – according to McGrath, MacMillan and Scheinberg (1992) – correlates negatively with entrepreneurship: "collective societies often limit private property [...] and tend to prohibit private access to resources" (Mitchell et al. 2000: 979); for Szanton (1998), Filipinos' low engagement in commerce depends on the moral pressure of obligatory sharing. Zanfrini and Sarli (2009: 295) define Filipinos as "culturally non prone to making investments".

Filipinos' limited managerial skills are an additional factor held responsible for low levels of entrepreneurship. This lack of expertise is attributed to pervasive corruption in the Philippines (which discourages capital investment) and most migrants' unemployment status at the time of migration (which entails both inexperience and a dearth of financial resources: Johnson, Muñoz and Alon 2007).

Filipino immigrants' weak engagement in business ventures has also been linked to their high employment opportunities, especially as regards women employed as domestic helpers. Enjoying both strong ties within the co-ethnic community and the support of the Catholic church, Filipino migrants – even if newly arrived – are easily incorporated into the mainstream labour market; and – according to resource disadvantage theory – the shift towards self-employment is considered the last option to be pursued when alternative employment cannot be found (Min 1986; Lodigiani 1995; Crane 2004; Zanfrini 2006).

Filipino migrants are used to borrowing money and accessing credit, especially in order to send remittances regularly to their families in the Philippines (Basa, De Guzman and Marchetti 2012). Filipinos' strong sense of belonging to an extended family pushes them to take care of their relatives, and supplying financial support helps satisfy households' daily consumption needs, promote children's education and procure health care for elderly parents. Moreover, Filipino migrants consider migration as temporary, and remittances may be invested in business activities that will support their family and themselves once they return home (Yang 2008; Ang, Sugiyarto and Jha 2009). The relevance of financial support for the extended family is well-exemplified by Filipino migrants' "double" engagement in the labour market, insofar as they are often active both in "regular" domestic work and informal business activities. The purpose of this twofold effort is to send a larger amount of remittances to families back home (Parreñas 2001; Fresnoza-Flot and Pécoud 2007).

As regards access to credit, Basa, De Guzman and Marchetti (2012) study indebted Filipino migrants in Italy and their access to credit by analysing the loans they contracted. Results show that the primary source of financing is Italian financial institutions, which lend money at a legal but very high interest rate to compensate for the migrants' lack of collateral. Italian banks and micro-credit organizations are another financial source, the secondary nature of which stems from the strict personal requirements that need to be satisfied and the smaller size of prospective loans. Relatives and friends are a marginal, but still quite common, source of financing. The greatest advantage of resorting to the extended family is that contracted loans are interest-free. Loans are based on the traditional *paluwagan* system: all members (friends, relatives, co-workers, neighbours) of a mutual help group save the same amount of money, put it in a common fund and take turns (rotating credit) in accessing the pooled savings. Finally, another residual (illegal) source of loans is informal lenders, usually co-national usurers charging high interest rates, to whom Filipino migrants without a regular residence permit and/or a regular work contract are more likely to resort.

Chinese migrant entrepreneurship

Empirical sociological research has provided ample evidence of Chinese immigrants' high propensity towards (prosperous) entrepreneurship, especially as compared to other non-European immigrants' (Light 1972; Portes and Sensenbrenner 1993; Busenitz and Lao 1996; Fairlie and Meyer 1996; Bates 1997; Oliveira 2003).

In explaining the nature of Chinese entrepreneurship, some scholars underscore the relevance of the millenary Confucian tradition, which promotes values consistent with thriving enterprises, such as hard work, deference, perseverance and diligence (Anderson and Lee 2008; Statman and Weng 2010; Allen 2017).[7] Additionally, Confucianism encourages a forward-looking culture fostering individuals' orientations towards future rewards and the virtue of frugality (Hofstede 2001). Parsimony and postponement of gratification are extremely widespread among Chinese immigrants (Zhou 1992; 2004): expenses are aimed at satisfying basic needs (food and housing) over luxury items, thus contributing to the accumulation of family savings, which (in the long term) may be invested in starting up small businesses.

Confucian culture also bestows relevance to the family, the basic unit of life and production in traditional Chinese society. Strong solidarity ties guarantee family members' ability to rely on mutual forms of emotional, practical and financial support. Intra-family loyalty allows a potential entrepreneur to bear more risks, and resorting to family workers helps reduce operational costs. Most Chinese businesses are indeed family-controlled, and kin are usually tireless providers of unpaid (or underpaid) labour and promoters of trustworthy relationships, thus reducing transaction and management costs (Zhou 2004; Zhou and Lin 2005; Chunxia 2010).

Chinese may also enjoy co-ethnic support and ethnic resources: collectivism is a typical trait of Chinese society. Several scholars ascribe Chinese immigrants' entrepreneurship to their "Chineseness", i.e., cultural traits founded on shared collective responsibility, solidarity, reciprocal trust and mutual loyalty.[8] Chinatowns are classical examples of ethnic enclaves whose members may count on a sizeable stock of social capital used by immigrant entrepreneurs to start up small ethnic activities (such as restaurants or garment factories)[9] (Light 1972; Nee and Nee 1973; Zhou 2004; Anderson and Lee 2008; Zhou and Cho 2010).

Family and the co-ethnic community are also primary sources of financial support. Most Chinese entrepreneurs finance their businesses either using their own savings or borrowing interest-free money from relatives and/or friends. A common strategy for bankrolling a new business is to pool financial resources lent by both family and co-ethnic members (Light and Bonacich 1988; Zhou 1992; Oliveira 2003; Wong 2013). Multiple financial sources rooted in the collectivist community help account for higher levels of entrepreneurship and lower degrees of risk aversion (Statman and Weng 2010).

In Chinese communities, access to credit is widely guaranteed by an alternative (or integrative) informal, ethnic-based financing source, such as rotating credit associations (*hui*) (Light 1972; Light and Bonacich 1988; Bates 1997; Kushnirovich and Heilbrunn 2008). Rotating credit clubs have a long tradition in China (dating back at least to the seventh century BCE) and conform to stringent ethnic-based norms (immigrant borrowers must be Chinese, hail from a specific geographic area, be known within the community and behave properly). The *hui* model, used for both saving and borrowing, represents an effective borrowing alternative to commercial banks, especially as immigrant Chinese entrepreneurs are frequently discriminated by the latter due to cultural differences, communication difficulties and lack of collateral.

Field work and study participants

The data used here are drawn from a survey conducted within the broader framework of a research project on "Intergenerational Transfers and Immigrant Population" at the University of Bologna.[10] Field work was carried out between November 2014 and November 2015, on 489 individuals coming (or born to parents) from four distinct areas: the Maghreb (Morocco, Tunisia and Algeria), the Philippines, China and Italy itself. Respondents were recruited via a snowball technique among adults residing in the province of Bologna (in Northeastern Italy); only one respondent from any given household was allowed to participate in the study.

The immigrant population in Italy is unequally distributed across its regions and more highly concentrated in the North. Maghrebis – especially Moroccans – are one of the major immigrant groups in the Bologna province and comprise one of the earliest (hence deeply-rooted) migrant flows towards Italy.[11] Immigrants from the Philippines are also one of the most populous and early non-native communities in Bologna, dating back to the early 1980s; they continue to be employed, typically, as domestic workers.[12] Chinese-origin migrants, featuring rapid growth over the last 20 years, display a strong entrepreneurial aptitude (Ceccagno 2003; Battilani and Fauri 2018) and a settlement behaviour featuring a high degree of geographic concentration (Bergamaschi 2011).[13]

The respondent recruitment strategy is of a clearly non-probabilistic nature and therefore does not authorize any claim to representativeness. A comparison of the socio-demographic profiles of the four respondent groups and the corresponding communities in the Emilia-Romagna region is nevertheless informative (Table 8.1). The Italian group, obviously, is a sort of benchmark against which immigrant-origin groups can be compared. In all four groups, respondents tend to be relatively young (as compared to the reference population from which they are drawn) and, roughly, equally distributed between males and females, although the latter are over-represented in the Filipino group. Almost all Maghrebis participating in the study are Moroccans (for a more extensive overview of these groups' socio-demographic characteristics: Albertini, Gasperoni and Mantovani 2019; on immigrant business groups in Italy: Strangio 2018).

The questionnaire included, besides a central section comprising a set of vignettes aimed at capturing norms and values shaping decision-making in difficult scenarios (see below), an initial section and a final one with closed-ended items regarding individuals' socio-demographic characteristics and ties with family members (for a more detailed account of the research project, see Mantovani, Gasperoni and Albertini 2018).

The vignette

Ascertaining individuals' authentic preferences, value orientations and norm expectations is notoriously difficult: a significant gap usually separates what an individual really believes and what she is willing to state in a public context (e.g., during an interview). A range of phenomena known to social researchers – such as acquiescence and social desirability – can induce a respondent to express opinions and attitudes that do not correspond to his genuine convictions (Marradi and Gasperoni 2002; Roccato 2003).

Table 8.1 Socio-demographic profile of respondent groups and corresponding reference populations (percentage values unless otherwise specified)

	Italians		*Maghrebis*		*Filipinos*		*Chinese*	
	Pop.	*Sample*	*Pop.*	*Sample*	*Pop.*	*Sample*	*Pop.*	*Sample*
Gender[a]								
Male	48	50	52	52	46	36	49	50
Female	52	50	48	48	54	64	51	50
Age[b]								
Mean	54	41	38	34	40	38	36	31
Median	53	41	35-39	30	35-39	38	35-39	26
(Min-Max age range)	(18-75+)	(18-84)	(18-75+)	(18-79)	(18-75+)	(18-68)	(18-75+)	(18-54)
Mean permanence in Italy (years)	–	–	n.a.	15.1	n.a	16.8	n.a.	11.9
(N)		(144)		(143)		(83)		(119)

a Population data refers to the Province of Bologna. Source: Istat 2015 (demo.istat.it).
b Population data refers to people of 18 years of age and more residing in the Province of Bologna. Source: Istat 2015 (demo.istat.it) for Italians; Census 2011 (http://dati-censimentopopolazione.istat.it/Index.aspx) for Maghrebis, Filipinos and Chinese.
n.a. = not available.

Exploring the self-perceived moral and material obligations of people engaged in a migratory project can be even more difficult (Font and Mèndez 2013; Gu 2013): besides the potential practical obstacles related to immigrants' limited linguistic competence and reluctance to interact with presumptive "officials", researchers and immigrants may subscribe to divergent norms and values, and immigrants may for a host of reasons perceive the need to censor their views. In such circumstances, using direct questions would be inappropriate and give rise to misleading results.

The data used in this study were collected via a technique based on narration of episodes and the observation of reactions to them. Finch speaks of *vignettes*: "short stories about hypothetical characters in specified circumstances, to whose situation the interviewee is invited to respond" (1987, 105). Marradi, using another term, describes a *story* as "an episode constructed and presented in such a way as to stimulate a reaction by the respondent, inducing him to take a position on the topic and thus reveal his value options in a more complete and less supervised way than he would usually do when answering a direct question" (2005, 29). A major advantage of this technique is its non-directive nature, providing the opportunity to collect data concerning beliefs and norms underpinning, for example, the identification of appropriate sources of financial support. Respondents are not asked to state what they personally would do in a given situation, but rather what the characters depicted in the vignette ought to do. Due to the distance it places between respondents and vignette characters, the impersonal stimulus reduces social desirability bias and encourages less guarded reactions and a more spontaneous disclosure of value orientations. Although vignettes represent hypothetical scenarios, they aspire to reproduce realistic situations to which respondents can easily relate. This makes it more likely for interviewees to express grounded, reasoned views based on experience and rooted in a precise cultural identity.

The vignette analysed in this study invites respondents to imagine a situation in which a young couple (sharing the respondents' native or specific immigrant origin) – experiencing economic difficulties after a long period of unemployment – decides to open a grocery shop. Undertaking the new enterprise, however, unequivocally requires an initial financial outlay well beyond the couple's means. Respondents are asked to whom the couple should turn for economic help and to elaborate on the reasons for their choices. The goal of the vignette is to capture the salience of family members, friendship and community networks, and banks (or other possible backers) as potential sources of financial aid, as well as to identify the underlying norms and value orientations justifying such preferences. Here is the text of the vignette:

> [Male name] is a young immigrant from [country of origin]. He and his wife have two children, aged 6 to 8. Due to the economic crisis the two spouses have lost their job in the clothing company where they worked. After more than a year of unemployment they have decided to

try to open a small grocery store. [Male name] and his wife have some savings, but to open the shop they need an additional €15 thousand. Whom should they ask for this financial help?

[Subsequent probe, to be repeated] Is there anybody else to whom [male name] and his wife could or should turn to for a loan?

The vignette clearly exemplifies a situation in which the primary motive to start up a small business is not related to the most widespread pull factors, such as achieving independence, making money or being one's own boss. On the contrary, the featured couple opts for self-employment because a major push factor is in play: unemployment (Renzulli, Aldrich and Moody 2000). The vignette's realism is bolstered by other features. Firstly, falling into unemployment was very common at the time of fieldwork, in the aftermath of the 2008 economic crisis, which affected immigrants to a greater degree than native Italians (Fellini 2018). Secondly, self-employment is a strategy common among immigrants seeking to escape unemployment and achieve integration in the destination society (Light 1972). Thirdly, opening a grocery store is a viable, "true-to-life" opportunity, since retailing is a widespread venture, featuring comparatively low entry barriers and costs (Butler and Greene 1997; Edwards et al. 2016). Finally, four distinct versions of the vignette were used: one for each respondent group. More specifically, the vignette was adapted to each respondent group: the male spouse's name identifies him as a member of the ethnic group to which the respondent belongs (Antonio for Italian respondents, Omar for Maghrebis, Reynaldo for Filipinos, Jian Jun for Chinese).

The realism of the vignette's scenario is further underscored by the fact that small and medium entreprises are the backbone of the Italian economy (Chiesi 2011) and self-employment is widespread among both the immigrant and (especially) the native populations. With respect to other European Union (EU) countries, Italy has a higher self-employment rate among natives as compared to immigrants. Far from being a second choice, self-employment is a rational strategy implemented by low-educated and low-skilled Italians aiming for upward social mobility (Fullin 2013). In 2015, according to official statistics (dati.istat.it), there were an estimated 4.9 million self-employed workers in the country, accounting for 29 per cent of all workers, significantly more than in any other EU country (except Greece). In the same year, 9.2 per cent of all retail entrepreneurs in Italy were of non-EU nationality, for a total of 210,000 workers (Direzione Generale dell'Immigrazione e delle Politiche di Integrazione 2016).

Interviewers were instructed to probe the reasons underlying respondents' reactions to the vignette, including reasons why (or why *not*) funding is sought from specific sources. Up to seven potential sources of financial support, along with motivations and other comments, were recorded.

Reactions were subsequently coded and assigned to the categories that are employed in the following analyses and reported in frequency distributions displayed in Tables 8.2 to 8.6. These categories include: family members, with a distinction being drawn between ascendant kin (parents, aunts, uncles), lateral kin (siblings, cousins) and others (or generic references to relatives); friends and local community; banks and other market-based sources; welfare programmes; other, residual strategies. Also, motivations and comments were explored in order to identify underlying rationales, norms and values. Multiple coding was allowed; many respondents highlighted more than one funding source and/or reason to use them.

The role of blood

Family members are mentioned as potential suppliers of financial aid by a majority of respondents in *each* of the four groups defined by area of origin, but this simple fact conceals significant differences along several dimensions (Table 8.2[14]), including the respondents' ethnicity, the type of family member cited, and the comparative salience of the reaction (as revealed by response order: it is reasonable to assume that the initial responses reflect a more spontaneous, "natural" propensity with respect to subsequent answers that entail additional cognitive energy).

Almost all Chinese and Italian respondents (94 and 92%, respectively) state that they would resort to kinship members, against 71 per cent of Maghrebi and 52 per cent of Filipino respondents. The apparent similarity among the

Table 8.2 Incidence of responses mentioning family members as potential funding sources, by respondents' area of origin, type of family member and response order (percentage values; base = number of respondents)

	Italy	*Maghreb*	*Philippines*	*China*
Any family member				
– Initial response	39	34	17	81
– First two responses	81	65	47	94
– All responses	92	71	52	94
Ascendant family				
– Initial response	31	20	12	38
– First two responses	69	36	25	53
– All responses	78	38	29	55
Lateral family				
– Initial response	6	9	1	39
– First two responses	20	27	18	72
– All responses	40	32	22	78
Other kin references				
– Initial response	2	5	4	4
– First two responses	9	17	12	13
– All responses	24	26	17	37
(N)	(144)	(143)	(83)	(119)

first two groups is significantly weakened if one also considers response order. A great majority of Chinese respondents (81%) mention a family member immediately, in their initial reaction to the vignette; in the other three groups only a minority does so. In the latter, nevertheless, blood relations, if referred to at all, are strongly concentrated among the first two responses.

The apparent similarity between Chinese and Italian respondents is also belied by the type of family members to whom they would turn for financial aid. The Chinese are more likely to ask siblings for help, both in general (78%) and in their initial reactions (39%), compared to Italians (40%), who are also quite loath to adopt an opening strategy of seeking out brothers and sisters (only 6%). Respondents originating from the Phillipines or the Maghreb are also disinclined to move laterally within their kinship networks; in the two groups, not unlike Italians, among those who *do* mention family members less than half cite brothers or sisters. (Of course, the likelihood of turning to siblings could be influenced by family size and structure: a person might not contemplate asking siblings for help if she hasn't any.)

Italians are highly likely to suggest that the vignette's main characters seek out assistance from one of their parents. If all responses are considered, 78 per cent of Italian respondents, against 55 per cent of Chinese ones, identify ascendant family members as prospective lenders. The Filipino and Maghrebi respondents are less likely (29 and 38%, respectively) to recommend reaching out to parents.

In each of the four respondent groups, *other* relatives are brought up less often than parents or siblings and quite rarely indeed in the initial reactions to the vignette. But, again, differences among groups emerge. The Chinese are more prone to speak of more distant blood relations (37%), the Filipinos appreciably less so (17%), with the Italians and the Maghrebis falling somewhere in between.

An exploration of the content of reactions to the vignette contributes to detecting recurring topics relating to family-based financial assistance. Some comments reveal hierarchical patterns dictating whether family members should be consulted before, after or simultaneously with friends.[15]

> They should ask their family first, if the family can help. First parents, then brothers and sisters. Then they can turn to friends. (M-m92)

> For the Chinese it's normal to ask friends and relatives for loans: we help each other out. (C-m65)

Other comments point to within-family hierarchies, shaping which kinds of relatives should be consulted first. Typically, as we have already seen, ascendant ties prevail over lateral kin.

> First you ask parents, then brothers and sisters, uncles, aunts and cousins, but it depends on the relationship. Sometimes the relationship with uncles and aunts is tighter than with siblings ... Relatives living in Italy [are] more willing. (C-w91)

> They need to ask for money from their family ... from the nearest family ties to the least close. (M-m78)

> They should seek help from the most direct relatives, like parents and siblings; since Filipino families are rather large, they have a greater chance of obtaining money. (F-m89)

> They should turn to their parents, the only relatives it is possible to turn to. (I-w51)

Some respondents go so far as to profess a policy of sibling avoidance, in that brothers and sisters might have similar needs and it would not be fair to undermine them.

> He shouldn't ask his brothers because they could have similar problems. (I-m58)

> It's best not to ask brothers and sisters or other relatives [besides parents] because they might have the same kind of problems or may have them in the future. (I-w51)

Nevertheless, there are instances in which requests directed at siblings are recommended over those made to parents.

> Antonio should turn first to his brothers and sisters, and then – if they don't have the means – to his parents. (I-w57)

Another recurrent feature involves the opportunity of turning to kin that actually possess *sufficient resources*. The type of kin relationship is of secondary importance; the tangible ability to provide a loan is paramount.

> You can ask a close relative that has greater economic means. (F-m95)

> Firstly, relatives that have economic means ... it depends on their economic situation. (C-w76)

> They could ask relatives and friends for economic help ... calculating the economic means of the people they turn to. (M-m97)

> Within the family he should ask who is economically more well off. (I-m95)

> As far as relatives are concerned, the choice needs to take into account the relative that has more economic means and is more willing to lend money; it could even be a cousin. (M-m95)

> It depends on the relatives' economic conditions: if they too have problems, it will be difficult [for the couple] to open their mouths and ask for help. (C-m89)

Lending ability is sometimes linked to geographic proximity and the constraints of transnational families. Pertinent comments imply that family members who do not already reside in Italy would be less able or less willing to help.

> Relatives, if they live in Italy or at least in Europe. In the described situation the parents are still in China, so probably [they should turn to] older brothers and sisters, or uncles if they're already immigrants. (C-w88)

> They could turn to ... family, but it depends if it's in Morocco and on its economic resources. (M-w92)

> Perhaps first the wife's relatives. At least for me that's the way it is, because my wife's parents live in Italy and are more willing. (C-w91)

> If you have a family that can lend a hand, you can ask them. But it has to be here, not in Morocco: they can't manage from over there. (M-m87)

Several respondents provided good reasons for *not* relying on family members for help. In some cases, this exclusionary stance is motivated by the sizeable burden that the loan would place on relatives (or friends).

> I certainly wouldn't advise them to turn to their families, because the sum of €15 thousand is too much. (M-w82)

> Asking someone for €15 thousand is demanding. It's preferable to seek a loan from a bank. (F-w53)

> You don't ask friends for more than €200... not even relatives. (F-w47)

> You can't ask relatives or friends because it's not easy to start a business: it's not €3-4 thousand. (M-m69)

In at least one case, the financial burden is an issue that directly impacts the aspiring borrowers: a Filipino respondent suggests avoiding families and friends because it would be costly.

> Asking friends isn't safe, and relatives aren't safe either, because they charge high interest and perhaps suddenly need the money back. (F-w95)

Most reactions alluding to potential expenses underline the fact that aid supplied by family members would entail the advantage of being interest-free or indeed, in certain circumstances, even a gift.

> Firstly they need to ask their family for the money ... It would be an interest-free loan, because interest is forbidden by religion and it would cause a scandal in the family. (M-m78)

> Brothers, first the oldest. It would be a gift: he's a blood brother. (M-w95)

> If the family is well off, the economic help could be requested as a gift. (M-m70)

> Reynaldo and his wife should ask their parents for the money. In this case the money should be given as a gift. (F-m89)

> Antonio should turn to relatives ... If there are no other brothers or sisters, [the money] could be given as a gift. (I-m68)

For some respondents, the family is a fall-back option, to be exploited only if it is not possible to borrow money from banks (or because the underlying assumption is that banks will deny any loan request).

> Antonio should borrow money from a bank. If he doesn't meet the requirements, then he could turn to his family, in particular his parents. (I-m92)

> If the bank doesn't approve a loan, Reynaldo should ask his and his wife's parents for the money. (F-w75)

> Antonio should resort to a bank, but since he's unemployed I don't think the bank would help him. Therefore he should ask a relative. (I-m93)

> Since it's difficult for a bank to grant a loan, they should turn to their family. (M-m94)

> They should ask [relatives] for a loan because it's impossible to borrow money from a bank. (C-m84)

Finally, another recurrent idea mentioned spontaneously has to do with explicit gender preference. Usually this means seeking assistance from a male family member (or a relative of the male member of the needy couple). Yet there are also instances in which females are given priority.

> They should ask a male sibling. We turn to a brother because he's more important, he's the one who controls everything, he's the boss. (M-w65)

Their families. In this case, the first person they should ask is Omar's father. (M-m89)

The first person I'd ask is my dad: the man is usually the one who works e takes care of the family's economic spending. (M-w81)

Antonio can ask for help firstly from his family, specifically his parents or secondly his wife's parents – a less appropriate solution. (I-w80)

In the following order: parents, brothers and sisters, cousins, reliable friends. Firstly Antonio's, then his wife's. (I-m55)

First they turn to female [relatives], but they can also ask Reynaldo's father. (F-m88)

The Muslim religion says that you must always first speak with your mother, about any topic. (M-m76)

The role of buddies

Many respondents spontaneously mentioned friends or the local community (usually identified on ethnic or religious bases, at least for the immigrant-origin respondent groups), which share with family ties their non-institutional, informal, non-market nature. This potential loan source, however, was rarely mentioned in initial reactions to the vignette (no more than 10% of responses in any group: Table 8.3) and, eventually, by a majority of cases only in the Chinese group (82%). Comparatively averse, as seen above, to turning to family members, Filipinos are also none too enthusiastic about asking friends or their community for financial support.

So, on the whole, unless one considers the Chinese respondents, amity and community are not among the primary prospective conduits to attaining financial help; and, even when they are, they do not qualify as the first choices. There are, nevertheless, exceptions.

Except for friends, no one else comes to mind. (F-w89)

Table 8.3 Incidence of responses mentioning friends or the local ethnic community as potential funding sources, by respondents' area of origin (percentage values; base = number of respondents)

	Italy	*Maghreb*	*Philippines*	*China*
– Initial response	3	10	10	9
– First two responses	12	27	19	45
– All responses	39	37	24	82
(N)	(144)	(143)	(83)	(119)

Some of the individual comments cited above, in relation to kin relationships, also mentioned friends, and other reactions also shed light on their role. For instance, friendships are mentioned as the context within which diversification strategies (deemed as mandatory due to the considerable sum required) can be implemented.

> In Italy [Chinese immigrants] usually have relatives and friends. €15 thousand isn't that large a sum. They can ask for loans a bit here and a bit there. (C-w91)

> Maybe they could scrape together €3-4-5 thousand from a friend, then 3-4-5 thousand from another. (M-w96)

> Ask good friends for half, a bank for the other half. (C-w92)

> The sum is large and so you divide it up into smaller amounts, making it easier for people to come up with the money. (C-w88)

> If you put together 10-15 people you can achieve a useful sum. (M-w65)

Immigrant-origin respondents occasionally evoke their ethnic communities (often mentioning their religious foundations) as a source of solidarity, and forms of rotating credit associations are implicitly cited by some Maghrebis.

> The mosque could provide help. In theory every Muslim worker should give a percentage [of his earnings] to the mosque. People often go there to ask for help. (M-m91)

> They could ask for a loan from the church, from the religious community they belong to. (F-w68)

> Islamic communities take up collections in case someone is in need. (M-m91)

> They can seek help from friends in the mosque, as a gift. (M-w70)

> In some areas there are Moroccan communities that help each other, for example in Lombardy and Emilia-Romagna, not in the South. (M-w90)

In at least one instance, ethnic identity is cited as a veritable obstacle to obtaining assistance.

> If he were from Pakistan or Bangladesh or China, the community would have helped him. In Morocco no one helps anyone. (M-m68)

The role of banks

Resorting to banks (or other market-based, credit-granting organizations) is spontaneously cited as a means for obtaining financial aid for starting up a business. For many respondents, indeed, it is the default option, i.e., mentioned in the immediate reactions to the vignette (Table 8.4). Among the Filipino, Italian and Maghrebi respondents, banks are named as the primary loan source more often (55, 52 and 40%, respectively) than either family ties or friendship and community networks; when other responses, starting from the second, are taken into account, banks appear among prospective lenders for a strong majority of cases in these three groups. The centrality of banks is particularly striking among the Filipinos: even when all answers are considered, banks remain more "popular" than kin. On the other hand, Chinese respondents distance themselves markedly from the other participants in the study: only one in ten mention banks in their initial reactions to the vignette, and three in four never get around to contemplating them as potential providers of capital.

The reasons underlying preference for banks include their integrity, the straightforward nature of the transaction, the amount of money required and the desire not to expose family members to risk of default.

> Banks, because you can be sure they won't screw you. (F-w95)

> They need to turn to banks. Unfortunately they won't obtain the money, but banks are the only solution. (M-m72)

> They can only resort to banks: it's too much money [for any other option]. (F-w47)

> The couple needs to ask the bank – and no one else, not even relatives – for a loan: there's the danger that the couple will not be able to repay the loan. (F-m70)

In many ways, banks are such an obvious choice that there is no need to supply detailed justifications for turning to them (this is especially

Table 8.4 Incidence of responses mentioning banks or other market-based institutions as potential funding sources, by respondents' area of origin (percentage values; base = number of respondents)

	Italy	*Maghreb*	*Philippines*	*China*
– Initial response	52	40	55	10
– First two responses	68	50	64	16
– All responses	78	62	66	25
(N)	(144)	(143)	(83)	(119)

true for Italians). Good reasons are more often provided for *not* using banks (or for anticipating the latter's likelihood of refusing a loan). Many respondents stress the fact that institutional borrowing is a typically cumbersome procedure – requiring collateral, co-sponsors, under-signers and so on – and ultimately thwarts successful outcomes. This can translate into specific difficulties for immigrant-origin loan-seekers, due to cultural obstacles, immigrants' irregular legal status or discriminatory practices among banks.

> Credit agencies don't help immigrants, as if they were afraid of them or didn't trust them. (M-m69)

> Usually banks here don't grant loans to Chinese. (C-m89)

> With banks it's difficult because you're a foreigner. (C-m95)

> For Chinese here it's difficult to borrow money from a bank. Even if the bank allows it, Chinese don't prefer this solution due to language problems and because the procedure is too complicated and long. (C-w89)

> They should ask a bank for a loan, provided that their residency permit allows it. (M-m78)

Another barrier to seeking financial aid from banks is common among Maghrebi respondents, who cite Islam's norms forbidding the charging and the payment of interest.

> As a Muslim he cannot resort to a bank. (M-m86)

> Our religion forbids us to charge interest. (M-w90)

> Banks are a last resort, because loans with interest are forbidden by the Islamic religion. (M-w87)

> I have no use for banks because interest is against Islam. (M-m87)

> The last choice would surely be a bank, because observant Muslims don't resort to banks because they charge interest on loans. (M-m92)

Despite this religious interdiction, as seen above, the Maghrebi group displays the most welcoming outlook towards banks, in part because some respondents cite Islamic banks.

> They could turn to banks, but only Islamic ones. But since there aren't any in Italy, that would be difficult. In any case, it would be an interest-free loan. (M-w92)

> If the bank is willing to grant them a loan, they should ask the bank. But [the loan would need to be] without interest, because that's how it works in their culture: there are banks that don't demand interest. (M-m85)

> The couple should ask for economic help from solidarity banks – essentially Muslim banks, operating in Arab countries. (M-m85)

Although banks may be viewed as archetypal lenders, some respondents also envisage other market-based solutions: making use of micro-credit initiatives, forming wider business partnerships, negotiating lines of credit from suppliers and selling off valuable possessions.

> Omar and his wife should turn to a micro-credit agency. (M-m80)

> A good idea might be to form a partnership with someone wanting to engage in a similar business ... and share the expenses. (M-m97)

> If you want to start a business you have to be willing to do anything: ask friends, a bit from suppliers, banks ... (C-w91)

> They should sell property in the Philippines so they can open the shop. (F-w75)

> The couple could sell property they have in Tunisia in order to obtain the money. (M-m92)

> They can sell valuable objects they have at home. (C-w92)

> His wife could sell her gold jewellery. (M-w81)

In a few cases, given the difficulties of borrowing money from a bank, even recourse to the black market and potential exposure to the extortionate practices of usury are evoked (but hardly endorsed; and, fortunately, nobody suggested carrying out a bank robbery or performing other illegal activities).

> They could also resort to a loan shark, but I don't recommend it. (I-m91)

> Since it's difficult for a bank to grant them a loan ... as an alternative: loan sharks. (M-m94)

Other solutions for raising money (or not)

A non-negligible share of reactions do not fit into any of the preceding categories, i.e., involve neither family members, nor friendship and community networks, nor market-based credit outlets. These residual reactions basically fall into two sets. The first entails seeking out financial assistance from

Table 8.5 Incidence of responses mentioning welfare initiatives or "exit strategies", by respondents' area of origin (percentage values; base = number of respondents)

	Italy	*Maghreb*	*Philippines*	*China*
Public sector / welfare solutions				
– Initial response	6	15	13	0
– First two responses	11	22	14	0
– All responses	15	27	17	1
"Exit"				
– Initial response	0	1	5	0
– First two responses	1	2	6	0
– All responses	2	2	6	0
(N)	(144)	(143)	(83)	(119)

welfare services and other public sector sources; the second consists merely in encouraging the vignette's characters to "give up", and forgo the idea of opening a new business.

Welfare solutions, suggested by a minority of respondents (Table 8.5), are mentioned more frequently by Maghrebi participants (27%) and, to a lesser extent, by Filipinos (17%) and Italians (15%). The prospect of turning to public institutions for help appears to be totally alien to the Chinese group. The underlying pattern, as concerns preferences across the four groups, is quite similar to that observed above for banks and other market-based strategies.

Individual comments show that respondents picture three distinct types of potential resources. Some express the (relatively vague) idea that public authorities ("the State") should be available to offer funding. Access to aid is justified by the fact that respondents have been regularly paying taxes and thus behaved as good citizens and financed public services.

> The State should help them because they've paid taxes ... In the event of need, the State should intervene providing economic aid. (F-w67)

> From the State. By working they've contributed to the Italian State's coffers, even if the Italian State doesn't take this into account. (M-m79)

> They should resort to the State in order to have access to funds supporting youth. (I-w92)

Secondly, social services and other opportunities provided by local (typically municipal) governments are mentioned in a more specific way, thus revealing a certain degree of institutional awareness and competence among respondents.

> Support should be sought from the city government's social services. (M-w94)

> Help should be requested from the State, in particular from city governments. (M-w75)

> The young couple could ask the city government for help, perhaps requesting an advance payment to start supporting the shop. The city could also rent out a venue to the couple. (M-w82)

> The city government, via social workers, [should help]. I think the city government provides funds for people who want to open small retail businesses, with limited collateral and rather accessible even for non-Italian citizens. (F-w57)

> They need to turn to the city government, because it helps start up shops by providing incentives. (F-m67)

> The couple should seek help from social services ... or NGOs that support foreigners in difficult circumstances. (M-m85)

> They should try to obtain social help (for example State or regional funds for small businesses) or ask social workers what authority is most suited for their situation. (M-w88)

Thirdly, the European Union is identified as a source of financial aid via targeted programmes. Only Italian respondents expressly cited European institutions as possible funding sources.

> They could draw a sum from European Union funds. (I-m80)

> [Antonio] should collect information concerning the existence of European funding for his kind of situation. (I-m85)

> Since he is relatively young, he could be supported by regional or European Union funding. (I-w63)

Of course, welfare programmes and social services are not necessarily fully public in nature and can be described as third sector initiatives. Yet the respondents' comments tend to strongly emphasize the public dimension of these activities.

Finally, a very small minority of respondents state that the unemployed couple described in the vignette should contemplate an "exit strategy", i.e., simply resign themselves to not opening a shop (Table. 8.5). For immigrant-origin respondents, accepting this recommendation would sometimes lead to the couple's abandoning the migratory project and returning to their origin country; other less extreme perspectives merely encourage them to persist in their job search. Some comments underline the fact that the size of the required loan is too large and would lead to insolvency: incurring debt should be out of the question.

> They should go back to the Philippines instead of opening a shop. (F-w62)

> If they have no money and have lost their jobs, they need to go back to Morocco. (M-w63)

> If nobody is willing to give money to Antonio, he should look for another job as an employee. (I-m64)

> If he has faith in God, he should settle for what he has and continue to look for a job in order to open a shop with his own means. (M-m36)

> It's too much money and the loan would be too large to pay back. (F-m69)

> They should not open the shop: it's too risky and the loan they need is too large. They should look for another job. (F-w92)

It should be noted that these few defeatist reactions *may* be interpreted as examples of the reformulation strategy that people occasionally adopt in order to dodge dilemmas: a respondent simply disavows the vignette's "ground rules" so as not to be obliged to make the difficult or distasteful choices the vignette thrusts upon her (Marradi 2005, 38). Respondents, after all, were asked to *whom* the unemployed spouses can turn for financial help, not *whether* obtaining such help is actually feasible. In this context, however, the reactions encouraging surrender appear sincere, pertinent and not determined by any underlying dissonance.

Overview of findings

The main findings emerging from the preceding analyses can be summarized as follows (and in Table 8.6, which refers to *all* responses, not respondents' initial reactions alone). Kin networks represent an almost universal source of financial assistance for Chinese and Italian respondents, and for a strong majority of Maghrebis. Chinese and Italian perceptions of family relationships diverge, however, in so far as the former tend to encourage contacting lateral kin (siblings), whereas the latter prefer ascendant family (parents). Moreover, Chinese respondents also tend to mention a greater variety of types of relatives, thus further bearing testament to the centrality of family for this participant group.

Among Chinese respondents, friendship and community networks are almost as frequently cited as family. Indeed, the tendency to rely on such sources of support is perhaps the most distinctive feature of this group; none of the other three groups comes close to expressing a strong propensity to rely on amity and community links. The Filipino respondents – markedly less inclined to seek help from family members, friends or the local community – are the most distant from the Chinese along these two dimensions.

A countervailing pattern distinguishes the remaining two major lending sources. The Chinese are much less prone to recommend use of banks, other market-based solutions or welfare services and programmes. The Filipino, Maghrebi and Italian groups, on the other hand, manifest a greater propensity to resort to the market as a primary source of aid, as compared to both the Chinese and the family. Similarly, the same three groups are also more likely to draw upon public sector services and programmes.

Figure 8.1 – which highlights the transition from initial reactions to all responses for the three major funding sources – calls attention to differences among respondent groups. Chinese respondents support family-centred strategies from the beginning, then transfer their preferences to community-centred solutions, relegating the market to a marginal position. Among Filipinos there emerge an initial prevalence of the market and a significant but only partial resurgence of kin relations. Maghrebi and Italian dynamics resemble each other: initial prominence of the market, followed by a strong comeback and eventual prevalence of family and a partial upswing for community.

In order to obtain a multivariate representation of the four groups' response profiles, a multiple correspondence analysis was performed. Figure 8.2 depicts the semantic space – corresponding to the first (horizontal axis) and second (vertical axis) components emerging from the analysis – which has seven active variables corresponding to the seven white dots: each variable took on the value "Yes" if the corresponding funding source was mentioned in respondents' first two reactions to the vignette, the value "No" if it was not cited; only the "Yes" values are represented in Figure 8.2.[16] If two white dots are near each other, the corresponding capital procurement opportunities tend to elicit similar reactions (i.e., they are both mentioned or both not mentioned).

Table 8.6 Incidence of responses mentioning a set of funding sources, by respondents' area of origin (all responses considered; percentage values; base = number of respondents)

	Italy	*Maghreb*	*Philippines*	*China*
Ascendant family	78	38	29	55
Lateral family	40	32	22	78
Other or generic family	24	26	17	37
Total family	92	71	52	94
Friendship/community networks	39	37	24	82
Banks and other market sources	78	62	66	25
Public sector / welfare solutions	15	27	17	1
"Exit"	2	2	6	0
(N)	(144)	(143)	(83)	(119)

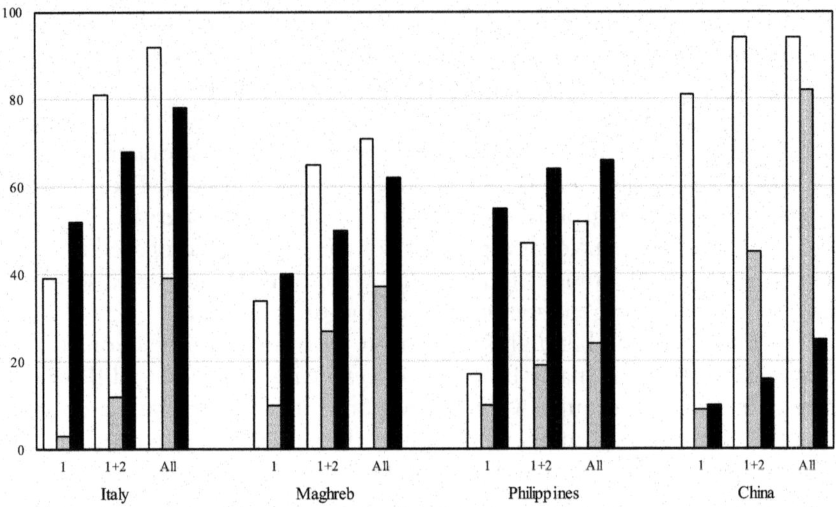

Figure 8.1 Incidence of first, first two and all responses mentioning a set of financial aid sources, by respondents' area of origin (white bars = family, grey = friends and community, black = market; percentage values; base = number of respondents)

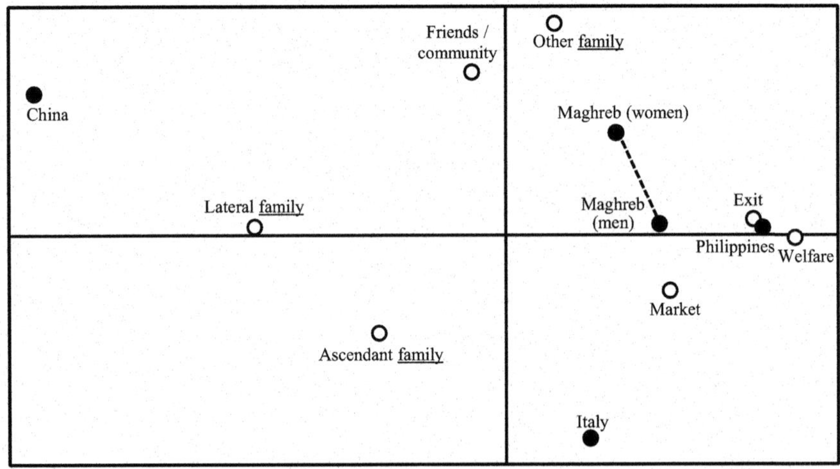

Figure 8.2 Perceptual map of financial aid sources (multiple correspondence analysis), with display of centroids of area-of-origin groups (weighted data)

If two white dots are distant, their corresponding sources of financial support tend to produce divergent reactions (one is brought up, the other is not). The ensuing semantic space shows that the main dimension (the horizontal axis) is defined by the contraposition of (on the right-hand side) a cluster comprising market-based schemes, welfare solutions and exit strategies and (on the left) a looser collection of family- and community-centred approaches.

Centroids of selected respondent groups (black dots) can be placed in the same semantic space. Their location mirrors the corresponding groups' proximity to (or distance from) the resource-seeking strategies emerging from their reactions to the vignette. The perceptual map highlights the gap separating the Chinese group from the other three, and the comparative homogeneity shared by the latter (and especially the convergence of Filipinos and Maghrebis).

On the basis of results not shown here, other respondent characteristics (such as employment status and level of education) do not appear to exert appreciable influence. One partial exception is visualized in Figure 8.2: whereas in other groups respondents' gender does not generate divergent reaction profiles, this is not true for the Maghrebis. In the latter group, in fact, men express a stronger tendency than women to resort to banks and welfare programmes.

Concluding remarks

This study employs a non-directive vignette technique in order to delve into native Italians' and immigrant-origin residents' value orientations as regarding appropriate funding sources for starting a new business. This methodological approach provides a double-barelled opportunity to both engage in structured data collection and statistical ("quantitative") analysis and identify (via a "qualitative" approach) authentic, spontaneously expressed motivations and value dimensions governing reactions to the vignette.

The findings reveal sharply defined differences in the outlooks of the four respondent groups, which arguably reflect essential cultural specificities (and are indirectly coherent with the middleman minority theory, which draws attention to how different ethnic origins correspond to different attitudes and bevahiours towards business). The intense, almost exclusive Chinese focus on kin relationships is extremely consistent with the influence of Confucianism and the importance it places on family. Similarly, the secondary, but extensive, relevance accorded by Chinese to amity and community networks reflects the group's characterization as an ethnic enclave cultivating co-ethnic social capital, counteracting the apparent irony of a powerful inclination towards business ventures accompanied by a sturdy aversion to formal, market-based capital procurement strategies (and to welfare initiatives).

Although Chinese and Italian respondents share a similar proximity to family, Maghrebis in some ways express the set of views least distant from the Italians': the market is, initially, the preferred venue for seeking out financial support, but the family ultimately becomes the main source of support. The North Africans' willingness to engage with banks might be a sign of integration in their host country, perhaps mediated by the existence of opportunities for obtaining credit without violating *riba*-avoidance norms. The Maghrebi group is also the only one displaying an appreciable gender-based difference, possibly reflecting a higher degree of deference, among women, for Islamic injunctions against charging and paying interest.

Filipino-origin immigrants are also relatively open to market-based funding opportunities, but against a backdrop typified by a lack of alternatives. Their propensity to turn to family is by far the weakest among the groups involved in this study and apparently challenges the cultural centrality of kin, but is consistent with the idea that intra-family support flows *back* to the origin country; immigrants help relatives who remain in the Phillipines, and not vice versa. The group's co-ethnic component of loan-seeking is also relatively weak, which fits the overall pattern of low entreprenuerial likelihood among Filipino immigrants.

Other topics identified in the initial review also emerge from respondents' comments. Two such topics worthy of note are banks' (actual or anticipated) discriminatory practices towards immigrants and the limited role given to financial assistance programmes set up by public authorities, both of which end up encumbering entrepreneurial aspirations.

Another way to interpret the differences across groups relates to the fact that the Chinese group features *imbalance*, a combination of family- and ethno-centric approaches reinforced by marginalization of the market as a source of start-up capital. Conversely, the other groups' profiles display greater equilibrium and reveal a comparatively robust tendency to envision opportunities in all of the major contexts: family, community, market, welfare. This could be further construed to imply that the Chinese community engages in self-reliance, even self-exclusion from the destination society, resulting in a relatively low level of integration. On the contrary, the Filipino and (especially) Maghrebi groups – with their more marked awareness and willingness to engage with market and public institutions – display a greater degree of integration and more vigorously resemble the Italian benchmark group.

Besides the ample evidence of within-group homogeneity and between-group heterogeneity, the results also substantiate differentiation, conflict and ambiguity *within* each respondent group, indicating that underlying cultural features hardly wield overwhelming influence on individual expectations and convictions, as the intersectional approach suggests.

Finally, the opportunity to observe respondents' freely exhibited rationales and comments lead to the identification of largely unforeseen motifs. First and foremost, many reactions encompass negative, exclusionary motivations: study participants offer good reasons for *not* turning to given potential lenders. Moreover, many topics evoked by participants are unanticipated: sibling avoidance/deference in seeking help within family; the idea that if one of the members of the unemployed couple is an only child, he/she may deserve parental support in the form of a gift rather than a loan; the notion that seeking help among kin relations should be a fall-back option, to be activated only when bank loans prove difficult to obtain; the immediate cogency of risk diversification strategies; the fact that formal credit-granting institutions are not the only market-based solution to be envisaged (the others include selling off personal assets, formation of partnerships, even resorting to loan sharks); the realism underpinning the recommendation of exit strategies (forgoing self-employment and even sacrificing the migratory project). Each of these topics would probably not have been uncovered by more direct data collection techniques.

Notes

1 Typical examples of middleman minority entrepreneurs include immigrant-origin Jews, Italians, Japanese, Chinese, and Koreans running small businesses in poor native- and immigrant-minority neighbourhoods (Light 1972; O'Brien and Fugita 1982; Min 1996; Lee 2002).

2 In traditional entrepreneurship literature, individualism (not collectivism) is a typical cultural value that helps explain attitudes towards business creation (Hofstede 1991; 2001). In individualistic societies, individuals act in their own interest (or in the interest of their immediate family members) and show a keen proclivity towards entrepreneurial innovation. On the contrary, "collective societies often limit private property [...] and tend to prohibit private access to resources" (Mitchell et al. 2000: 979). The familism characterizing these societies is a form of nepotism that is detrimental to efficiency and productivity in modern business organizations (Wong 2013). Nonetheless, other entrepreneurship studies suggest that individualism and collectivism are not opposite extremes of a continuum, as commonly described, and both, albeit neither encouraging nor discouraging entrepreneurship, influence its development (Tiessen 1997).

3 This external dimension is part of the wider "opportunity structure" contemplated by the *mixed embeddedness approach*, which takes into account not only immigrant entrepreneurs' social embeddedness in co-ethnic networks, but also their institutional embeddedness as regards the economic (labour market conditions) and political (laws, rules and policies aimed at fostering or discouraging immigrants' entrepreneurship) contexts (Kloosterman, Rath and van der Leun 1999; Kloosterman and Rath 2001).

4 Recently, intersectional approaches have revealed that different patterns towards ethnic entrepreneurship might be observed "within" the same ethnic group, in that other key dimensions – such as social class and gender – may be responsible for differing degrees of access to financial and social resources (Romero and Valdez 2016; Valdez 2016).

5 A major limit of these studies is that a variety of national and ethnic groups is included under the Muslim label, and their shared religion may conceal specific cultural traits.

6 Muslim entrepreneurs are predominantly men. In most Muslim countries, working in the public sphere is perceived as inappropriate for women (Tucker 2007). Islamic values as well as Moroccan collectivistic family ideology also assume that men are the primary source of financial assistance, whereas women must perform traditional roles as wives, mothers, and homemakers (Mizrachi 2005).

7 The positive influence of Confucianism on entrepreneurship has been underlined since the second half of the twentieth century, in concomitance with the Asian economic boom. Before then, most scholars considered Confucianism as a firm barrier against entrepreneurship due to the particularly low social status conferred upon merchants and traders, limited support for inventiveness, a lack of capitalist spirit, and other features (Zhu 2015; Usman 2016).

8 An additional explanation of Chinese entrepreneurship tendencies is not ethnic-based and linked to the block mobility hypothesis, stemming from discrimination experienced in the mainstream labour market (Light 1972).

9 The reconfiguration of Chinatowns as ethnic enclaves is at the centre of a current debate (Luk and Pan 2005; Zhou and Lin 2005). Chinese entrepreneurs conduct business activities involving not only co-ethnic members, but also the native community, as both suppliers and clients (Oliveira 2003; Battilani and Fauri 2018).

10 This work was supported by a FARB grant from the University of Bologna (project code FFBO121274).

11 In the 2014–2015 period, 15.2 per cent of the 117,122 non-Italians residing in Bologna came from the Maghreb, and nearly 8 out of 10 Maghrebis were Moroccans. Morocco was the major country of origin of immigrants in the province of Bologna until 2008, when Romania achieved the same status.

12 In 2015 Filipinos accounted for 5.3 per cent of the non-Italian population in the province of Bologna, thus comprising its seventh largest immigrant group.

13 In 2015 4.8 per cent of non-Italian residents in the province of Bologna were of Chinese origin.

14 The percentage values reported in Table 8.2 and later tables correspond to the incidence of given response categories among all *respondents* within the corresponding group, not among all *reactions*.

15 Every cited comment in this chapter ends with a text in parentheses: a capital letter identifying the respondent subgroup (M = Maghrebi, F = Filipino, C = Chinese, I = Italian), a hyphen, and then a lower case letter for gender (m = man, w = woman) attached to the final two digits of year of birth. For example, "(I-w67)" denotes a respondent who is an Italian woman born in 1967.

16 The first two components account, respectively, for 29 and 16 per cent (45% overall) of total inertia. Before performing the multiple correspondence analysis, cases were re-weighted in order to assign the same collective weight to each of the area-of-origin groups, thus equalizing their contributions to the perceptual map.

References

Agbayani-Siewert P. (1994). Filipino American Culture and Family: Guidelines for Practioners. *Families in Society*. 44: 429–438.

Alaslani M. and Collins J. (2017). The Blocked Mobility Hypothesis and Muslim Immigrant Entrepreneurship in Sydney, Australia. *Review of Integrative Business & Economics Research*, 6(3): 333–357.

Albertini M., Gasperoni G. and Mantovani, G. (2019). Whom to Help and Why? Family Norms on Financial Support for Adult Children among Immigrants. *Journal of Ethnic and Migration Studies*. 45(10): 1769–1789.

Aldén L. and Hammarstedt M. (2016). Discrimination in the Credit Market? Access to Financial Capital among Self-Employed Immigrants. *Kylos*. 69(1): 3–31.

Allasino E., Reyneri E., Venturini A. and Zincone G. (2004). *Labour Market Discrimination against Migrant Workers in Italy*. International Migration Paper 67. Geneva: International Labour Office.

Allen L. (2017). Confucianism and Entrepreneurship in ASEAN Context. In Mandal P. and Vong J. (eds.). *Entrepreneurship in Technology for ASEAN*. Berlin: Springer Science+Business Media, 161–173.

Anderson A.R. and Lee E.Y.C. (2008). *From Tradition to Modern: Attitudes and Applications of Guanxi in Chinese Entrepreneurship* (openair.rgu.ac.uk).

Ang A.P., Sugiyarto G. and Jha S. (2009). *Remittances and Household Behavior in the Philippines*. Manila: Asian Development Bank.

Ariff M. (1988). Islamic Banking. *Asian-Pacific Economic Literature*. 2(2): 48–64.

Avola M. and Cortese A. (2012). Mobilità e carriere di immigrati imprenditori. *Quaderni di Sociologia*. 58: 7–40.

Ayub M. (2002). *Islamic Banking and Finance: Theory and Practice*. Karachi: State Bank of Pakistan.

Basa C., De Guzman V. and Marchetti S. (2012). *International Migration and Over-Indebtedness: The Case of Filipino Workers in Italy*. London: International Institute for Environment and Development.

Bates T. (1997). Financing Small Business Creation: The Case of Chinese and Korean Immigrant Entrepreneurs. *Journal of Business Venturing*. 12(2): 109–124.

Bates T., Lofstrom M. and Servon L.J. (2011). Why Have Lending Programs Targeting Disadvantaged Small Business Borrowers Achieved So Little Success in the United States?. *Economic Development Quarterly*. 25(3): 255–266.

Battilani P. and Fauri F. (2018). Chinese Migration to Italy: Features and Issues. In Fauri F. and Tedeschi P. (eds.), *Labour Migration in Europe. Volume I: Integration and Entrepreneurship among Migrant Workers – A Long-Term View*. Basingstoke: Palgrave Macmillan, 11–42.

Baycan-Levent T. and Nijkamp P. (2009). Characteristics of Migrant Entrepreneurship in Europe. *Entrepreneurship and Regional Development*. 21(4): 375–397.

Bergamaschi, M. (2012). Distribuzione territoriale e modelli insediativi della popolazione straniera a Bologna. *Sociologia urbana e rurale*. 99: 117–134.

Bonacich E. (1973). A Theory of Middleman Minorities. *American Sociological Review*. 38(5): 583–594.

Butler J. and Greene P. (1997). *Ethnic Entrepreneurship: The Continuous Rebirth of American Enterprise*. In Sexton D.L. and Smilor R.W. (eds.). *Entrepreneurship 2000*. Chicago: Upstart, 267–289.

Busenitz L.W. and Lau C.M. (1996). A Cross-Cultural Cognitive Model of New Venture Creation. *Entrepreneurship Theory and Practice*. 20(4): 25–40.

Cavalluzzo K. and Wolken J. (2005). Small Business Loan Turndowns, Personal Wealth, and Discrimination. *The Journal of Business*. 78(6): 2153–2178.

Ceccagno A. (2003). New Chinese Migrants in Italy. *International Migration*. 41(3): 187–213.

Cetindamar D., Gupta V.K., Karadeniz E.E. and Egrican N. (2012). What the Numbers Tell: The Impact of Human, Family and Financial Capital on Women and Men's Entry into Entrepreneurship in Turkey. *Entrepreneurship & Regional Development*. 24(1–2): 29–51.

Chiesi A.M. (2011). Il ruolo degli imprenditori immigrati nello sviluppo della piccola impresa in Italia. In CNEL (ed.). *Il profilo nazionale degli immigrati imprenditori in Italia*. Rome: CNEL, 8–31.

Chunxia W. (2010). The Influence of Confucian Culture on Business Management: A Case Study of Chinese Entrepreneurs in Macau. *International Journal of Business Anthropology*. 1(2): 117–134.

Collins J. (2000). Ethnicity, Gender and Australian Entrepreneurs: Rethinking Marxist Views on Small Business. *Journal of Social Change and Critical Inquiry*. 2: 137–149.

Cooney T., Manning J., Arisha A. and Smyth P. (2011). *Muslim Entrepreneurship in Ireland*. Dublin: Dublin Institute of Technology.

Crane K. (2004). *Governing Migration: Immigrant Groups' Strategies in Three Italian Cities Rome, Naples and Bari*. Rome: Psychoanalytic Institute for Social Research.

Dallalfar A. (1994). Iranian Women as Immigrant Entrepreneurs. *Gender and Society*. 8(4): 541–561.

Deakins D., Majmudar M. and Paddison A. (1997). Developing Success Strategies for Ethnic Minorities in Business: Evidence from Scotland. *New Community*. 23: 325–342.

Direzione Generale dell'Immigrazione e delle Politiche di Integrazione (2016). *Sesto rapporto annuale. I migrant nel mercato del lavoro in Italia*. Rome: Ministry of Labour and Social Policies.

Edwards P., Ram M., Jones T. and Doldor S. (2016). New Migrant Businesses and their Workers: Developing, but Not Transforming, the Ethnic Economy. *Ethnic and Racial Studies*. 39(9): 1587–1617.

el Bouk F., Vedder P. and te Poel Y. (2013). The Networking Behavior of Moroccan and Turkish Immigrant Entrepreneurs in Two Dutch Neighborhoods: The Role of Ethnic Density. *Ethnicities*. 13(6): 771–794.

El-Massidi M.O. (2008). *Access to Capital in the Absence of Religiously Appropriate Financial Products: A Case Study on Muslim Business Owners in Sacramento*. University of California, https://escholarship.org/uc/item/09f6691x.

Espiritu Y.L and Wolfe D.L. (2001). The Paradox of Assimilation: Children of Filipino Immigrants in San Diego. In Rumbaut R.G. and Portes A. (eds.). *Ethnicities: Children of Immigrants in America*. New York: Russell Sage Foundation, 157–186.

Evans D.S. and Jovanovic B. (1989). An Estimated Model of Entrepreneurial Choice under Liquidity Constraints. *Journal of Political Economy*. 97(4): 808–827.

Fairlie R.W. (2005). Entrepreneurship among Disadvantaged Groups: Women, Minorities and the Less Educated. In Parker S. (ed.). *The Life Cycle of Entrepreneurial Ventures. International Handbook Series on Entrepreneurship. Vol 3*. Boston: Springer, 437–478.

Fairlie R.W. and Lofstrom M. (2015). *Immigration and Entrepreneurship*. CESIFO Working Paper no. 529.

Fairlie R.W. and Meyer B.D. (1996). Ethnic and Racial Self-Employment Differences and Possible Explanations. *Journal of Human Resources*. 31(4): 757–793.

Fellini I. (2018). Immigrants' Labour Market Outcomes in Italy and Spain: Has the Southern European Model Disrupted during the Crisis? *Migration Studies*. 3(1): 53–78.

Fielden S. and Davidson M.J. (2012). BAME Women Business Owners: How Intersectionality Affects Discrimination and Social Support. *Gender in Management: An International Journal*. 27(8): 559–581.

Finch J. (1987). The Vignette Technique in Survey Research. *Sociology*. 21(1): 105–114.

Font J. and Méndez M. (eds.) (2013). *Surveying Ethnic Minorities and Immigrant Populations: Methodological Challenges and Research Strategies*. Amsterdam: Amsterdam University Press.

Fresnoza-Flot A. and Pécoud A. (2007). Emergence of Entrepreneurship Among Filipino Migrants in Paris. *Asian and Pacific Migration Journal*, 16(1): 1–28.

Fullin G. (2013). Quanto diversi? E in che cosa? Lavoratori autonomi immigrati e autoctoni a confronto. In Colombo A. (ed.). *Stranieri in Italia. Figli, lavoro, vita quotidiana*. Bologna: Il Mulino, 187–224.

Glazer N. and Moynihan D.P. (1970). *Beyond the Melting Pot: The Negroes, Puerto Ricans, Jews, Italians, and Irish of New York City*. Cambridge: MIT Press.

Gu C.-J. (2013). *Interviews*. In Gold S.J. and Nawn S.J. (eds.). *Routledge International Handbook of Migration Studies*. London: Routledge, 506–521.

Hamid S.A. and Sa'ari C.Z. (2011). Reconstructing Entrepreneur's Development based on al-Qur'an and al-Hadith. *International Journal of Business and Social Science*. 2(19): 110–116.

Haynes G.W., Rowe B.R., Walker R. and Gong-Soog H. (2000). The Differences in Financial Structure Between Women- and Men-Owned Family Businesses. *Journal of Family and Economic Issues*. 21(3): 209–226.

Hofstede G. (1991). *Culture and Organizations: Software of the Mind*. London: McGraw-Hill.

Hofstede G. (2001). *Culture's Consequences: Comparing Values, Behaviors, Institutions and Organizations across Nations*. Thousand Oaks: Sage.

Hosler A. (1998). *Japanese Immigrant Entrepreneurs in New York City: A New Wave of Ethnic Business*. New York: Garland.

Ilahiane H. (2014). Mediating Purity: Money, Usury and Interest, and Ethical Anxiety in Morocco. *Human Organization*. 73(4): 315–325.

Iqbal M. and Molyneux P. (2005). *Thirty Years of Islamic Banking: History, Performance and Prospects*. London: Palgrave Macmillan.

Jarvis R. (2000). Finance and the Small Firm. In Carter S. and Jones-Evans D. (eds.), *Enterprise and Small Business: Principles, Practice and Policy*. London: Prentice-Hall.

Johnson J., Muñoz J.M. and Alon I. (2007). Filipino Ethnic Entrepreneurship: An Integrated Review and Propositions. *International Entrepreneurship and Management Journal*. (3)1: 69–85.

Khan F. (2010). How "Islamic" is Islamic Banking? *Journal of Economic Behavior & Organization*. 76: 805–820.

Kibria N. (1994). Household Structure and Family Ideologies: The Dynamics of Immigrant Economic Adaptation among Vietnamese Refugees. *Social Problems*. 41(1): 81–96.

Kidwell R., Hoy F. and Ibarreche S. (2012). "Ethnic" Family Business or Just Family Business? Human Resource Practices in the Ethnic Family Firm. *Journal of Family Business Strategy*. 3(1): 12–17.

Kloosterman R.C. (2010). Matching Opportunities with Resources: A Framework for Analysing (Migrant) Entrepreneurship from a Mixed Embeddedness Perspective. *Entrepreneurship and Regional Development*. 22(1): 25–45.

Kloosterman R. and Rath J. (2001). Immigrant Entrepreneurs in Advanced Economies: Mixed Embeddedness Further Explored. *Journal of Ethnic and Migration Studies*. 27(2): 189–201.

Kloosterman R., van der Leun J. and Rath J. (1999). Mixed Embeddedness: (In) formal Economic Activities and Immigrant Businesses in the Netherlands. *International Journal of Urban and Regional Research*. 23(2): 253–267.

Kontos M. (2003). Self-Employment Policies and Migrants' Entrepreneurship in Germany. *Entrepreneurship & Regional Development*. 15: 119–135.

Kushnirovich N. and Heilbrunn S. (2008). Financial Funding of Immigrant Businesses. *Journal of Developmental Entrepreneurship*. 13(2): 167–184.

Lee J. (2002). *Civility in the City: Blacks, Jews, and Koreans in Urban America*. Cambridge: Harvard University Press.

Light I. (1972). *Ethnic Enterprise in America: Business and Welfare Among Chinese, Japanese, and Blacks*. Berkeley: University of California Press.

Light I. and Bonacich E. (1988). *Immigrant Entrepreneurs: Koreans in Los Angeles, 1965-1982*. Berkeley: University of California Press.

Light I. and Gold S. (2000). *Ethnic Economy*. San Diego: Academic.

Lodigiani R. (1995). Il caso filippino. In Ambrosini M., Zandrini S. and Lodigiani R. (eds.). *L'integrazione subalterna: peruviani, eritrei e filippini nel mercato del lavoro milanese*. Milan: Fondazione Cariplo-ISMU.

Luk C.M. and Pan M.B. (2005). Ethnic Enclave Reconfiguration: A "New" Chinatown in the Making. *GoeJournal*. 64(1): 17–30.

Maas M. (2011). *Filipino Immigrant Entrepreneurship in the Netherlands: Beyond Business*. Radboud University, PhD Dissertation.

Mangiafico L. (1988). *Contemporary American Immigrants: Patterns of Filipino, Korean and Chinese Settlement in the United States*. New York: Praeger.

Mantovani D., Gasperoni G. and Albertini, M. (2018). *L'uso di "storie" per indagare gli obblighi di sostegno nelle famiglie di immigrati*. In Gasperoni G., Albertini M. and Mantovani D. (eds.). *Fra genitori e figli. Immigrazione, rapporti intergenerazionali e famiglie nell'Europa contemporanea*. Bologna: Il Mulino, 193–220.

Marlow S. and Patton D. (2005). All Credit to Men? Entrepreneurship, Finance and Gender. Entrepreneurship. *Theory and Practice*. 29: 717–735.

Marradi A. (2005), *Raccontar storie. Un nuovo metodo per indagare sui valori*: Rome: Carocci.

Marradi A. and Gasperoni G. (eds.) (2002). *Costruire il dato 3. Le scale Likert*. Milan: Franco Angeli.

Masurel E., Nijkamp P., Tastan M. and Vindigni G. (2002). Motivations and Performance Conditions for Ethnic Entrepreneurship. *Growth and Change*. 33(2): 238–260.

McGrath R.G., MacMillan I.C. and Scheinberg S. (1992). Elitists, Risk-Takers, and Rugged Individualists? An Exploratory Analysis of Cultural Differences between Entrepreneurs and Non-Entrepreneurs. *Journal of Business Venturing*. 7: 115–135.

Merz E., Oort F.J., Ozeke-Kocabas E. and Schuengel C. (2009). Intergenerational Family Solidarity: Value Differences Between Immigrant Groups and Generations. *Journal of Family Psychology*. 23(3): 291–300.

Min P.G. (1986). Filipino and Korean Immigrants in Small Business: A Comparative Analysis. *Amerasia Journal*. 13(1): 53–71.

Mitchell R.K., Smith B., Seawright K.W. and Morse E.A. (2000). Cross-Cultural Cognitions and the Venture Creation Decision. *Academy of Management Journal*. (43)5: 974–993.

Mizrachi B. (2005). The Henna Maker: A Moroccan Immigrant Woman Entrepreneur in an Ethnic Revival. In Keister L.A. (ed.). *Entrepreneurship: Research in the Sociology of Work*, 15: 257–277.

Nee V. and Nee B.B. (1973). *Longtime Californ': A Documentary Study of an American Chinatown*. Palo Alto: Stanford University Press.

O'Brien D.J. and Fugita S.S. (1982). Middleman Minority Concept: Its Explanatory Value in the Case of the Japanese in California Agriculture. *Pacific Sociological Review*. 25(2): 185–204.

OECD/European Union (2019). *The Missing Entrepreneurs 2019: Policies for Inclusive Entrepreneurship*. Paris: OECD.

Oliveira R.C. (2003). *Immigrants' Entrepreneurial Opportunities: The Case of the Chinese in Portugal*. Milan: Fondazione ENI Enrico Mattei.

Parreñas, R.S. (2001). *Servants of Globalization. Women, Migration and Domestic Work*. Palo Alto: Stanford University Press.

Piperopoulos P. (2010). Ethnic Minority Businesses and Immigrant Entrepreneurship in Greece. *Journal of Small Business and Enterprise Development*. 17(1): 139–158.

Portes A. and Sensenbrenner J. (1993). Embeddedness and Immigration: Notes on the Social Determinants of Economic Action. *American Journal of Sociology*. 93(6): 1320–1350.

Portes A. and Zhou M. (1992). Gaining the Upper Hand: Economic Mobility among Immigrant and Domestic Minorities. *Ethnic and Racial Studies*. 15(4): 491–522.

Rath J. and Kloosterman R. (2000). Outsiders' Business: A Critical Review of Research on Immigrant Entrepreneurship. *International Migration Review*. 34(3): 657–681.

Rath J. and Schutjens V. (2015). Migrant Entrepreneurship: Alternative Paradigms of Economic Integration. In Triandafyllidou A. (ed.). *Routledge Handbook of Immigration and Refugee Studies*. New York: Routledge, 96–103.

Renzulli L.A., Aldrich H. and Moody J. (2000). Family Matters: Gender, Networks, and Entrepreneurial Outcomes. *Social Forces*. 79(2): 523–546.

Reyneri E. and Fullin G. (2008). New Immigration and Labour Markets in Western Europe: A Trade-Off between Unemployment and Job Quality?. *Transfer European Review of Labour and Research*. 14(4): 31–57.

Roccato, M. (2003). *Desiderabilità sociale e acquiescenza*. Milan LED.

Romero M. and Valdez Z. (2016). Introduction to the Special Issue: Intersectionality and Entrepreneurship. *Ethnic and Racial Studies*. 39(9): 1553–1565.

Sanders J. and Nee V. (1996). Social Capital, Human Capital, and Immigrant Selfemployment: The Family as Social Capital and the Value of Human Capital. *American Sociological Review*. 61(2): 231–249.

Semi G. (2006). Il ritorno dell'economia di Bazar. Attività commerciali marocchine a Porta Palazzo, Torino. In Decimo F. and Sciortino G. (eds.). *Reti migranti*. Bologna: Il Mulino, 89–113.

Servon L.J., Fairlie R.W., Rastello B. and Seely A. (2010). The Five Gaps Facing Small and Microbusiness Owners: Evidence from New York City. *Economic Development Quarterly*, 24(2): 126–142.

Siddiqui N.M. (2004). *Riba, Bank Interest and the Rationale of Its Prohibition*. Jeddah: Islamic Development Bank-Islamic Research and Training Institute.

Solano G. (2016). *Immigrant Self-Employment and Transnational Practices: The Case of Moroccan Entrepreneurs in Amsterdam and Milan*, University of Amsterdam and University of Milan Bicocca, PhD dissertation.

Chong B.S. and Liu M.-H. (2009). Islamic Banking: Interest-Free or Interest-Based? *Pacific-Basin Finance Journal*. 17: 125–144.

Statman M. and Weng J. (2010). Investments across Cultures: Financial Attitudes of Chinese-Americans. *Recent Research*. 11(1): 37–44.

Strangio D. (2018). Entrepreneurship and Immigrant Business Groups in the Italian Labour Market. In Fauri F. and Tedeschi P. (eds.). *Labour Migration in Europe. Volume I: Integration and Entrepreneurship among Migrant Workers – A Long-Term View*. Basingstoke: Palgrave Macmillan, 109–126.

Szanton D.L. (1998). Contingent Moralities: Social and Economic Investment in a Philippine Fishing Town. In Hefner R.W. (ed.). *Market Cultures: Society and Morality in the New Asian Capitalisms*. Boulder: Westview, 257–267.

Tienda M. and Raijman R. (2004). Promoting Hispanic Immigrant Entrepreneurship in Chicago. *Journal of Developmental Entrepreneurship*. 9(1): 1–21.

Tiessen J.H. (1997). Individualism, Collectivism, and Entrepreneurship: A Framework for International Comparative Research. *Journal of Business Venturing*. 12(5): 367–384.

Tseng Y.F. (1997). Ethnic Resources as Forms of Social Capital: A Study on Chinese Immigrant Entrepreneurship in Los Angeles. *Taiwanese Sociological Review*. 1: 169–205.

Tucker H. (2007). Undoing Shame: Tourism and Women's Work in Turkey. *Journal of Tourism and Cultural Change*. 5: 87–105.

Usman U. (2016). Confucianism Ethic and the Spirit of Capitalism. *Academic Journal of Islamic Studies*. 1(2): 177–187.

Valdez Z. (2008). The Effect of Social Capital on White, Korean, Mexican, and Black Business Owners' Earnings in the US. *Journal of Ethnic and Migration Studies*. 34(6): 955–973.

Valdez Z. (2016). Intersectionality, the Household Economy, and Ethnic Entrepreneurship. *Ethnic and Racial Studies*. 39(9): 1618–1636.

van Delf H., Gorter C. and Nijkamp P. (2000). In Search of Ethnic Entrepreneurship Opportunities in the City: A Comparative Policy Study. *Environment and Planning C: Government and Policy*. 18(4): 429–451.

Waldinger R.D., Aldrich H. and Ward R. (1990). *Ethnic Entrepreneurs: Immigrant Business in Industrial Society*. Newbury Park: Sage.

Williams C.C. (2008). The Motives of Off-the-Books Entrepreneurs: Necessity- or Opportunity-Driven? *International Entrepreneurial Management Journal*. 5(2): 203–217.

Wingfield A.H. and Taylor T. (2016). Race, Gender and Class in Entrepreneurship: Intersectional Counterframes and Black Business Owners. *Ethnic and Racial Studies*. 39(9): 1679–1696.

Wong B. (2013). The Role of Ethnicity in Enclave Enterprises: A Study of the Chinese Garment Factories in New York. In Ng F. (ed.). *Asian American Issues Relating to Labor, Economics, and Socioeconomic Status*. New York and London: Routledge, 108–118.

Yang D. (2008). International Migration, Remittances, and Household Investment: Evidence from Philippine Migrants' Exchange Rate Shocks. *Economic Journal*. 118(528): 591–630.

Yoon I. (1995). The Growth of Korean Immigrant Entrepreneurship in Chicago. *Ethnic and Racial Studies*. 18(2): 315–335.

Zanfrini L. (2006). Il consolidamento di un "mercato del lavoro parallelo". Una ricerca sugli immigrati disoccupati in Lombardia. *Sociologia del lavoro*. 101: 141–172.

Zanfrini L. and Sarli A. (2009). *Migrants' Associations and Philippine Institutions for Development: Italian Report*. Milan: Quaderni Ismu.

Zhou M. (1992). *Chinatown: The Socioeconomic Potential of an Urban Enclave*. Philadelphia: Temple University Press.

Zhou M. (2004). The Role of the Enclave Economy in Immigrant Adaptation and Community Building: The Case of New York's Chinatown. In Butler J.S. and Kozmetsky G. (eds.). *Immigrant and Minority Entrepreneurship: The Continuous Rebirth of American Communities*. Westport: Praeger, 37–60.

Zhou M. (2006). Revisiting Ethnic Entrepreneurship: Convergences, Controversies, and Conceptual Advancements. *International Migration Review*. 38(3): 1040–1074.

Zhou M. and Cho M. (2010). Noneconomic Effects of Ehtnic Entrepreneurship: Evidence from Chinatown and Koreatown in Los Angeles, USA. *Thunderbird International Business Review*. 52(2): 83–96.

Zhou M. and Lin M. (2005). Community Transformation and the Formation of Ethnic Capital: Immigrant Chinese Communities in the United States. *Journal of Chinese Overseas*. 1(2): 260–284.

Zhu Y. (2015). The Role of *Qing* (Positive Emotions) and *Li* (Rationality) in Chinese Entrepreneurial Decision Making: A Confucian *Ren-Yi* Wisdom Perspective. *Journal of Business Ethics*. 126: 613–630.

Zubairu U., Dauda C., Paiko I. and Sakariyau O. (2015). The Moral Entrepreneur. *Terengganu International Management and Business Journal*. V(2): 22–30.

9 Mothering from afar

The subjective well-being of Eastern European migrants in Italy

Francesca Tosi

Introduction

With as many as 270 million migrants worldwide – 3.5 per cent of the global population (United Nations, Department of Economic and Social Affairs, Population Division 2017) – many individuals today are involved in family care at a distance. Migrants create transnational families to maximize resources and opportunities in the global economy to be shared among the household members, while maintaining a feeling of collective unity and a sense of responsibility to each other's well-being (Bryceson and Vuorela 2002; Parreñas 2005). As a result, the concept of family itself is redefined so as to overcome distances and political differences between countries. By challenging conventional notions of family life as delimited by geographical proximity, split families become functional and visible again in a transnational setting (Baldassar, Baldock and Wilding 2007; Sørensen and Vammen 2014; Ducu 2016).

However, the benefits generated via emigration can come at great emotional cost. Prolonged physical separation between family members may lead to a renegotiation of affective ties and sometimes to the onset of conflicts and new tensions, which reverberate both in migrants' and in *left-behinds*' lives, including that of the children growing up with parental absence.[1] Besides the hardships migrants are usually confronted with while settling in destination countries, transnational parents also face the difficult trade-off of improving children's livelihoods on the one hand, and caring for them on the other (Carling, Menjívar and Schmalzbauer 2012). Among the factors that interrelate with their ability to fulfil the parental role, gender takes on special relevance. Both emigrated women and men sustain their children's basic needs through material provision and remittances; however, mothers in particular are also expected to continue providing emotional bonds from afar (Parreñas 2005). In fact, while it is true that all migrant parents engage in transnational parenting practices as one way of trying to mitigate the costs of separation (Zentgraf and Chinchilla 2012), parenting and family care responsibilities still are strongly gendered in many societies, which makes migrant mothers live the parent-child relationship differently from fathers (Dreby 2006; Fresnoza-Flot 2009; Parreñas 2005; 2015). Sense of guilt, distress and fear of social stigma are commonly reported feelings by migrant mothers who leave the care of their children in the hands of others, especially by those who experience longstanding absence from home (Schmalzbauer 2004; Bernhard, Landolt and Goldring 2008).

To the present day, empirical evidence on how transnational parenthood mediates the well-being of migrant women relies heavily on ethnographic evidence and qualitative research, also due to the scarcity of quantitative data on transnational migrant lives at both large- and small-scale survey levels. Some scholarly initiatives have recently contributed to fill this gap in some regions of the world – see for instance the *Migrations between Africa and Europe* (MAFE) project (Beauchemin 2018). However, many aspects of the phenomenon remain unclear and hardly measurable, and in most countries quantitative investigations have never been carried out on the matter. The opportunity to conduct an evaluation using suitable statistical information is thus to be valued, as it would allow the extent to which transnational motherhood affects migrants' living conditions and their chances to live decent and fulfilling existences in host countries to be fully captured.

The goal of this chapter is to provide the first quantitative evidence on the relationship between transnational motherhood and subjective well-being of migrant women in Italy. To that aim, an empirical analysis will be carried out by exploiting the Italian National Institute of Statistics' (Istat) Survey on Social condition and integration of foreign citizens 2011–2012 (Istat 2016). The empirical analysis will focus on a sub-group of migrant women who immigrated in Italy from selected Eastern European countries. The reason to do so is twofold. First, qualitative research carried out in the Italian context (Piperno 2007; Solari 2010; Vianello 2009; Ducu 2014; Ambrosini 2019) shows that migrant mothers experience distress from the tension between the economic opportunities enjoyed in Italy and the promotion of their left-behind families' well-being. Lone transnational mothers from Eastern European countries like Romania and Ukraine and mainly employed in care work seem to be especially concerned by such a tension and are reported to suffer from isolation, both during and after their stay in the host country (Ducu 2014; Marchetti and Venturini 2014). Second, Eastern Europeans – Romanians, Ukrainians and Moldovans in particular – are among the most populous female immigrant groups in Italy and tend to emigrate as single mothers in a later stage of life (Marchetti and Venturini 2014). Hence, their case is both highly informative on the transnational motherhood phenomenon and relevant for policy purposes. Yet, to the best of the author's knowledge, no quantitative appraisal of the well-being of transnational mothers living in Italy has ever been carried out to date.

The empirical analysis presented in this chapter will examine 12 health-related subjective well-being indicators – related to both the physical and mental health domains – deriving from the 12-Items Short-Form Survey instrument (SF-12) (Ware, Kosinski and Keller 1996; Ware and Gandek

1998) implemented in the Istat survey. By applying heteroskedastic ordered regression modelling (Williams 2010; 2016), it is possible to evaluate how transnational motherhood and subjective well-being are interconnected while: i) explicitly considering that both subjective evaluations and mothering functions may vary over the life course (Cabraal and Singh 2013; Bonizzoni and Boccagni 2014; Sørensen and Vammen 2014; Wall and Bolzman 2014; Tosi and Impicciatore 2019), depending on mothers' and children's life stages; and ii) correcting for unobserved culture-specific notions of well-being and parenting (Zentgraf and Chinchilla 2012). In order to control for possible confounders, a large set of explanatory variables – including socio-demographic and individual characteristics, socio-economic conditions and migration background – will also be considered in the models.

The remainder of this chapter is organized as follows: the next sections explore the relevant literature on transnational motherhood and migrant well-being, focusing on female migration flows between Italy and Eastern Europe. Then, the empirical analysis is described, by illustrating the data and the methods used to analyse the relationship between maternal care across borders and migrant subjective well-being, and by presenting the main findings. The last section concludes by proposing some elements for discussion and ideas for further research.

Transnational relations and family well-being

Transnational linkages are at the very root of international mobility patterns. Migration decisions, choice of destination, the establishment of channels of transactions are all deeply linked with transnational family ties. Such bonds are multifaceted and dynamic (Ambrosini 2019), as they transform and redefine themselves over time under the constraint of geographical distance. In the literature on transnationalism, one of the major interpretative trends of such relations stresses the risk of rupture and disintegration of families, the hardship they are confronted with, and the negative consequences family members undergo due to separation (Hochschild 2000; Parreñas 2001). A more recent strand of research focuses instead on how transnational families manage to maintain their functionality and to build an identity of their own (Baldassar et al. 2007; Baldassar and Merla 2014). However, one thing the literature agrees upon is that costs and benefits of family separation via migration vary according to the contexts in which they occur (Zentgraf and Chinchilla 2012). Moreover, gains and losses to migration also involve non-monetary aspects of well-being and impact different members of the family in different ways (Cooke 2008; Amit and Riss 2014). Left-behind children, for instance, are reported to suffer from lower psychological well-being under some circumstances (Mazzucato et al. 2015), as well as from lower self-rated health (Cebotari, Mazzucato and Siegel 2017), and weaker educational performance (Cebotari and Mazzucato 2016). As regards to migrant parents, several domains pertaining to both the material and the psychological spheres of life are known to be determinants of migrant well-being, including employment, housing, education and health conditions (D'Isanto, Fouskas and Verde 2016; OECD 2017). Psychological aspects are also being acknowledged as crucial components of the general sense of "being well", especially for migrants who face the challenges set by social integration and language acquisition (Amit 2010; 2012). As reported in the literature, subjective evaluations by migrant parents in particular seem exactly to point at consistently lower levels of life satisfaction (Haagsman, Mazzucato and Dito 2015; Dito, Mazzucato and Schans 2017; Mazzucato et al. 2017). Therefore, to look at transnational parenting practices and at how perceived and measurable costs and benefits of separation impact the actors involved appears to be one valid analytical approach to tackle the matter. To this regard, Zentgraf and Chinchilla (2012) stress that several factors characterizing the contexts of departure may affect transnational family members' well-being at both the micro and the macro-level of analysis. Pre-migration family structures and local childcare traditions are relevant variables in determining how separation will affect both migrants' and their children left behind's lives – see for instance the protective role played in childrearing by extended families that is typical of many sending societies (Åkesson, Carling and Drotbohm 2012; Suárez-Orozco, Todorova and Louie 2012). However, factors like geographical distance (Banfi and Boccagni 2011), migrant legal status in the country of arrival (Calavita 2005; Menjívar 2006; Falicov 2007; Fresnoza-Flot 2009), migrants' social class (Bryceson and Vuorela 2002; Menjívar 2006) and extension of social networks (Vianello 2009; Marchetti 2013; 2017) and gender relations (Parreñas 2005; Dreby 2006) are also able to shape the transnational parental experience and deserve to undergo in-depth investigation.

Transnational motherhood and the gendered experience of parenting across borders

Female migration is a context of socially defined moralities (Åkesson, Carling and Drotbohm 2012) and, worldwide, migrant women are affected to a larger extent than men by gendered notions of appropriate mobility, occupation and living conditions (Sørensen and Vammen 2014). It follows that transnational parenthood is also affected in gender-specific ways, as it consists in rather distinct experiences for women and men who migrate to help sustain their children back home (Carling, Menjívar and Schmalzbauer 2012). In fact, although both migrant mothers and fathers usually stay in touch with their children and send gifts and money regularly, they are confronted with rather different parental experiences, both in the host country and in relation to their children (Dreby 2006).

In order to live up to societal caregiving expectations and obligations, migrant women strive to maintain emotional proximity to their children through intensive nurturing from a distance (Parreñas 2005), that is, putting into action all those practices – including sending gifts and remittances, making phone calls, arranging visits, and so forth – that Hondagneu-Sotelo and Avila (1997) first defined as *transnational motherhood*. If migrant fathers usually see the sending of remittances as their main care responsibility, mothers tend also to foster emotional contact with their children, by exerting control over them (Boccagni 2010; 2011; 2012), trying to maintain emotional intimacy and fulfilling parental responsibilities for children's social and emotional needs (Parreñas 2005; Dreby 2006). The increasing availability of low-cost forms of communication surely facilitates transnational mothers' obligations today (Peng and Wong 2013; Gonzalez and Katz 2016; Nedelcu and Wyss 2016). However, technology might not be sufficient to ease the negative feelings arising from being able to only care for one's children from afar, because it cannot entirely replace hands-on care (Asis 2002; Bernhard, Goldring and Landolt 2005; Horton 2009). Thus, on the one hand, transnational motherhood proves to challenge gender norms and social imaginaries of motherhood, according to which mothers who migrate internationally for wage work leave behind them a void that cannot be filled by other caregivers (Zentgraf and Chinchilla 2012). On the other hand, empirical research carried out in host countries (Abrego 2009) shows that the pressure placed on migrant mothers may affect their well-being by limiting their chances of integration and, under some circumstances, lead them to chronic poverty. In fact, a way transnational mothers find to cope with burdensome parental expectations is to remit as much income as possible, as demonstrated for instance by Lim (2009), Peter (2010) and by Solari (2010) for the Italian case. At the subjective well-being level, it is reported that moral expectations of motherly responsibilities and self-sacrifice may engender emotional distress, fear of social stigma, feelings of hopelessness and guilt (Hondagneu-Sotelo and Avila 1997; Aranda 2003; Bernhard, Goldring and Landolt 2005; Parreñas 2005; Baldassar 2007; Horton 2009; Vermot 2015). Of course, mothering functions are not fixed over the life course; rather, they change depending on the life stage of both mothers' and children's biography (Cabraal and Singh 2013; Bonizzoni and Boccagni 2014; Wall and Bolzman 2014). Furthermore, negative outcomes can also be alleviated by the existence of strong familial networks that allow mothers to migrate while leaving children with substitute caregivers whom they trust (Tizard 1991; Peng and Wong 2016).

Women who care: Eastern European migrants in Italy

Female migration and the experience of transnational motherhood are profoundly linked to the concepts of global care chains (Hochschild 2000; Ehrenreich and Hochschild 2003) and of circulation of care (Baldassar and Merla 2014). Even if from different perspectives, these two concepts stress the contradictory characteristics of care migration by shedding light on the gains and losses – both economic and emotional – generated by the interplay between international migration (especially of mothers), care work and the creation of transnational families.[2]

Care-related international migration represents today one of the major mobility trends at the global level, driven by the continuing growth of the care economy. The reasons behind such tendency are manifold and include the increasing withdrawal of the State from the provision of care, in particular for the elderly; demographic ageing in wealthy countries and the growing participation of the female global population in the labour market (Farris 2015; Lutz 2018). According to the International Labour Organization (ILO 2015), private households worldwide employ a total of 67.1 million people, of which nearly 73 per cent are women.[3] In Western Europe, migrant care workers are thought to account for nearly 2 million people, even though in Italy alone it is estimated that in one household out of ten there is a migrant worker who takes care for the children or the elderly (Ambrosini 2013). It follows that care giving in private households has become the largest employment sector for migrant women during the last decades (Lutz 2018), also due to the permanent demand for a low paid, flexible and highly-gendered workforce (Di Bartolomeo and Marchetti 2016). In the literature, some authors analyse these trends from a macro-level perspective to provide theoretical explanations of the transnational social asymmetry involving receiving households in host countries and families left behind in sending societies (Hochschild 2000; Parreñas 2001; Williams 2012; Baldassar and Merla 2014). Other scholars emphasize instead their micro-level implications, focusing in particular on their impacts in the everyday life of migrant women – often transnational mothers – who continue to be retained by the care sector due to its unregulated and poor working conditions (Farris 2015).

In Europe, East-West migration mainly consists in care labour migration directed especially towards Southern European states (Bettio, Simonazzi and Villa 2006). After the sudden transition to a capitalist economy, women in post-Soviet countries have taken charge of the economic needs of their households by becoming transnational breadwinners (Solari 2010; Di Bartolomeo and Marchetti 2016). Being at the crossroads of the migration routes between the former Western and Eastern blocks and the Mediterranean migration route connecting North Africa and the Middle East with Europe (Bonifazi et al. 2008; Colucci 2018), Italy has become one of the most important destinations of extra-European migration flows and is consistently chosen as a top destination by Eastern European women involved in the transnational care chain (Vianello 2009; Solari 2010; Boccagni and Ambrosini 2012; Marchetti 2013; Marchetti and Venturini 2014).

Based on this evidence, several studies have focused on transnational maternal practices of Eastern European women living in Italy and on how mothering across borders affects the life of these migrant women. In the almost entirely qualitative literature on the topic, mixed evidence emerges on how mothering from afar interrelates with migrant women's subjective well-being. For instance, Romanian migrant mothers report feeling discriminated by their community of origin, which commonly associates female absence from the household with family disruption (Ducu 2009; 2014; 2016). These mothers attempt to follow normative gender roles regarding motherhood by planning frequent trips back home and daily telephone calls, and sending money and gifts to their children (Piperno 2007; Vianello 2009). Nevertheless, they face accusations of carelessness and abandonment, and of putting family integrity at risk, while their breadwinning role is not fully acknowledged by the community of origin. On the other hand, migration provides these women with the opportunity to economically provide for their children, which engenders feelings of self-confidence and trust in their own capabilities. In some cases, communities in the home country may also organize support for emigrated mothers by helping non-migrant members of transnational families to fulfill care duties. In that regard, Piperno (2007) emphasizes the positive role of home country-based welfare actors, particularly schools and NGOs, in helping transnational mothers from Romania and Ukraine to raise their children from afar. Such kind of support helps to mitigate mothers' negative feelings arising from the loss of trust and control of their children and, at times, from the struggle to be acknowledged as mothers by their own children, while also suffering from experiences with racism and discrimination in the host country (Pirwitz 2019). Solari (2010) offers additional insights on transnational motherhood by Ukrainian older women who engage in circular mobility between the home country and Italy. These women express a sense of pride connected with being able to support their children and extended family by remitting income, paying for their education, housing and medical services. At the same time, they are often put in a bad light by the public discourse for substituting hands-on care with "easy money" children sometimes spend in a less than careful way. In Italy, they might feel doubly marginalized from the highly demanding Italian care labour market, and from the pressure to take on family responsibilities at a distance (Vianello 2009; Castagnone et al. 2007), while being negatively stigmatized by the Ukrainian community.

In sum, evidence from field research points at the existence of a contradictory relationship between mothering from afar and migrant mothers' subjective well-being. On the one hand, transnational mothers report to suffer from the double burden of distance from home and stigmatization. On the other hand, their ability to produce stable income to be remitted back home entails processes of emancipation and self-confidence acquisition. Although conveying rich information on transnational mothers' living conditions, the relevant literature relies entirely upon qualitative research, which leaves important knowledge gaps to be filled. Hence this chapter proposes an original contribution by carrying out a quantitative appraisal of the well-being of transnational mothers living in Italy who come from Eastern European countries. To that end, it endeavours to empirically answer the following question: How is transnational motherhood related with the subjective well-being of migrant women in Italy?

Empirical analysis

The data used in this chapter is the Istat Survey on *Social Condition and Integration of Foreign Citizens 2011–2012* (Istat 2016), which is representative of households with at least one foreign member legally residing in the national territory. The selected sub-sample of 4,346 observational units corresponds to migrant women between 15 and 64 years of age who were born in one of the following countries: Romania (N = 2,100), Albania (N = 931), Ukraine (N = 643), Poland (N = 412) and Moldova (N = 260). These five nationalities alone represent 46 per cent of the total female foreign resident population and 85.2 per cent of the total Eastern European female resident population in Italy.[4]

In the data, the transnational mother profile is reconstructed by developing an *ad hoc* identification strategy to target women having at least one child who:

(i) was born before the last migration to Italy took place;
(ii) did not immigrate to Italy with their mother; and
(iii) is currently living in the origin country.

Such an identification strategy is then used to create a family status indicator variable that categorizes migrant women into the following three groups: childless women, non-transnational mothers (non-TNM) and transnational mothers (TNM).

In order to investigate migrant women's subjective well-being, the empirical analysis focuses on 12 health-related subjective well-being indicators drawn from a set of questionnaire items best known as 12-Items Short-Form Survey (SF-12). The SF-12 instrument was designed to assess self-perceived general health and well-being statuses in the context of epidemiological studies (Ware et al. 1996; Ware and Gandek 1998).[5] It covers a wide range of health-related concepts, ranging from bodily pain to social functioning, pertaining to two broader domains: physical health and mental health (Table 9.1). In the empirical literature on individual well-being, it is also commonly used as a quality of life measure (Diener 1984; Diener et al. 1985; Kahneman and Krueger 2006).

Well-being is a multidimensional concept and subjective evaluations could be influenced by several objective conditions. Among the most relevant ones there is age, which plays a crucial role in determining migrant well-being regardless of the existence of a parent-child bond and the kind of family or childcare arrangement (Tosi and Impicciatore 2019). In addition,

Table 9.1 12-items short-form survey indicators

Domain	*Indicators*	*Variable*	*Type*	*Modalities*
Physical Health	General Health: Self-rated health	GH1	Ordinal	1 = Excellent 2 = Very good 3 = Good 4 = Fair 5 = Poor
	Physical Functioning: Limited in moderate activities (such as moving a table, pushing a vacuum cleaner, bowling, or riding a bike)	PF2	Ordinal	1 = Yes, Limited a lot 2 = Yes, Limited a little 3 = No, Not limited at all
	Physical Functioning: Hard to climb several flights of stairs	PF4	Ordinal	1 = Yes, Limited a lot 2 = Yes, Limited a little 3 = No, Not limited at all
	Role-Physical: Accomplished less as a result of physical health	RP2	Dichotomic	1 = No 2 = Yes
	Role-Physical: Limited in the kind of work or other activities as a result of physical health	RP3	Dichotomic	1 = No 2 = Yes
	Bodily Pain: Pain interferes with normal work	BP2	Ordinal	1 = Not at all 2 = A little bit 3 = Moderately 4 = Quite a bit 5 = Extremely
Mental Health	Vitality: Full of energy	VT2	Ordinal	1 = All of the time 2 = Most of the time 3 = A good bit of the time 4 = Some of the time 5 = A little of the time 6 = None of the time
	Social Functioning: Health or emotional problems interfere with social activities (such as visiting friends and relatives)	SF2	Ordinal	1 = All of the time 2 = Most of the time 3 = A good bit of the time 4 = Some of the time 5 = A little of the time 6 = None of the time

(*continued*)

Table 9.1 (Cont.)

Domain	*Indicators*	*Variable*	*Type*	*Modalities*
	Role-Emotional: Accomplished less as a result of emotional problems	RE2	Dichotomic	1 = No 2 = Yes
	Role-Emotional: Not careful as a result of emotional problems	RE3	Dichotomic	1 = No 2 = Yes
	Mental Health: Calm and peaceful	MH3	Ordinal	1 = All of the time 2 = Most of the time 3 = A good bit of the time 4 = Some of the time 5 = A little of the time 6 = None of the time
	Mental Health: Down-hearted and blue	MH4	Ordinal	1 = All of the time 2 = Most of the time 3 = A good bit of the time 4 = Some of the time 5 = A little of the time 6 = None of the time

Notes: Ordinal variables whose modalities were originally collected in reverse order were recoded so as to assign lower values to worse health outcomes and higher values to better health outcomes. Dichotomic response questions were also transformed into dummy variables (0–1), where null values denote the absence of good health and positive values denote better health conditions. For all indicators, the categories "Does not know" and "Did not answer" were recoded to missing.

Source: Author.

as seen in the literature (Cabraal and Singh 2013; Bonizzoni and Boccagni 2014; Wall and Bolzman 2014), mothering functions are not fixed over the life course, as they heavily depend on the life stage of the mother's biography. For these reasons, the age of the mother is considered one particularly important explanatory variable to be taken into consideration in the empirical investigation. Second, national cultures may reinforce attitudes and expectations towards maternal care (Parreñas 2005; Vianello 2009; Solari 2010; Ducu 2014). Also, coming from a certain country of origin could play a role in determining subjective well-being levels, both for the existence of culture-specific notions of what a "good life" is, and because of the peculiarity of each migration background.

In order to take all those interconnections into account and given the ordinal nature of the outcomes under consideration, in this chapter the subjective well-being of migrant women is evaluated by applying heteroskedastic ordered modelling, also known as heterogeneous choice modelling (Williams 2010; 2016), to each of the 12 health-related subjective well-being indicators.[6] Statistically, heteroskedastic ordered modelling helps to deal with data with residual variances differing across cases. It does so by simultaneously fitting two equations: one for the determinants of the outcome, or choice, and another for the determinants – in this specific case, the variable *age* – of the residual variance. Such modelling strategy avoids standard errors to be wrong and parameter estimates to be biased due to the incorrect assumption that well-being levels are independently related to the life course. In addition, heteroskedastic ordered models can also be employed to relax the assumption of independently and identically distributed errors among the sample units through the specification of clustered standard errors. In this case, the clusters are specified as individuals' countries of origin so as to acknowledge that observational units sharing the same nationality might look and behave alike concerning both their mothering practices and subjective well-being evaluations. Finally, besides implementing the *family status* indicator as the main explanatory variable of interest, the models control for a set of possible confounders by including independent variables accounting for individual characteristics (country of origin, age, marital status and the presence of chronic illnesses), socio-economic conditions (educational level and activity status, distinguishing between unemployed, legally and illegally employed migrants) and migration background (length of stay in Italy, the reason for migration, frequency of visits to the home country).

Formally, for each health-related subjective well-being indicators $j=(1,2,\ldots,J)$, where $J=12$, let denote $x=(x_1,\ldots,x_k)$ as the vector of explanatory variables at the individual level i, with $i=(i_1,\ldots,i_n)$, where the k values of x are said to be the determinants of the observed outcome of interest y. The outcome (choice) equation is specified as in (1), whereas the variance equation can be written as in (2), where z is a vector of m values for the i th observation that are related to error variances, and γ represents the coefficient associated with each m value (Williams 2010; 2016). In this model, m values correspond to age values (in years), under the assumption that as age increases, the error variances may also increase, while γ shows the extent to which the age variable affects the variance.[7]

For an ordered variable y with 1 to C categories and θ_c cutpoints, where $c=(1,\ldots,C-1)$, on the underlying latent variable y^*, the full heteroskedastic ordered model with logit link is specified as in (3).[8]

$$y_i^* = \sum_k x_{ik}\beta_k + \epsilon_i \qquad (1)$$

$$\sigma_i = \exp\left(\sum_m z_{im}\gamma_m\right) \tag{2}$$

$$P(y_i > c) = \text{invlogit}\left\{\frac{\sum_k x_{ik}\beta_k - \theta_c}{\exp\left(\sum_m z_{im}\gamma_m\right)}\right\} = \text{invlogit}\left(\frac{\sum_k x_{ik}\beta_k - \theta_c}{\sigma_i}\right) \tag{3}$$

where

$$\text{invlogit}(x) = \text{inverse logit function of } x = \frac{\exp(x)}{\{1+\exp(x)\}}$$

$$\exp\left(\sum_m z_{im}\gamma_m\right) = \exp\{\ln(\sigma_i)\} = \sigma_i$$

$$\theta_0 = -\infty \text{ and } \theta_C = \infty.$$

As a final step, the regression analyses are replicated by excluding the subsample of childless women so as to better study the variability in subjective well-being levels within the group of migrant parents only. That also allows the number of children to be included as an additional control variable.

Findings

Transnational mothers account for 17.8 per cent of female Eastern European migrants living in Italy – almost one in every five women. Thus, compared to the share of transnational parents over the total migrant population – 13.6 per cent, as estimated in Tosi and Impicciatore (2019) – women from Eastern Europe seem to be a group particularly concerned by maternal care across borders. Among them, non-transnational mothers represent the modal group (46.7%), whereas childless women are estimated to be 35.6 per cent. By any means, the distribution among the three groups differs depending on the country of origin. Ukrainian nationals show by far the largest group of transnational mothers (39.5%), followed by Moldovans (22.3%), Poles (19.0%) and Romanians (15.9%). Albanian women represent a noticeable exception, with only 1.3 per cent of transnational mothers (Table 9.2). That is likely due to their specific and longstanding migration pattern to Italy, mainly motivated by the will to reunify with their first-migrant male partners (Table 9.3).

Transnational mothers are usually older than migrant women who live along with their children in Italy. Among those who have at least

Table 9.2 Family status of Eastern European migrant women by country (row %)

Country	*Childless*	*Non-TNM*	*TNM*	*Total*	*(N)*
Romania	39.1	45.0	15.9	100	(2,100)
Albania	25.8	72.9	1.3	100	(931)
Ukraine	35.6	24.9	39.5	100	(643)
Poland	41.7	39.2	19.0	100	(412)
Moldova	29.8	47.9	22.3	100	(260)
Total	35.6	46.7	17.8	100	(4,346)

Notes: Sample weights applied.

Source: Own elaborations on Istat survey on Social condition and integration of foreign citizens 2011–2012.

Table 9.3 Reason why leaving the home country by country of origin (column %)

	Romania	*Albania*	*Ukraine*	*Poland*	*Moldova*
Find a job	9.9	4.1	14.3	18.0	10.9
Earn more money	12.0	2.5	20.1	14.6	14.0
Quality of life for themselves/family	31.5	12.7	37.8	26.1	38.8
Affective ties	32.1	64.1	15.5	19.4	21.4
Family problems/ threatens	3.3	0.8	4.5	1.1	4.7
Education	1.6	3.4	0.3	2.2	0.1
War/conflicts/ environmental disaster	0.1	2.2	0.1	0.5	0.3
Persecution	0.2	1.1	0.3	0.5	0.4
Travel/adventure	3.8	0.7	2.8	10.5	3.0
Not my choice	3.4	6.8	2.3	1.9	4.1
Other	2.2	1.8	2.0	5.3	2.3
Total	100.0	100.0	100.0	100.0	100.0
(N)	(2,100)	(931)	(643)	(412)	(260)

Notes: Sample weights applied. Respondents could indicate more than one option while answering the question.

Source: Own elaborations on Istat survey on Social condition and integration of foreign citizens 2011–2012.

one left-behind child, 71.2 per cent are 45 to 64 years of age, while only 18.3 per cent of non-transnational mothers are older than 44 (Table 9.4). Moreover, only one in every five of them reports being married and currently living with their partner: 53.5 per cent declare instead to be widowed, legally separated, or divorced, while 27.8 per cent is in a couple at a distance. Regarding the occupational conditions, transnational mothers appear

Table 9.4 Socio-demographic characteristics of Eastern European migrant women by family status (column %)

	Childless	*Non-TNM*	*TNM*	*Total*	*(N)*
Age class					
15-34	65.0	44.0	4.6	33.1	(1,867)
35-44	17.9	37.7	24.2	34.0	(1,268)
45-64	17.1	18.3	71.2	32.9	(1,211)
Total	100.0	100.0	100.0	100.0	(4,346)
Marital Status					
Not in a couple	74.5	27.5	53.5	34.7	(2,207)
In a couple	21.4	70.0	18.6	55.9	(1,845)
Couple at a distance	4.1	2.5	27.8	9.5	(294)
Total	100.0	100.0	100.0	100.0	(4,346)
Activity status					
Legally employed	52.4	43.3	73.9	51.7	(2,149)
Illegally employed	8.8	8.2	7.6	8.0	(443)
Not employed	38.7	48.5	18.5	40.3	(1,754)
Total	100.0	100.0	100.0	100.0	(4,346)

Notes: Sample weights applied.

Source: Own elaborations on Istat survey on Social condition and integration of foreign citizens 2011–2012.

to be stably integrated into the Italian labour market, as 81.5 per cent of them declare to be employed, of which nine out of ten (90.7%) work in legal employment and only 9.3 per cent are illegally employed. This comes as no surprise, given that Eastern European women make up the greatest part of the domestic and care workers, a vivid and demanding economic sector in Italy as highlighted earlier in this chapter. In fact, such an extensive participation into the host labour market might be linked to their specific parenting condition: migrant women with different family statuses show considerably lower proportions of occupied individuals – only 51.5 per cent of non-transnational mothers and 61.2 per cent among the childless – and, among the latter, the proportion of those working in illegal employment is higher (15.9% among migrant mothers living with their children and 14.4% among women with no children).

As regards to health-related subjective well-being, summary statistics presented in Table 9.5 underline that, compared to childless women and to women living with their children in Italy, transnational mothers consistently report lower levels of well-being across both dimensions of physical and mental health. In 11 out of 12 indicators, transnational mothers show significantly worse well-being outcomes, as verified by the independent groups t-test.[9] In particular, when ordinal indicators are analysed (GH1, PF2, PF4, BP2, VT2, SF2, MH3 and MH4), migrant mothers with left-behind

Table 9.5 Summary statistics of SF-12 well-being indicators by family status group

Indicator	*Family status*	*N*	*Median*	*Mean*	*SD*	*Min*	*Max*
Physical Health							
GH1	Childless	1,580	4	4.26*	0.74	1	5
	Non-TNM	1,956	4	4.15*	0.74	1	5
	TNM	738	4	3.89*	0.76	1	5
PF2	Childless	1,540	3	2.92*	0.31	1	3
	Non-TNM	1,918	3	2.91*	0.35	1	3
	TNM	722	3	2.85*	0.41	1	3
PF4	Childless	1,553	3	2.95	0.25	1	3
	Non-TNM	1,929	3	2.94	0.27	1	3
	TNM	725	3	2.87*	0.39	1	3
RP2	Childless	1,537	1	0.95	0.22	0	1
	Non-TNM	1,917	1	0.93	0.26	0	1
	TNM	724	1	0.90*	0.30	0	1
RP3	Childless	1,545	1	0.95*	0.22	0	1
	Non-TNM	1,923	1	0.94*	0.24	0	1
	TNM	727	1	0.90*	0.30	0	1
BP2	Childless	1,548	5	4.77*	0.68	1	5
	Non-TNM	1,932	5	4.72*	0.72	1	5
	TNM	726	5	4.63*	0.79	1	5
Mental Health							
VT2	Childless	1,553	5	4.73*	1.17	1	6
	Non-TNM	1,931	5	4.67*	1.18	1	6
	TNM	731	5	4.51*	1.16	1	6
SF2	Childless	1,541	6	5.38	0.94	1	6
	Non-TNM	1,924	6	5.42	0.87	1	6
	TNM	725	6	5.31*	0.92	1	6
RE2	Childless	1,547	1	0.94	0.23	0	1
	Non-TNM	1,925	1	0.93	0.25	0	1
	TNM	727	1	0.91*	0.29	0	1
RE3	Childless	1,547	1	0.93	0.25	0	1
	Non-TNM	1,925	1	0.93	0.25	0	1
	TNM	726	1	0.93	0.25	0	1
MH3	Childless	1,552	5	4.73	1.17	1	6
	Non-TNM	1,932	5	4.64	1.20	1	6
	TNM	730	5	4.44*	1.19	1	6
MH4	Childless	1,552	5	4.92	1.11	1	6
	Non-TNM	1,930	5	4.95	0.98	1	6
	TNM	729	5	4.69*	0.97	1	6

Notes: Sample weights applied. Stars (*) indicate that means are significantly different across groups as per the independent group t-test computed with Stata 15.

Source: Own elaborations on Istat survey on Social condition and integration of foreign citizens 2011–2012.

children report lower mean levels of subjective well-being. Similarly, in most of the dichotomic indicators considered (RP2, RP3 and RE3), trans-national mothers report lower mean subjective well-being levels than migrant women in other family statuses. The only indicator that appears to be homogeneously distributed across the different groups is the RE2 (Role-Emotional: Accomplished less as a result of emotional problems) indicator. Compared to migrant women with different family statuses, the substantially equal levels of perceived capability of accomplishing everyday tasks reported by transnational mothers could be explained by the relatively more satisfactory employment conditions experienced by the latter. In fact, their involvement in the Italian care labour market could work as a protective factor, as labourers who work under more secure employment conditions might feel less exposed to economic uncertainty and perceive that their physical and emotional efforts are being rewarded by their ability to provide material support to their children.

With the aim of evaluating if transnational mothers' experience is associated with lower subjective well-being levels by considering all possible confounders, estimates from heteroskedastic ordered models are reported in Figure 9.1.[10] The odds ratios of the *family status* indicator confirm that, other things being equal, being a transnational mother is negatively associated with numerous subjective well-being indicators for Eastern European migrant women.

Concerning the physical health domain, women with left-behind children are less likely to rate their own general health (GH1) positively compared to childless women. On the other hand, the existence of a parent-child bond *per se* seems to not make any difference when determining subjective well-being levels, as indicated by the non-significant odds ratio associated with being a parent who lives with all their children in Italy. In terms of physical functioning (PF2), compared to women who do not have children, transnational mothers are more likely to feel limited by their physical health in carrying out moderate activities. Again, the same negative outcome does not apply to mothers in general, as non-transnational mothers' physical functioning self-assessment is not statistically different from that of childless women. The two dichotomic indicators (RP2 and RP3) also point at a highly significant difference between transnational mothers and other migrant women. Compared to migrants who do not have children at all, women who practice childcare from a distance face a reduced probability to self-evaluate as well-functioning as a result of their physical health.

As regards to the mental health domain, three out of six indicators shed light on transnational mothers' relative greater emotional vulnerability, especially in terms of their emotional role functioning (RE2 and RE3). Migrants who practice motherhood across borders are less likely than childless migrants to self-evaluate as well-functioning in response to emotional problems (accomplished less), and more likely to evaluate themselves as not having problems of carelessness while carrying out their work or other activities. Transnational motherhood is also associated with weaker mental health in the recurrent feeling of sadness and discouragement

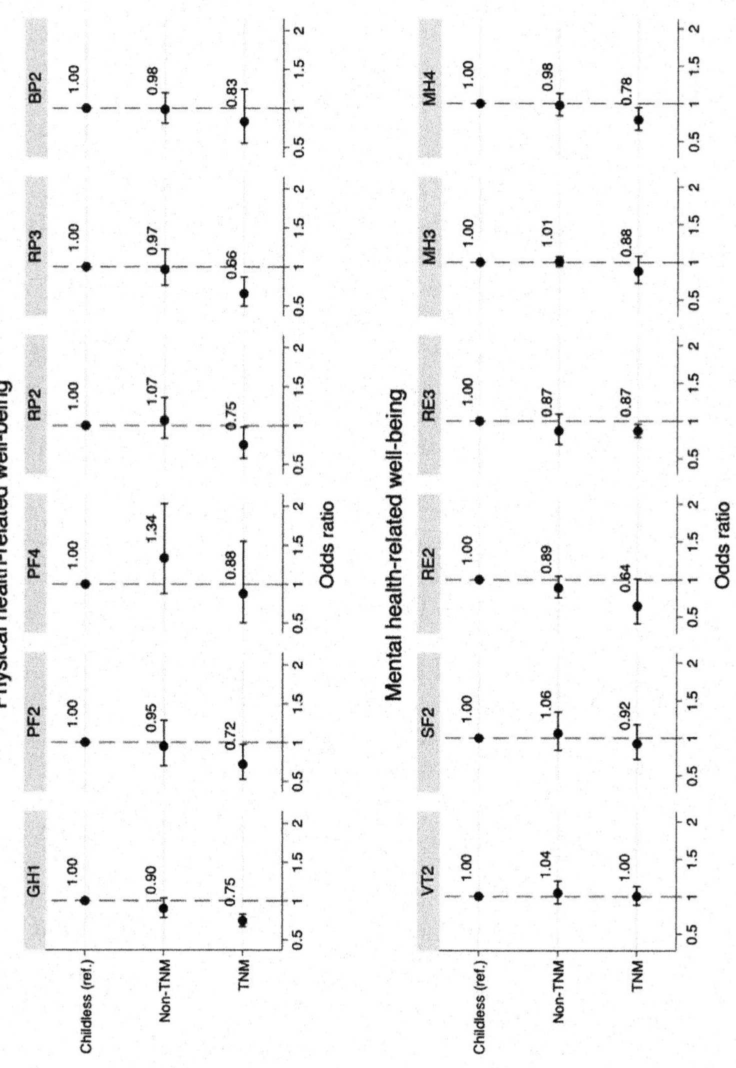

Figure 9.1 Odds ratios of migrant women's subjective well-being (heteroskedastic ordered model estimates)

Notes: Bands are 95% confidence intervals. All controls applied.

Source: Own elaborations on Istat survey on social condition and integration of foreign citizens 2011–2012.

(MH4): according to the estimates, transnational mothers are less likely to be exempt from feeling blue and downhearted compared to childless migrants.

Transnational motherhood seems thus to expose migrant women to lower health-related quality of life outcomes. Such evidence is particularly significant when migrants with left-behind children are compared to migrants who do not have children at all. However, what role transnational relations play *per se* in determining migrant mothers' subjective well-being needs to be further clarified. To address that, the regression analyses were replicated by rerunning the models using the data on the sub-group of migrant mothers only and by including the number of children as an additional control.

Figure 9.2 graphically presents the odds ratios of the *family status* indicator computed for each of the 12 indicators.[11] As far as physical health is concerned, transnational mothers fare worse than migrant women who live with their children in Italy, *ceteris paribus*. The former are less likely than the latter to rate positively their own general health (GH1) and face a reduced probability to self-evaluate as well-functioning from a physical standpoint (PF2 and PF4). Moreover, migrants who practice motherhood across borders are at higher risk of experiencing interference with their normal work due to bodily pain (BP2). Finally, looking at the odds ratios associated with two dichotomic deprivation indicators (RP2 and RP3), transnational mothers are more likely than non-transnational mothers to report having accomplished less during the last month and to self-evaluation as being limited in the kind of work or other regular daily activities they carry out, as a result of physical health problems.

Regarding mental health-related well-being, transnational mothers are less likely to be exempt from seeing their social activities limited by emotional problems (SF2). They also are at higher risk of feeling blue and downhearted (MH4) compared to migrant mothers with no left-behind child. Lastly, the analysis of emotional role functioning indicators also shows that transnational mothers are less likely to report that emotional problems did not interfere with their capability to accomplish one's tasks (RE3); and that they also face a greater risk (as per the reduced probability in the RE3 indicator) of self-evaluating as carrying out regular daily activities less carefully than usual as a result of feeling depressed or anxious.

Conclusions

To adopt a transnational perspective is crucial to achieve a better understanding of migration and migrant lives. Such a purpose requires embracing the concept of emotional and relational *homing* (Boccagni 2017) so as to include all the intangible ties and motivations that go beyond the mere geographical proximity.

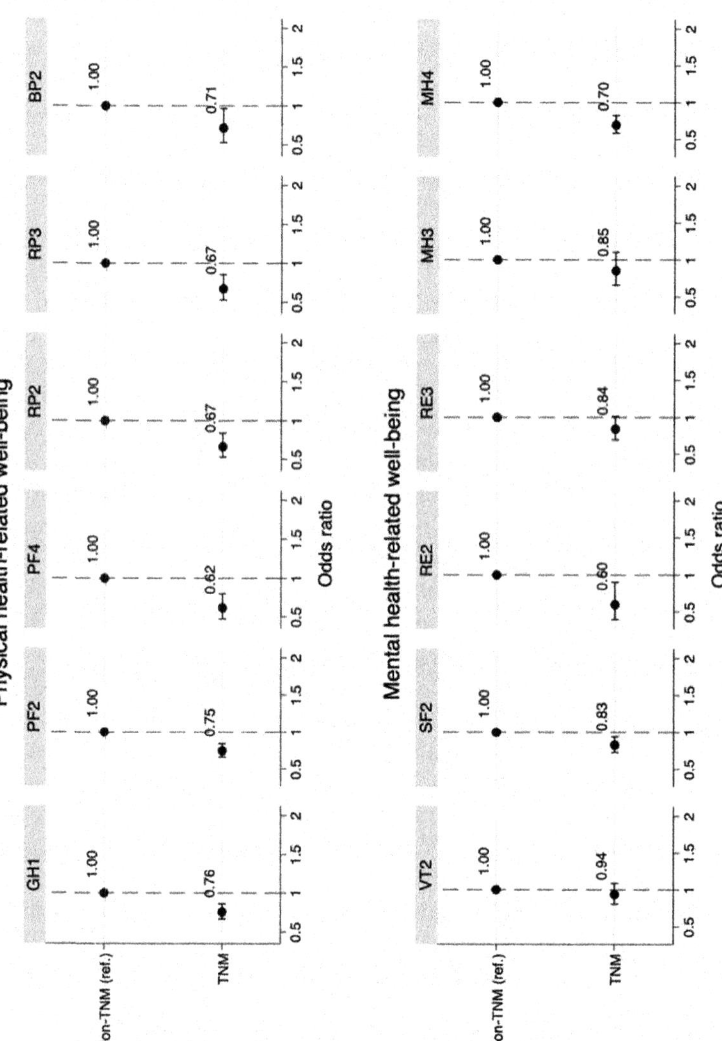

Figure 9.2 Odds ratios of migrant mothers' subjective well-being (heteroskedastic ordered model estimates)

Notes: Bands are 95% confidence intervals. All controls applied.

Source: Own elaborations on Istat survey on social condition and integration of foreign citizens 2011–2012.

The international literature on transnationalism, mostly originating in ethnographic research carried out in different times and regions of the world, has ascertained that transnational parenting is a strongly gendered experience. Due to the existence of gender norms and social imaginaries of motherhood and fatherhood, women and men receive different incentives to emigrate and to engage in parental care practices from afar. Mothers who migrate for wage work while leaving the children in the care of others are often severely judged by their transnational community. Such a pressure engenders feelings of guilt, distress, fear of social stigma and loss of emotional contact with their children, all of which undermine transnational mothers' health and psychological well-being.

Worldwide, female migration from poor countries is profoundly intertwined with the increasing demand coming from wealthy and ageing societies for low-cost and flexible care labour. Some observers understand migrant women as part of a global care chain, which employs their labour but leaves them deprived on the emotional side (Hochschild 2000; Parreñas 2001). Some others see them instead as key actors in the circulation of care (Baldassar and Merla 2014). Anyhow, economic and emotional gains and losses to migration are deeply interconnected in the life of women who leave their family behind to become breadwinners in the global economy of care. Nevertheless, policy makers from host societies are seldom interested in understanding the nature and the consequences of such interplay, including if and how it affects the everyday life of migrants living in their countries and striving for achieving socio-economic integration.

Starting from these premises, this chapter has examined the relationship between transnational motherhood and migrant subjective well-being in Italy by focusing on the available micro-level statistical information on the social condition and integration of Eastern European female nationals (Istat 2016). By reviewing the existing qualitative literature on transnational motherhood involving Eastern European migrants in Italy, mixed evidence has emerged on how mothering across borders affects migrant mothers' lives. On the one hand, the experience of migration allows mothers to concretely provide economic and material means for their left-behind families. It also contributes to the generation of processes of emancipation and acquisition of self-confidence within the household, where the newly achieved breadwinning role allows women to participate in family care as equal with their partners (Ducu 2009; 2014; 2016). On the other hand, mothering from afar puts Eastern European migrant women in a bad light in the eyes of their transnational community, which often blames them for being absent and accuses them of causing suffering and possibly harm to their own children (Castagnone et al. 2007; Piperno 2007; Vianello 2009; Solari 2010). Empirical results – generated through heteroskedastic ordered modeling (Williams 2010; 2016) applied to 12 health-related subjective well-being indicators (Ware et al. 1996; Ware and Gandek 1998) – stress that transnational mothers do suffer from lower subjective well-being in several domains, pertaining to both the physical and the mental health spheres. The disadvantage experienced by transnational Eastern European mothers manifests clearly with respect to both childless migrants and migrant mothers who live with their children in Italy – individual characteristics, socio-economic conditions and migration background being equal. Physically, transnational mothers are more likely to report lower self-assessed general health or problems at work due to bodily pain, and to self-evaluate as being limited in the kind of work or other regular daily activities they carry out as a result of health problems. As regards mental well-being, transnational motherhood is associated with weaker perceived psychological health, greater emotional vulnerability, and the tendency to feel sad and discouraged.

On a general note, the struggle with the emotional difficulties of transnational motherhood is not to be seen as fixed for all women and all circumstances. In fact, they may improve or worsen depending on a number of contextual factors, like immigration regimes of receiving societies (Calavita 2005; Menjívar 2006; Falicov 2007) and childrearing arrangements in the countries of origin (Tizard 1991; Suárez-Orozco, Todorova and Louie 2012; Åkesson, Carling and Drotbohm 2012; Peng and Wong 2016). Most of that information is unfortunately still unavailable at the statistical level in many countries, due to the structural inadequacy of existing international migration data (Willekens et al. 2016). To address that, migration data science would need to promote radical improvement in data production and collection by implementing two main advancements: firstly, by assuming the transnational perspective in survey design, so as to make practices and linkages across borders visible and understandable, especially in regard to family relations. Secondly, by adopting a gender-sensitive perspective, in order to increase awareness on the gendered nature of many aspects and phases of migration – from aspirations and constraints to mobility in countries of origin, to expectations and integration in the host societies. That would considerably improve the general understanding of men's and women's experiences in all kinds of mobility, which in turn could hopefully reverberate in the design and implementation of enhanced migration and social integration policies.

Acknowledgements

The author gratefully acknowledges Fondazione Alsos and the research programme *Migrazioni e migranti in Italia 2018–2020* for supporting this research as part of the project "Transnational Parenthood and Migrant Well-Being in Italy", and thanks to the Italian National Institute of Statistics (Istat) for having granted access to the micro-data used in this chapter. The ideas and views expressed here should not under any circumstances be regarded as stating an official position of Istat. Special thanks are also due to Roberto Impicciatore, Rosella Rettaroli and Livia Elisa Ortensi, who provided insight and expertise that greatly assisted the research, and to Pierpaolo Ascari, Gaia Cottino, Ilaria Fiorentini, Vincenzo Galatà, Silvia Luraschi, Lidia Manzo, Selenia Marabello, Davide Mazzoni, Mattia Messena, Rosalba Nodari,

Valeria Piro, Silvia Pitzalis, Giuliana Sanò, Valeria Tonioli, Carolina Vesce and Matteo Deleidi for fruitful discussion.

Notes

1 Although there is great diversity in family arrangements across the globe, the transnational family literature often focuses on nuclear families composed by a couple with young children where at least one adult member is living abroad (Mazzucato et al. 2015).
2 See Lutz (2018) for a critical discussion of these theories.
3 Official statistics probably severely underestimate the phenomenon, as ILO itself stresses (ILO 2013). The inadequacy of quantitative data on the matter is also due to the fact that care provision is a privatized employment sector which is rarely subjected to institutional control and regulation (Lutz 2018).
4 Source: Foreign resident population on 1 January 2020 (data last extracted on 13 May 2020 from I.Stat).
5 The SF-12 is a subset of the SF-36, a survey questionnaire developed for the Medical Outcomes Study (MOS), a multi-year study of patients with chronic conditions. The 12-items survey instrument aims at reducing survey length and respondent burden while guaranteeing minimum standards of precision for purposes of group comparisons involving multiple health dimensions (Ware et al. 1996; Ware and Gandek 1998).
6 All estimates were computed using Stata 15 by means of the *oglm* package (Williams 2010; 2016).
7 The underlying assumption is that variation in health status is greater in an older population as compared with a younger and healthier population. Such an assumption has also been empirically validated by means of the *hettest* command in Stata 15, which performs three versions of the Breusch-Pagan (Breusch and Pagan 1979) and the Cook-Weisberg (Cook and Weisberg 1983) tests for heteroskedasticity. Results of the tests are made available by the author upon request.
8 Such model specification is equally valid for both ordered variable outcomes and dichotomic variable outcomes, provided that the latter are coded in an ordered fashion (e.g., 0–1) (Williams 2010).
9 The independent groups t-test compares the means of two groups to assess whether they are statistically different from one another. Results are made available by the author upon request.
10 The complete set of estimates from the heteroskedastic ordered models is made available by the author upon request.
11 The complete set of estimates from the heteroskedastic ordered models for the sub-population of migrant mothers is made available by the author upon request.

References

Abrego L. (2009). Economic Well-Being in Salvadoran Transnational Families: How Gender Affects Remittance Practices. *Journal of Marriage and Family*. 71(November): 1070–1085.

Åkesson L., Carling J. and Drotbohm H. (2012). Mobility, Moralities and Motherhood: Navigating the Contingencies of Cape Verdean Lives. *Journal of Ethnic and Migration Studies*. 38(2): 237–260.

Ambrosini M. (2013). *Irregular Migration and Invisible Welfare*. Basingstoke: Palgrave Macmillan.

Ambrosini M. (2019). *Famiglie nonostante. Come gli affetti sfidano i confini*. Bologna: Il Mulino.

Amit K. (2010). Determinants of Life Satisfaction Among Immigrants from Western Countries and from the FSU in Israel. *Social Indicators Research*. 96: 515–534.

Amit K. (2012). Social Integration and Identity of Immigrants from Western Countries, the FSU and Ethiopia in Israel. *Ethnic and Racial Studies*, 35(7), 1287–1310.

Amit K. and Riss I. (2014). The Subjective Well-Being of Immigrants: Pre- and Post-migration. *Social Indicators Research*. 119(1): 247–264.

Aranda E.M. (2003). Global Care Work and Gendered Constraints. The Case of Puerto Rican Transmigrants. *Gender & Society*. 17(4): 609–626.

Asis M.M.B. (2002). From the Life Stories of Filipino Women: Personal and Family Agendas in Migration. *Asian and Pacific Migration Journal*. 11(1): 67–94.

Baldassar L. (2007). Transnational Families and the Provision of Moral and Emotional Support: The Relationship between Truth and Distance. *Identities*. 14(4): 385–409.

Baldassar L., Baldock C.V. and Wilding R. (2007). *Families Caring across Borders: Migration, Ageing and Transnational Caregiving*. Basingstoke: Palgrave Macmillan.

Baldassar L. and Merla L. (eds.). (2014). *Transnational Families, Migration and the Circulation of Care: Understanding Mobility and Absence in Family Life*. New York and Abingdon: Routledge.

Banfi L. and Boccagni P. (2011). Transnational Family Life and Female Migration in Italy: One or Multiple Patterns? In Kraler A., Kofman E., Kohli M. and Schmoll C. (eds.), *Gender, Generations and the Family in International Migration*. Amsterdam: Amsterdam University Press, 287–311.

Beauchemin C. (ed.). (2018). *Migration between Africa and Europe*. Cham: Springer International Publishing.

Bernhard J.K., Goldring L. and Landolt P. (2005). Transnational, Multi-Local Motherhood: Experiences of Separation and Reunification among Latin American Families in Canada. *Early Childhood Education Publications and Research*. Paper 6. http://digitalcommons.ryerson.ca/ece/6.

Bernhard J.K., Landolt P. and Goldring L. (2008). Transnationalizing Families: Canadian Immigration Policy and the Spatial Fragmentation of Care-giving among Latin American Newcomers. *International Migration*. 47(2): 3–31.

Bettio F., Simonazzi A. and Villa P. (2006). Change in Care Regimes and Female Migration: The "Care Drain" in the Mediterranean. *Journal of European Social Policy*. 16(3): 271–285.

Boccagni P. (2010). Private, Public or Both? On the Scope and Impact of Transnationalism in Immigrants' Everyday Lives. In Baubock R. (ed.), *Diaspora and Transnationalism: Concepts, Theories and Methods*. Amsterdam: Amsterdam University Press, 185–203.

Boccagni P. (2011). Migrants' Social Protection as a Transnational Process: Public Policies and Emigrant Initiative in the Case of Ecuador. *International Journal of Social Welfare*. 20(3): 318–325.

Boccagni P. (2012). Practising Motherhood at a Distance: Retention and Loss in Ecuadorian Transnational Families. *Journal of Ethnic and Migration Studies*. 38(2): 261–277.

Boccagni P. (2017). *Migration and the Search for Home: Mapping Domestic Space in Migrants' Everyday Lives*. New York: Palgrave Macmillan.

Boccagni P. and Ambrosini M. (2012). *Cercando il benessere nelle migrazioni. L'esperienza delle assistenti familiari straniere in Trentino*. Milano: Franco Angeli.

Bonifazi C., Okolski M., Schoorl J. and Simon P. (eds.). (2008). *International Migration in Europe: New Trends and New Methods of Analysis*. Amsterdam: Amsterdam University Press.

Bonizzoni P. and Boccagni P. (2014). Care (and) Circulation Revisited: A Conceptual Map of Diversity in Transnational Parenting. In Baldassar L. and Merla L. (eds.). *Transnational Families, Migration and the Circulation of Care: Understanding Mobility and Absence in Family Life*. New York and Abingdon: Routledge, 78–93.

Breusch T.S. and Pagan A.R. (1979). A Simple Test for Heteroscedasticity and Random Coefficient Variation. *Econometrica*. 47(5): 1287–1294.

Bryceson D.F. and Vuorela U. (2002). Transnational Families in the 21st Century. In Bryceson D.F. and Vuorela U. (eds.). *The Transnational Family: New European Frontiers and Global Networks*. Oxford: Berg Press, 3–30.

Cabraal A. and Singh S. (2013). Contested Representations of Remittances and the Transnational Family. *South Asia: Journal of South Asia Studies*. 36(1): 50–64.

Calavita K. (2005). *Immigrants at the Margins: Law, Race, and Exclusion in Southern Europe. Cambridge Studies in Law and Society*. Cambridge: Cambridge University Press.

Carling J., Menjívar C. and Schmalzbauer L. (2012). Central Themes in the Study of Transnational Parenthood. *Journal of Ethnic and Migration Studies*. 38(2): 191–217.

Castagnone E., Eve M., Petrillo R.E. and Piperno F. (2007). *Le migrazioni di cura dalla Romania e dall'Ucraina in Italia: Percorsi e impatto sui paesi di origine*. Fieri Working Papers No. 34. Roma: Cespi-Fieri.

Cebotari V. and Mazzucato V. (2016). Educational Performance of Children of Migrant Parents in Ghana, Nigeria and Angola. *Journal of Ethnic and Migration Studies*. 42(5): 834–856.

Cebotari V., Mazzucato V. and Siegel M. (2017). Child Development and Migrant Transnationalism: The Health of Children Who Stay Behind in Ghana and Nigeria. *Journal of Development Studies*. 53(3): 444–459.

Colucci M. (2018). *Storia dell'immigrazione straniera in Italia: dal 1945 ai nostri giorni*. Roma: Carocci.

Cook D. and Weisberg S. (1983). Diagnostics for Heteroscedasticity in Regression. *Biometrika*. 70(1): 1–10.

Cooke T.J. (2008). Migration in a Family Way. *Population, Space and Place*. 14(4): 255–265.

D'Isanto F., Fouskas P. and Verde M. (2016). Determinants of Well-Being among Legal and Illegal Immigrants: Evidence from South Italy. *Social Indicators Research*. 126(3): 1109–1141.

Di Bartolomeo A. and Marchetti S. (2016). Migrant Women's Employment in Paid Reproductive Work through the Crisis: The Case of Italy (2007-2012). *Investigaciones Feministas*. 7(1): 57–74.

Diener E. (1984). Subjective Well-being. *Psychological Bulletin*. 95(3): 542–575.

Diener E., Emmons R.A., Larsen R.J. and Griffin S. (1985). The Satisfaction With Life Scale. *Journal of Personality Assessment*. 49(1): 71–75.

Dito B.B., Mazzucato V. and Schans D. (2017). The Effects of Transnational Parenting on the Subjective Health and Well-Being of Ghanaian Migrants in the Netherlands. *Population, Space and Place*. 23(3): 1–15.

Dreby J. (2006). Honor and Virtue: Mexican Parenting in the Transnational Context. *Gender and Society*. 20(1): 32–59.

Ducu V. (2009). Women in the Lives of Romanian Transnational Families. *Studia Universitatis Babes Bolyai - Politica*. LIV(1-2): 191–201.

Ducu V. (2014). Transnational Mothers from Romania. *Romanian Journal of Population Studies*. VIII(1): 117–141.

Ducu V. (2016). Experiences from "Home" – Belonging to a Transnational Family. *Romanian Journal of Population Studies*. X(1): 91–104.

Ehrenreich B. and Hochschild A.R. (eds.). (2003). *Global Woman: Nannies, Maids, and Sex Workers in the New Economy*. New York: Henry Holt and Company.

Falicov C.J. (2007). Working with Transnational Immigrants: Expanding Meanings of Family, Community, and Culture. *Family Process*. 46(2): 157–171.

Farris S.R. (2015). Migrants' Regular Army of Labour: Gender Dimensions of the Impact of the Global Economic Crisis on Migrant Labor in Western Europe. *Sociological Review*. 63(1): 121–143.

Fresnoza-Flot A. (2009). Migration Status and Transnational Mothering: The Case of Filipino Migrants in France. *Global Networks*. 9(2): 252–270.

Gonzalez C. and Katz V.S. (2016). Transnational Family Communication as a Driver of Technology Adoption. *International Journal of Communication*. 10: 2683–2703.

Haagsman K., Mazzucato V. and Dito B.B. (2015). Transnational Families and the Subjective Well-Being of Migrant Parents: Angolan and Nigerian Parents in the Netherlands. *Ethnic and Racial Studies*. 38(15): 2652–2671.

Hochschild A.R. (2000). Global Care Chains and Emotional Surplus Value. In Hutton W., Giddens A. and Myers N. (eds.). *On the Edge: Living with Global Capitalism*. London: Jonathan Cape, 130–146.

Hondagneu-Sotelo P. and Avila E. (1997). "I'm Here, but I'm There". The Meanings of Latina Transnational Motherhood. *Gender & Society*. 11(5): 548–571.

Horton S. (2009). A Mother's Heart is Weighed Down with Stones: A Phenomenological Approach to the Experience of Transnational Motherhood. *Culture, Medicine and Psychiatry*. 33(1): 21–40.

ILO (2013). *Domestic Workers Across the World: Global and regional statistics and the extent of legal protection*. Geneva: International Labour Office.

ILO (2015). *Global Estimates on Migrant Workers: Results and Methodology*. Geneva: International Labour Office.

Istat (2016). *Condizione e integrazione sociale dei cittadini stranieri 2011-2012 - Aspetti metodologici dell'indagine*. Roma: Istat.

Kahneman D. and Krueger A.B. (2006). Developments in the Measurement of Subjective Well-Being. *Journal of Economic Perspectives*. 20(1): 3–24.

Lim S.-L. (2009). "Loss of Connections is Death". Transnational Family Ties Among Sudanese Refugee Families Resettling in the United States. *Journal of Cross-Cultural Psychology*. 40(6): 1028–1040.

Lutz H. (2018). Care Migration: The Connectivity between Care Chains, Care Circulation and Transnational Social Inequality. *Current Sociology*. 66(4): 577–589.

Marchetti S. (2013). Dreaming Circularity? Eastern European Women and Job Sharing in Paid Home Care. *Journal of Immigrant and Refugee Studies*. 11(4): 347–363.

Marchetti S. (2017). Networks Beyond Nationalities? Relationships amongst Eastern European Women Workers in Italy Facing the Economic Crisis. *Journal of Ethnic and Migration Studies*. 43(4): 633–651.

Marchetti S. and Venturini A. (2014). Mothers and Grandmothers on the Move: Labour Mobility and the Household Strategies of Moldovan and Ukrainian Migrant Women in Italy. *International Migration*. 52(5): 111–126.

Mazzucato V., Cebotari V., Veale A., White A., Grassi M. and Vivet J. (2015). International Parental Migration and the Psychological Well-Being of Children in Ghana, Nigeria, and Angola. *Social Science & Medicine*. 132(May): 215–224.

Mazzucato V., Dito B.B., Grassi M. and Vivet J. (2017). Transnational Parenting and the Well-Being of Angolan Migrant Parents in Europe. *Global Networks*. 17(1): 89–110.

Mazzucato V., Schans D., Caarls K. and Beauchemin C. (2015). Transnational Families Between Africa and Europe. *International Migration Review*. 49(1): 142–172.

Menjívar C. (2006). Liminal Legality: Salvadoran and Guatemalan Immigrants' Lives in the United States. *American Journal of Sociology*. 111(4): 999–1037.

Nedelcu M. and Wyss M. (2016). "Doing Family" through ICT-Mediated Ordinary Co-Presence: Transnational Communication Practices of Romanian Migrants in Switzerland. *Global Networks*. 16(2): 202–218.

OECD (2017). Migrants' Well-Being: Moving to a Better Life? In OECD (eds.). *How's Life? 2017: Measuring Well-Being*. Paris: OECD Publishing.

Parreñas R. (2001). Mothering from a Distance: Emotions, Gender, and Intergenerational Relations in Filipino Transnational Families. *Feminist Studies*. 27(2): 361–390.

Parreñas R. (2005). *Children of Global Migration: Transnational Families and Gendered Woes*. Stanford: Stanford University Press.

Parreñas R. (2015). *Servants of Globalization: Migration and Domestic Work*. Stanford: Stanford University Press.

Peng Y. and Wong O.M.H. (2013). Diversified Transnational Mothering via Telecommunication: Intensive, Collaborative, and Passive. *Gender and Society*. 27(4): 491–513.

Peng Y. and Wong O.M.H. (2016). Who Takes Care of My Left-Behind Children? Migrant Mothers and Caregivers in Transnational Child Care. *Journal of Family Issues*. 37(14): 2021–2044.

Peter K.B. (2010). Transnational Family Ties, Remittance Motives, and Social Death among Congolese Migrants: A Socio-Anthropological Analysis. *Journal of Comparative Family Studies*. 41(2): 225–243.

Piperno F. (2007). From Care Drain to Care Gain: Migration in Romania and Ukraine and the Rise of Transnational Welfare. *Development*. 50(4): 63–68.

Pirwitz A. (2019). Romanian Migrants in Western Europe: Expectations, Challenges and the Importance of their Networks. *Philologica Jassyensia*. 1(1): 221–230.

Schmalzbauer L. (2004). Searching for Wages and Mothering from Afar: The Case of Honduran Transnational Families. *Journal of Marriage and Family*. 66(December): 1317–1331.

Solari C. (2010). Resource Drain vs. Constitutive Circularity: Comparing the Gendered Effects of Post-Soviet Migration Patterns in Ukraine. *Anthropology of East Europe Review*. 28(1): 215–238.

Sørensen N.N. and Vammen I.M. (2014). Migration and Development: Rethinking Recruitment, Remittances, Diaspora Support and Return. *New Diversities*. 16(2): 89–108.

Suárez-Orozco C., Todorova I.L.G. and Louie J. (2012). Making up for Lost Time: The Experience of Separation and Reunification among Immigrant Families. *The New Immigration: An Interdisciplinary Reader*. 41(4): 179–196.

Tizard B. (1991). Employed Mothers and the Care of Young Children. In Phoenix A., Woollett A. and Lloyd E. (eds.). *Motherhood: Meanings, Practices and Ideologies*. Thousand Oaks: Sage, 178–194.

Tosi F. and Impicciatore R. (2019). *Transnational Parenthood and Migrant Subjective Well-Being in Italy*. Paper presented at the British Society for Population Studies (BSPS) Annual Conference 2019, Cardiff University, September 11.

United Nations, Department of Economic and Social Affairs, Population Division. (2017). *International Migration Report 2017*.

Vermot C. (2015). Guilt: A Gendered Bond within the Transnational Family. *Emotion, Space and Society*. 16(August): 138–146.

Vianello F.A. (2009). *Migrando sole. Legami transnazionali tra Ucraina e Italia*. Milano: Franco Angeli.

Wall K. and Bolzman C. (2014). Mapping the New Plurality of Transnational Families: A Life Course Perspective. In Baldassar L. and Merla L. (eds.). *Transnational Families, Migration and the Circulation of Care: Understanding Mobility and Absence in Family Life*. New York and Abingdon: Routledge, 77–93.

Ware J.E. and Gandek B. (1998). Overview of the SF-36 Health Survey and the International Quality of Life Assessment (IQOLA) Project. *Journal of Clinical Epidemiology*. 51(11): 903–912.

Ware J.E., Kosinski M. and Keller S.D. (1996). A 12-Item Short-Form Health Survey: Construction of Scales and Preliminary Tests of Reliability and Validity. *Medical Care*. 34(3): 220–233.

Willekens B.F., Massey D., Raymer J. and Beauchemin C. (2016). International Migration under the Microscope. *Science*. 352(6288): 897–899.

Williams F. (2012). Converging Variations in Migrant Care Work in Europe. *Journal of European Social Policy*. 22(4): 363–376.

Williams R. (2010). Fitting Heterogeneous Choice Models with Oglm. *Stata Journal*. 10(4): 540–567.

Williams R. (2016). Understanding and Interpreting Generalized Ordered Logit Models. *Journal of Mathematical Sociology*. 40(1): 7–20.

Zentgraf K.M. and Chinchilla N.S. (2012). Transnational Family Separation: A Framework for Analysis. *Journal of Ethnic and Migration Studies*. 38(2): 345–366.

10 Free or bounded?

Migration, ethnicity, social background and educational choices in four European countries

Eleonora Vlach

Introduction

The movement of individuals across national borders is one of the most relevant and debated phenomena of current Western societies. In 2018 more than five million people immigrated to OECD countries, 2 per cent more than in 2017 (OECD 2019). More than one million of them were asylum seekers, fleeing from war and unstable political conditions in their home countries. The difficulties faced by immigrant families, however, do not cease upon arrival. To the contrary: completely new challenges open up once the destination country is reached. Meeting these challenges is what scholars refer to by the term "integration". Moreover, difficulties faced by first generation immigrants upon arrival (such as language barriers, labour market discrimination, reduced social contacts – Kogan 2006; 2011; Heath and Cheung 2007; Ballarino and Panichella 2013) can be, and frequently are, transmitted to the second generation, even though their children are not immigrants *strictu sensu*. For example, parents with reduced command of the destination country's language might prefer to use their mother tongue at home. They might also experience difficulties in helping their children with homework. The resulting sub-optimal learning environment could translate into lower grades, lower educational degrees and consequently lower labour market opportunities. At the same time, immigrant parents are likely to transmit (through socialization) their extraordinary high ambition and sense of self-denial which enabled them to migrate in the first place. These dispositions can favour their offspring's educational aspirations despite lacking language proficiency. Acknowledging the pivotal importance of acquiring country-specific human capital for the chances of integration of migrants and their descendants, this chapter focuses on the educational choices of second generations. Analysing how many underage children of immigrants are not in full time education today, in fact, allows us to anticipate how widespread poverty and social exclusion might be within the population with migration background in the future (Rumberger and Lamb 2003; OECD 2005; Ballarino and Checchi 2006; Murray and Sundin

2008; Jonsson, Kilpi-Jakonen and Rudolphi 2014). The fact that children of immigrants are generally found at the bottom end of the educational distribution is a rather consistent finding across Western societies (OECD 2017). Yet, previous studies reported a great variation across migration generations (with second generations outperforming the first one), as well as across ethnicities (with some minorities consistently performing better than others, sometimes even better than natives). For some of these ethnic minorities the ethnic gap (i.e. the difference in outcomes between children of immigrants and their native peers) entirely disappears, once the socio-economic status (SES) of parents is controlled for. Nonetheless, this does not hold true for all minorities. Considering the complexity of the general picture deriving from previous studies, this chapter aims at adding to the literature by providing a more comprehensive assessment of sources of the ethnic gap in educational outcomes, taking into account the micro (individual) as well as the macro (institutional) level. The contribution to the debate is threefold.

In order to understand the mechanisms driving ethnic educational differentials, not only are immigrants contrasted to natives, but also the effect of specific ethnicities is considered. More precisely, a distinction between students' place of birth (outside or inside the destination country) and ethnicity background (operationalized as parental country of origin) is suggested, and its usefulness in providing a deeper understanding of the sources of the ethnic gap is empirically assessed.

In addition, analyses will not be confined to the sole decision to avoid early school leaving, but will also assess the chosen field of study in case of educational persistence. Many previous studies on the ethnic gap focused on academic achievement or educational attainment in vertical terms (e.g. completed years of education, secondary school enrolment or university participation) neglecting to a substantial extent the choice of majors. The question as to whether second generations' socio-economic status and previous achievement affect vertical and horizontal decisions similarly, is, thus, still left largely unanswered. However, the answer to this question has high social relevance, as in current Western societies featuring mass education, labour market opportunities increasingly depend on the chosen field of study rather than on the educational level alone.

Finally, the chapter contributes to the literature by comparing results from four European countries characterized by extremely different educational systems: England, Germany, the Netherlands and Sweden. Our current understanding of the role of institutional features in shaping immigrants' chances of integration is, in fact, far from being complete. On the one hand, previous international results converge in reporting that lower SES, lower grades and a migration background are all factors tending to depress educational success. On the other hand, the observed cross-country variation in the magnitude of the ethnic gap suggests that destination countries are differently successful in minimizing the existing obstacles to migrants' educational integration.

In the following section, the influence of micro-level dimensions such as migration, ethnicity, socio-economic status and academic achievement on the educational ethnic gap is assessed, and the underlying mechanisms explained. Successively, the features of the four national contexts compared in this study, both in terms of migration histories and educational systems, will be briefly summarized. The data, variables and analytical strategy employed for the analyses are described in a dedicated paragraph, before reporting the results of the analyses. The last section concludes with discussing findings, limitations and policy implications.

Theoretical background

By undersigning the Treaty of Amsterdam in 1997, European Union Member States committed themselves to actively fight inequality based on ethnic origin, religious belief, gender, sexual orientation, age and disability. Twenty years later, promoting children of immigrants and children of native equal educational opportunities is still an important goal for the European Union. Recent empirical evidence, in fact, suggests that students keep on being affected by structural constraints in taking their educational choices. As the latter translate into a differential risk of unemployment, poverty and social exclusion, understanding the mechanisms that structure educational choices is of paramount importance.

The influence of socio-economic background

One of the most important sources of educational inequality is considered to be the lack of cultural and economic resources within the family of origin. According to Boudon (1974), the socio-economic status of parents affects offspring's educational choices in two ways: i) favouring competencies development and thus better grades (primary effect); ii) supporting costly yet prestigious educational choices, independently from prior achievement (secondary effect). The joint operating of these two mechanisms results in an unequal distribution of educational degrees between individuals, to the favour of children of advantaged parents. Focusing our attention on educational choices, and following a rational action theory approach, we can interpret observed differentials as originating from distinctive evaluations of the utility of alternatives. The perceived utility (U) of a specific degree is:

$$U = (P \cdot B) - (C_d + C_i) \tag{1}$$

where P is the probability of success (i.e. the likelihood of obtaining the degree), B are the perceived benefits of the degree and C costs (direct expenses for educational materials d, and indirect costs of renounced labour market income i). On one side, thanks to higher availability of economic resources, students from wealthy families will perceive prestigious educational choices as more affordable in comparison to their less affluent peers (hence *C* will be smaller). On the other side, having the chance to rely on the support of academic educated parents, their achievements are likely to be higher (mechanism of primary effects). As a result, students from more advantaged families will look more confidently to their chances of gaining remunerative, yet demanding, degrees (*P* will be higher for them). Lastly, the perceived benefits of prestigious degrees will be remarkable for them (*B* will be higher), as any lower alternative will imply decreasing living standards with respect to those experienced growing up in a high status family.

For children of less advantaged families, all the opposite applies. The opposite also applies to children of immigrants as, due to language barriers, lack of country-specific human capital and discrimination on the labour market, their parents are overrepresented within less remunerated and stable occupations. According to this reading, the educational ethnic gap detectable in descriptive comparisons depends on the overlap between having immigrant parents and having fewer socio-economic resources at their disposal (composition hypothesis). Azzolini (2012), for example, found the immigrant-native gap in the transition to Italian upper secondary education halving after controlling for SES. Similarly, both in Sweden and in the Netherlands young Turks' drop-out risk is reduced to 1/3 once family background is considered (Jonsson, Kilpi-Jakonen and Rudolphi 2014).

The influence of migration background

If previous studies highlighted the central role of parental resources in explaining the educational ethnic gap, they had also to conclude that a part of this gap remains unexplained, especially for some ethnic groups. This unexplained part can be conceived as the autonomous effect of migration background on educational choices. Migration background is, however, a rather broad umbrella-term, which can include immigrants, their children and their nephews. In order to better analyse the sources of the ethnic gap, the two dimensions underlying this term (migration and ethnicity) should be gauged separately. The mechanisms that explain the autonomous effect of each, in fact, are different.

According to the studies of Portes and Rumbaut (1996), migration is an experience to which a great increase in psychological stress is connected, both for parents and involved children. Padilla and Durán (1995) highlight that experiencing a completely new society is usually accompanied by alienation. This is true especially when migration takes place during school years, and when origin and destination countries are particularly different from one another (in terms of language, norms, values). The traumatic experience of migration can, in addition, translate into decreased sense of self-efficacy (i.e. the perception of being able to steer one's own destiny), and increased tendency of attributing life experiences to circumstances beyond one's own control (Kao 1999). As recently shown by Triventi, Vlach and Pini (2020), such socio-psychological perceptions depress scholastic achievements, as they connect to lower motivations of investing in education to obtain a future gratification (Covington 1984; Bandura 1993; 1995).

However, a part of ethnic disadvantage not explained by parental SES can be found also for children of immigrants born at destination, who therefore did not experience any migration trauma. Thus, once the experience of migration is controlled together with SES in the models, the remaining gap can be attributed to ethnicity. Ethnicity refers to the individuals' lineage, i.e. the fact that one's own parents and ancestors are members of the ethnic majority of a country different than that in which one lives. Despite the literature frequently assigned to the dimension of ethnicity in general sub-optimal educational outcomes (Foster, Gomm and Hammersley 1996; Stevens and Dworkin 2014), not all ethnic groups underperform the ethnic majority of the country of destination (Portes and Rumbaut 2001; Riphahn 2003; Lutz 2007; Rothon 2007). Some ethnic groups fare significantly better than children of natives even in simple comparisons, as for example Asian students in America (Portes and Rumbaut 2001; Bennett and Xie 2003; Kao and Thompson 2003; Xie and Hsin 2013) and Europe (Fekjaer 2007; Storen and Helland 2010). Other groups report an initial penalty, which vanishes as soon as parental SES is taken into account, as in the case of young Turks in Germany (Relikowski, Schneider and Blossfeld 2009; Becker 2013). Others, however, show a particularly persistent penalty, as for students from Pakistan and Bangladesh, the Caribbean, North Africa and sub-Saharan Africa in England (Riphahn 2003; Phalet, Deboosere and Bastiaenssen 2007; Storen and Helland 2010; Heath and Brinbaum 2014; Stevens and Dworkin 2014).

Employing here Boudon's suggestion of decomposing total effects into direct and indirect effects might be particularly useful to grant a better understanding. Indirect effect of ethnicity has to be intended the effect that the variable exerts on achievements, which then translates into educational choices. Previous studies converge in reporting worse grades and lower achievements for ethnic minorities with respect to children of natives, which tend to persist even when parental SES is taken into account (Kao and Thompson 2003; Marks 2005; Fekjaer 2007; Vlach 2017; 2019). A convincing explanation is offered through cultural arguments, which interpret the gap as resulting from differences in parenting styles and parents' cultural assets, rather than parents' educational degrees. According to this interpretation, the cultural resources possessed by non-native parents represent less than an ideal match with norms, routines and expectations built in educational institutions (Rist 1970). Teachers, for example, will more easily recognize a type of cultural capital similar to their own in children of natives (Portes and Rumbaut 1996; Schnepf 2004). In addition, due to language barriers (Portes and Rumbaut 2001; Maki and McHugh 2014), immigrant parents might experience difficulties in getting involved in their children's school life, as well as in helping them with homework (Schneider and

Coleman 1993; Weiss, Caspe and Lopez 2006; Dalla Zuanna, Farina and Strozza 2009; Hoenig, Leopold and Shavit 2013; Mantovani and Gasperoni 2018), and in retrieving and effectively using information on the functioning of the school system of the destination country (Erikson and Jonsson 1996; Schnepf 2004; Kristen 2005; Herzog-Punzenberger and Schnell 2014; Barone et al. 2018). We therefore expect a negative indirect effect of ethnicity on educational outcomes.

When we turn our attention to the direct effect of ethnicity, however, we encounter what is known in the literature as ethnic paradox. While ethnic minorities tend to report lower academic achievements, their educational choices are on average more prestigious than those of the majority, especially when students with similar levels of socio-economic resources are compared. The paradox finds its origin in the higher educational aspiration shared by members of migrant families.

The positive effect of educational aspirations

Taking as a reference point a rational action theory framework and equation (1) above, the results of the literature on the ethnic paradox can be interpreted as highlighting an effect of ethnicity on the perceived benefits and probability of success of educational alternatives, everything else being equal. Two conflicting hypotheses aim to explain why children of immigrants feature higher educational ambitions (Becker and Gresch 2016). The first one is migration optimism. It suggests that, due to the economic, social and psychological costs involved, individuals that do put into practice a migration project represent a selected population, featuring specific characteristics with respect to co-nationals that do not migrate (Feliciano 2005a; 2005b; Ichou 2014; 2015). Most importantly, they share an above average ambition to ameliorate their living conditions, work ethic and sense of self-denial (Kao and Tienda 1995; Vallet 2006). However, upon arrival immigrant parents not rarely find themselves in lower remunerated and less prestigious jobs (Kogan 2007). Nonetheless, they often perceive it as being the "price of immigration" and expect to reach upward social mobility with their children, who are born in the destination country and master the language of the ethnic majority. Migration optimism explains why immigrant parents (and their children as well) might be less affected in their evaluation of the probability of success by eventual lower grades and learning difficulties. In other words, they will be comparatively less risk adverse. A concurrent argument, instead, focuses on the role of perceived benefits of educational alternatives (equation 1). According to this second interpretation of the ethnic paradox, children of immigrants perform more prestigious educational choices as they anticipate being discriminated against at the time of transition to the labour market. As employers are perceived by members of ethnic minorities as more likely to hire natives in the case of equal educational credentials, acquiring higher degrees represents a rational decision that may increase one's own competitive advantage (Riach and Rich 2002; Heath, Rothon and Kilpi 2008; Kilpi-Jakonen 2011).

Country-specific institutional features

The consideration that children of immigrants are on average keener than natives to make prestigious educational choices, let us understand how important the role of educational institutions might be in allowing higher aspirations to translate into choices and thus ameliorate ethnic minorities' educational opportunities. According to the studies of Jackson (2012; 2013), it is possible to juxtapose "choice driven" educational systems, considered more favourable to children of immigrants, to "exam-based" ones. Choice driven educational systems are comprehensive and provide universalistic and unstratified education till the end of mandatory schooling. These educational systems are typical in Anglo-Saxon and Nordic countries. Here enrolment into next grades is much more a matter of individual motivation rather than performance, as courses can be retaken and initial choices reversed. Exam-based systems, to the contrary, are highly selective systems typical of Continental Europe and German-speaking countries. These systems feature various parallel curricula (tracks), usually starting already at a very early point of the individual career (right after primary school). Despite being formally granted, shifts between tracks occur rarely. Moreover, track choice depends on prior performances (from the obligation to follow teachers' track assignment, to the need to pass a test of competencies).

Despite their high social relevance, studies on the effect of educational systems on children of immigrants' educational choices are still scarce (Crul and Schneider 2009; Jackson 2012; 2013; Jackson, Jonsson and Rudolphi 2012; Heath and Brinbaum 2014). Evidence collected so far converges in highlighting that choice driven educational systems favour a positive direct effect of ethnicity regardless of its negative indirect effect (mediated by achievements). To the contrary, in exam-based educational systems the indirect effect of ethnicity is expected to be stronger. Despite reporting higher aspirations as well, the trajectories of children of immigrants within exam-based educational systems will depend much more on their lower performance.

The discussion on the influence of educational systems in supporting or hindering children of immigrants' educational opportunities advises us on how the horizontal dimension of education (the track attended) is of importance for ethnic minorities' integration chances. In today's Western societies featuring mass education, participation into post-mandatory education is an experience shared by the majority of the population (Shavit and Blossfeld 1993; Bukodi and Goldthorpe 2013). As a result, labour market returns of educational degrees are now even more influenced by the specific curriculum attended within the same school level (Müller 2005; Reimer Noelke and Kucel 2008; Triventi 2013). Lucas (2001) suggested that most advantaged families with the aim of maintaining their socio-economic advantage, will not only exploit the vertical dimension of education, but increasingly also the horizontal one. Especially now that educational participation becomes more and more universal, privileged families will use their higher economic and cultural resources to ensure that their offspring occupy the comparatively best qualitative positions (prestigious tracks) within the same educational level. In order to obtain the more comprehensive picture of the educational integration chances of ethnic minorities that this chapter seeks to provide, not only the choice to remain in full time education at age 15–16 is examined in the next section, but also the track attended.

Contextual features of England, Sweden, Germany and the Netherlands

To perform our analyses, we take into consideration four countries, each of which features a specific history of immigration[1] and a specific system of education.[2]

England represents one of the countries with the oldest migration history between those here assessed, due to important migration inflows from former colonies (especially from East Asia) already before world wars in the twentieth century. Additional flows reached the country as a result of EU enlargements before Brexit in early 2020. Today the country reports an incidence of 9.3 per cent of individuals with a foreign passport on the total population (slightly above EU average of 7.8%), whereas less than 4.0 per cent of foreigners are non-EU citizens (Eurostat 2019). The five most represented nationalities in order of incidence are the Polish, Indian, Irish, Romanian and Italian. As anticipated above, England features a comprehensive educational system (or "choice based"). Education is universalistic and undifferentiated up to secondary school inclusive, whereas post-secondary education decisions are easily reversible. The system is pretty much decentralized: education in England is different from education in Scotland or Wales and, due to the importance of local stakeholders, school curricula might show differences at the sub-regional level as well.

The Netherlands also features a long-term immigration tradition due to the presence of ex-colonies. Eurostat data report that almost 94.0 per cent of the population in the country has a Dutch citizenship (2 percentage points more than the average of other EU Member States), whereas the population of foreign citizens is equally split between EU countries and extra-EU countries (Eurostat 2019). It has to be noticed that Antilleans enjoy a Dutch citizenship. Today the most represented nationalities are the Polish, Turkish, German, Syrian and English. The Netherlands features a stratified system of education. Here education is undifferentiated only until the end of lower secondary school at age 12, after which several tracks are available. On the basis of the track, different competencies are trained, either academic or professional. These curricula are, however, all decided at the state level (similarly to Sweden), implying that each student following a specific track across the country is expected to develop the same competencies.

Sweden experienced a great increase in incidence of immigrants more recently, with respect to the other countries addressed by this study. The main migration flows were those of asylum seekers, fleeing from unstable political conditions outside Europe. The 851,000 foreigners in the country represent today 8.9 per cent of the population, whereas only around one third of immigrants are EU-citizens, a rate slightly below the EU average (Eurostat 2019). The nationality with the highest incidence is the Syrian, followed by the Finnish, Polish, Somalian and Danish. Like England, Sweden too features a comprehensive educational system, characterized by universalistic and undifferentiated education throughout mandatory schooling. Differently to the former, however, the system is centralized. School curricula are thus decided centrally at the state level, and the same happens with state exams.

In today's Germany, there are more than 9 million persons without German citizenship, numbers that make the country one of the most important immigration destinations in Western Europe, especially for non-EU citizens. The latter represent 6.6 per cent of the German population (two percentage points more than the EU average – Eurostat 2019). The distribution of nationalities still hints at the active recruitments of manual workers from Southern Europe in the aftermath of the Second World War. The five most numerous nationalities are, in order of incidence: Turkish, Polish, Syrian, Italian and Romanian. Germany is the country featuring the most stratified and selective educational system in Europe. Students in Germany are divided into different tracks usually already at age 10, after four years of primary education. Assignment to track depends on prior achievement and reversibility of initial choices occurs rarely. To mitigate selectivity, so-called *Gesamtschulen* – which provide additional two years of unstratified and universalistic education – have been recently increasingly made available. In two of the 16 German Länder, tracking starts however at age 12. In fact, the responsibility of educational decisions in Germany lays at the *Länder* level and not at the federal state level.

Data and methods

Data

Analyses are performed on the Children of Immigrants Longitudinal Survey in Four European Countries (CILS4EU) (Kalter et al. 2014).[3] CILS4EU is an international survey with representative samples of students in England, Sweden, Germany and the Netherlands. Since 2010/11, students aged initially 13–14 years have been followed for three years in order to map their educational progresses. CILS4EU is particularly suitable to analyse children of immigrants' educational choices as the survey: i) oversampled children of immigrants (thereby providing the number of cases needed to disentangle the influence of multiple factors of inequality); ii) adopted the same survey strategy in each country, granting direct comparability of results (CILS4EU 2014).

In order to consider both primary and secondary effects (Boudon 2014), in the analysis of students' educational trajectories, we take advantage of the longitudinal design of CILS4EU. Analyses are carried out on students who took part in both first wave (when a competency test was administered) and third wave (collected right after the expected transition to post-mandatory schooling) (CILS4EU 2016). Despite panel attrition,[4] a common phenomenon in longitudinal studies, children of immigrants did not show a higher drop-out rate than natives (CILS4EU 2016). Thus, regarding the central aspect of our analysis, random withdrawal can be assumed.[5]

Variables

Table 10.1 reports the descriptive statistics of the variables employed in our analyses. As dependent variables we consider both educational participation and, conditional on it, track choice. More precisely, our first dependent variable represents the decision to remain in full-time education at age 15–16, i.e. after the completion of compulsory schooling. Because early school leavers are the part of the population with the highest risk of unemployment in the European Union (Eurostat 2019), this is a particularly suitable age to test potential occurrences of structural barriers. Following the strategy suggested by Jonsson and colleagues (2014) to achieve cross-country comparability, our first dependent variable is a dummy variable taking value 1 in case of regular transition to post-mandatory full-time education, and 0 otherwise. The latter code identifies, thus, students who enter the labour market (either directly or through internships), become NEET, or experience grade retention. The share of students in full time education at age 15–16 is higher in choice-based educational systems (92% and 89% respectively in England and in Sweden), whereas it reaches the lowest value in Germany (66% only). The results from the German case mirror the high selectivity of its educational system, but also the great availability of internships and on-the-job trainings (*Ausbildung*), which for many students in the country represents a suitable alternative to full-time education (Müller and Pollak 2010).

Our second dependent variable regards the type of full-time education chosen by students who regularly continued schooling. Here we follow the strategy proposed by Lessard-Phillips and colleagues (2014) to address track choices across countries. We use a dummy variable which takes value 1 in case of academic oriented education, and 0 for vocational education. The cross-country variation seems slightly lower than what has already been discussed regarding the choice to remain in full time education. More than 60 per cent of the students in each country attend academic education, apart from the Netherlands, where the share is around 50 per cent only.

Table 10.1 Variable distributions

	England	*Sweden*	*Netherlands*	*Germany*
Transition to post mandatory education				
Early school leavers	8.3	11.1	25.9	34.3
Continue to next level	91.7	88.9	74.1	65.7
Of which chose:				
Academic education	68.5	68.0	50.1	61.3
Vocational education	31.5	32.0	49.9	38.7
Migration experience				
No (born in specific country)	91.7	91.7	96.9	94.2
Yes (born in foreign country)	8.3	8.3	3.1	5.8
Ethnicity				
ENGLAND				
British (ethnic majority)	86.1			
India	1.7			
Pakistan and Bangladesh	3.2			
East Africa	1.5			
Africa (other)	2.0			
Caribbean and Latin America	0.5			
Asia (other)	2.9			
Europa	1.7			
Others	0.4			
SWEDEN				
Swedish (ethnic majority)		81.7		
Denmark, Finland and Norway		1.1		
Turkey		1.5		
Iran		0.9		
Former Yugoslavia		3.3		
America		1.2		
Africa		1.5		
Asia (other)		6.3		
Europa (other)		2.5		
NETHERLANDS				
Dutch (ethnic majority)			93.2	
Suriname			0.6	
Antilles			0.1	
Morocco			0.7	
Turkey			1.4	
Africa (other)			0.5	
America (other)			0.3	
Asia (other)			2.1	
Europe			1.1	
GERMANY				
German (ethnic majority)				82.1
Turkey				5.0
Former URSS				4.8
Former Yugoslavia				1.2
Poland				1.8
Southern Europe				1.2

Table 10.1 (Cont.)

	England	*Sweden*	*Netherlands*	*Germany*
Asia (other)				2.4
Africa				0.6
Others				0.9
Parents' highest degree				
Tertiary education	35.8	48.2	18.8	22.5
Upper secondary education	38.0	38.2	77.8	70.3
Primary or less	23.7	9.3	3.0	4.2
Do not know	2.5	4.3	0.4	3.0
Parental SES				
Mean ISEI	57.8	55.2	52.1	51.2
Standard deviation	20.4	20.2	19.4	19.8
Do not know	5.2	5.5	1.6	5.4
Sex				
Male	45.4	43.8	50.0	48.0
Female	54.6	56.2	50.0	51.9
Year of birth				
1995, 1994, 1993, 1992, 1991	34.2	3.5	38.0	58.0
1996, 1997, 1998	65.8	96.5	62.0	42.0
Linguistic competencies				
Mean	17.4	19.6	17.5	13.1
Standard deviation	3.0	4.8	4.2	4.3
N	1,961	2,460	2,376	3,339

Source: CILS4EU data, waves 1 and 3.

To provide a comprehensive view of sources of the educational ethnic gap, four dimensions are entered in our models as main explanatory factors. Firstly, the individual's migration background is disentangled into two independent dimensions. The first one is migration, which aims at capturing the direct experience of migration, independently from parents' nationality or the age at which the migration occurred. We operationalize it as a dummy variable, which takes value 0 if the student was born in the country where he/she attends school (i.e. the survey country), and 1 otherwise. First generation students are, thus, coded as 1 on this variable. The share of students that directly experienced a migration is highest in England and Sweden (8.3%) and lowest in the Dutch sample (around 3.0%), whereas Germany reports an average value (5.8%).

The second dimension is ethnicity. Ethnicity is operationalized according to the country of birth of the two parents. In the few cases where country of origin differs between parents, the country of birth shared by one parent with the son/daughter is considered. In cases where the country of origin was different for all three (student and parents), the maternal rule was followed. Ethnicity is coded as a country-specific categorical variable. However, for each country, the reference category in our models is constituted by being a member of the country's ethnic majority (e.g. being a child of German parents in Germany or of Swedish parents in Sweden – 82%; child of Dutch parents in the Netherlands – 93%; child of English parents in England – 86%). The country-specific operationalization of ethnicity will necessitate running separate models for each country.

The third dimension is parental socio-economic status. In our analyses, parental SES is operationalized with two variables. The higher educational degree between the two parents is employed as a proxy for the cultural capital available within the family. As a proxy for families' socio-economic resources, the more prestigious occupation between mother and father is used. The latter is measured by means of the International Socio-Economic Index of Occupational Status (Ganzeboom, De Graaf and Treiman 1992) and in accordance with the dominance approach (Erikson et al. 2005). Both parental education and occupation are self-reported by students. In order not to lose students for whom parental information is missing, a separate regressor (identifying missing cases) is added in the models.

The fourth dimension in our analyses is students' prior educational achievement. It takes the form of a continuous variable, reporting the score obtained by each student on a standardized test of linguistic competencies administered at the time of the first wave. To obtain the score, correct answers have been summed up and the sum was standardized at the country level. The result is a directly comparable measure of competencies, interpretable as number of standard deviations from the country mean.

In addition, our analyses also control for sex (a dummy variable where female is coded as 1), and age (being born before or in/after 1996). Moreover, in the full models a country-specific categorical variable, referring to the type of lower secondary education attended, is entered as an additional control variable.

Results

For our analyses of both vertical and horizontal education choices, binomial logistic regression models are employed. Due to country-specific immigration histories, which lead to different compositions of ethnicities in the student populations, models are run separately by country. Finally, to take into account the similarity of students attending the same school, standard errors are clustered accordingly.

Social origin, ethnicity and educational choices

In this session our attention is focused on the autonomous effects of migration and ethnicity on the transition to full-time post mandatory education, net of parental socio-economic resources. In line with the theoretical discussion, we expect the migration experience exerting negative secondary

Table 10.2 Estimated effect of migration on the propensity to continue in regular full-time education at age 15–16 across countries. Average marginal effects from logistic regression models with standard errors clustered at school level (in brackets)

Direct migration experience	*Model 1a*	*Model 2*	*Model 3*	*Model 4*
England	0.057***	–0.046	–0.057	–0.047
	(0.014)	(0.052)	(0.056)	(0.055)
Sweden	–0.012	–0.006	–0.020	0.042*
	(0.025)	(0.030)	(0.028)	(0.023)
Netherlands	–0.094	–0.368***	–0.374***	–0.160
	(0.151)	(0.125)	(0.131)	(0.125)
Germany	–0.002	–0.037	–0.036	0.038
	(0.056)	(0.066)	(0.067)	(0.060)

Source: CILS4EU data. Weighted results. Total observations: see Table 10.1. Complete models available upon request. Significance level: *** p<0.01; ** p<0.05; * p<0.1.

effects (thus negatively influencing choices net of achievements – Boudon 1974), and positive secondary effects for ethnicity instead. Additionally, we expect children of immigrants to be comparatively more constrained in their choices in Germany and the Netherlands, due to the higher selectivity and stricter stratification of the educational system in these countries.

Table 10.2 presents the results obtained from analysing migration. To facilitate interpretation, results are expressed as average marginal effects (AME).[6] The estimates can, thus, be read as the difference in percentage points in the probability of performing a regular transition to full-time education at age 15–16 for immigrant students compared to that of students born in the country where they are attending school.

Its bivariate effect (model 1a) reports a negative sign which, however, in Sweden, the Netherlands and Germany does not represent a statistically significant difference. In England migration seems to affect school choices positively. However, this is only due to a composition effect with ethnicity: once the latter is controlled for in model 2, the positive effect of migration vanishes.

In model 3, which additionally controls for parental SES, all countries show a negative yet not statistically significant influence for migration, except for the Netherlands. Hence, when we compare youth with the same ethnic background and the same level of cultural and economic capital within the family, only in the Netherlands we find immigrant students who fare worse than natives. Nonetheless, this difference fades away when we control for prior achievement, sex, age and lower secondary school attendance in model 4. Results from the complete models, thus, seem to contradict our expectations: no statistically significant negative effects remain at a 95 per cent confidence level, where Sweden even reports a marginally significant positive estimate. Our finding suggests that migration is not a source of higher risk of early school leaving and grade retention, once ethnicity, socio-economic background and prior achievement is taken into account.

We now move our attention to the second analysed aspect of migration background: ethnicity. Table 10.3 reports our findings regarding the variable operationalized as discussed in the previous session,[7] again expressed in the form of Average Marginal Effects. Contrary to migration, the influence exerted by ethnicity on the choice to remain in full time education at age 15–16 seems to be in line with initial expectations. Results regarding the bivariate effect of the variable (model 1b), however, seem to be rather mixed, with only a few ethnicities significantly outperforming country-specific ethnic majorities with their school choices. This is the case, for example, for Indians in England and Iranians in Sweden, as well as for other broader groups, which, due to lower numbers are more difficult to decompose and thus to interpret (such as Africans in Germany, Asian and Africans in England, as well as Europeans and Latin Americans in the Netherlands). Few ethnicities report a negative coefficient (these are, among others, students from Denmark, Finland and Norway in Sweden, Surinamese in the Netherlands and youth from former Yugoslavia in Germany). These penalties are, however, not statistically significant. Controlling for the migration experience (model 2) consolidates further (especially for the Dutch sample) our initial positive findings, as also happens once we take into consideration parental socio-economic resources (model 3). The more individual dimensions are controlled for in our models, the higher the number of ethnic minorities reporting an educational premium, and the greater the latter's magnitude and significance.

As we are going to discuss in more detail in the concluding session, the remarkable difference between models 2 and 3 for some ethnic groups can be considered as a sign of overlap between minority status and lack of socio-economic resources. This explains why children of Turkish and Polish immigrants in Germany, or Pakistani and Bangladeshi in England did not originally show a significant and positive difference to children of immigrants reported by other ethnic minorities.

Also, once prior achievement is controlled for, together with the other control variables (model 4), the image of a premium shows even more, in all countries but the Netherland. Overall, 52 per cent of the country-specific ethnic minority groups report a statistically significant positive influence of ethnicity, whereas minorities reporting a statistically significant penalty are zero. Everything else being equal, young Turks are more likely than the ethnic majority to perform a regular transition to full-time post mandatory education in both Germany and Sweden (respectively 12 and 6 percentage points more likely), whereas in the Netherlands they simply perform like children of natives. Iranians in Sweden, Antilleans in the Netherlands and Polish in Germany are also greatly outperforming their majority peers, showing a transition propensity 10 percentage points higher. Before discussing

Table 10.3 Estimated effect of ethnicity on the propensity to continue in regular full-time education at age 15–16 across countries. Average marginal effects from logistic regression models with standard errors clustered at school level (in brackets)

Ethnicity	*Model 1b*		*Model 2*		*Model 3*		*Model 4*	
England								
India	0.049**	(0.023)	0.058***	(0.019)	0.058***	(0.019)	0.056***	(0.021)
Pakistan& Bangladesh	0.012	(0.026)	0.025	(0.026)	0.040*	(0.022)	0.045**	(0.021)
East Africa	0.044	(0.031)	0.058**	(0.026)	0.056**	(0.026)	0.062***	(0.023)
Africa *(other)*	0.067***	(0.017)	0.077***	(0.017)	0.075***	(0.018)	0.078***	(0.018)
Asia *(other)*	0.083***	(0.011)	0.089***	(0.012)	0.088***	(0.012)	0.089***	(0.012)
Sweden								
Nordic country	−0.051	(0.092)	−0.057	(0.105)	−0.067	(0.102)	−0.111	(0.111)
Turkey	0.021	(0.036)	0.020	(0.037)	0.049	(0.032)	0.064**	(0.025)
Iran	0.088***	(0.019)	0.087***	(0.020)	0.095***	(0.020)	0.107***	(0.017)
Form. Yugoslavia	−0.015	(0.037)	−0.016	(0.037)	0.015	(0.031)	0.033	(0.028)
America	0.024	(0.052)	0.020	(0.054)	0.036	(0.052)	−0.055	(0.044)
Africa	0.023	(0.033)	0.021	(0.036)	0.052*	(0.029)	0.077***	(0.025)
Asia *(other)*	−0.049*	(0.027)	−0.054	(0.033)	−0.010	(0.029)	0.020	(0.025)
Europe *(other)*	−0.002	(0.045)	−0.006	(0.050)	0.038	(0.049)	0.018	(0.046)
Netherlands								
Suriname	−0.041	(0.197)	0.087	(0.126)	0.107	(0.093)	0.071	(0.064)
Antilles	0.146	(0.111)	0.205**	(0.092)	0.209**	(0.088)	0.127**	(0.060)
Morocco	0.007	(0.112)	0.040	(0.111)	0.105	(0.083)	0.059	(0.085)
Turkey	0.119	(0.105)	0.140	(0.101)	0.187**	(0.088)	0.081	(0.064)
Africa *(other)*	0.131	(0.136)	0.226**	(0.089)	0.249***	(0.068)	0.176**	(0.075)
America *(other)*	0.212**	(0.088)	0.261***	(0.079)	0.265***	(0.075)	0.183***	(0.061)
Asia *(other)*	−0.159	(0.184)	0.082	(0.111)	0.098	(0.091)	−0.081	(0.081)
Europe	0.209**	(0.081)	0.254***	(0.078)	0.253***	(0.076)	0.196***	(0.059)
Germany								
Turkey	0.009	(0.056)	0.013	(0.056)	0.090**	(0.044)	0.123***	(0.037)
Former USSR	0.051	(0.052)	0.068	(0.059)	0.100*	(0.056)	0.090	(0.067)
Form. Yugoslavia	−0.054	(0.081)	−0.046	(0.081)	0.023	(0.072)	0.077	(0.053)
Poland	0.079	(0.075)	0.089	(0.071)	0.159**	(0.062)	0.098**	(0.050)
Southern Europe	0.041	(0.109)	0.058	(0.107)	0.129	(0.092)	0.13	(0.083)
Asia *(other)*	−0.018	(0.098)	−0.006	(0.096)	0.048	(0.085)	0.046	(0.082)
Africa	0.196***	(0.069)	0.198***	(0.067)	0.240***	(0.056)	0.255***	(0.049)
Others	−0.157	(0.099)	−0.134	(0.099)	−0.085	(0.085)	−0.093	(0.106)

Source: CILS4EU data. Weighted results. Total observations: see Table 10.1. Complete models available upon request. Significance level: *** p<0.01; ** p<0.05; * p<0.1. As no variation in the dependent variable is detected for Caribbeans, Europeans and Other students in England, these students are excluded from Table 10.3.

cross-country differences, however, a closer look at the mechanisms driving these premia, as well as checking whether they translate into better track choices too, is important.

Disentangling the effect of ethnicity

In this session, the role played by previous competencies on the educational choices of children of immigrants will be further investigated by applying the decomposition technique (KHB) suggested by Karlson and Holm (2011) and Breen, Karlson and Holm (2013). By means of KHB decomposition, it is possible to split the total effect of ethnicity on track choices into two components: i) the direct net effect of ethnicity on the choice of the track (hence the "secondary effect" of ethnicity, adopting Boudon's terminology); ii) the effect of ethnicity that is mediated by its prior effect on achievements (hence its "primary effect").

Hence, while the coefficients of ethnicity presented in model 4 of Table 10.3 constitute the direct effect of this explanatory variable, Table 10.4 presents the results obtained by implementing KHB decomposition on the ethnic background variable, in order to obtain a measure of the indirect effect of this variable through achievements.

Our empirical findings support the idea of the existence of an ethnic paradox. While being a child of immigrants influences educational achievements, on average, negatively; it also fosters more prestigious educational choices.

Our decomposition exercise highlights two central aspects. Firstly, the negative indirect effect of ethnicity on educational choices (net of migration, parental cultural and economic capital, sex, age and type of lower secondary education) is generalized to all ethnicities (column 3 of Table 10.4). Interestingly enough, the only deviations from this pattern are shown by those ethnic minorities less affected by linguistic barriers: Indians in England and Scandinavians in Sweden. The command of the destination country's language seems to represent, thus, a protection against the risk of negative indirect effects. The deviation from the pattern shown by the Netherlands might be more dependent on lower case numbers and greater attrition of children of immigrants over waves (CILS4EU 2016), rather than constituting a substantive finding. Further research should replicate the current study on different data in order to better understand the interesting result of the Dutch sample.

A second central aspect is the total effect of the ethnic variable (column 1 of Table 10.4), which proves to be positive for 83 per cent of the country-specific ethnic minority groups, and positive and statistically significant for almost half of them. As we are going to comment further in the discussion session below, this means that having an ethnic background, net of parental resources and additional controls, does represent an advantage, or at least not a penalty, for the great majority of ethnicities, despite potential difficulties in

Table 10.4 Estimate of the total, direct and indirect effect of ethnicity

Ethnicity	*Total effect*		*Direct effect*		*Indirect Effect*
England					
India	0.058***	(0.020)	0.056***	(0.021)	0.0015
Pakistan and Bangladesh	0.041*	(0.022)	0.045**	(0.021)	−0.0040
East Africa	0.061***	(0.024)	0.062***	(0.023)	−0.0005
Africa *(other)*	0.077***	(0.018)	0.078***	(0.018)	−0.0014
Asia *(other)*	0.089***	(0.011)	0.089***	(0.011)	−0.0005
Sweden					
Nordic country	−0.095	(0.104)	−0.111	(0.111)	0.016
Turkey	0.042	(0.030)	0.064**	(0.025)	−0.022
Iran	0.095***	(0.019)	0.107***	(0.016)	−0.012
Former Yugoslavia	0.006	(0.033)	0.033	(0.028)	−0.027
America	0.037	(0.051)	0.055	(0.044)	−0.018
Africa	0.061**	(0.028)	0.077***	(0.025)	−0.016
Asia *(other)*	−0.005	(0.028)	0.020	(0.025)	−0.025
Europe *(other)*	−0.003	(0.050)	0.018	(0.046)	−0.016
Netherlands					
Suriname	0.073	(0.068)	0.071	(0.068)	0.002
Antilles	0.130**	(0.058)	0.127**	(0.059)	0.004
Morocco	0.068	(0.084)	0.060	(0.073)	0.008
Turkey	0.091	(0.065)	0.081	(0.065)	0.010
Africa *(other)*	0.179**	(0.079)	0.176**	(0.080)	0.002
America *(other)*	0.187***	(0.054)	0.183***	(0.056)	0.004
Asia *(other)*	−0.077	(0.078)	−0.081	(0.079)	0.003
Europe	0.197***	(0.044)	0.196***	(0.045)	0.006
Germany					
Turkey	0.085*	(0.036)	0.123***	(0.034)	−0.037
Former URSS	0.082	(0.068)	0.090	(0.068)	−0.007
Form. Yugoslavia	0.048	(0.055)	0.077	(0.053)	−0.029
Poland	0.087*	(0.051)	0.098*	(0.050)	−0.010
Southern Europe	0.098	(0.083)	0.103	(0.083)	−0.005
Asia *(other)*	0.013	(0.087)	0.046	(0.082)	−0.033
Africa	0.238***	(0.048)	0.255***	(0.045)	−0.016
Others	−0.103	(0.107)	−0.093	(0.107)	−0.010

Source: CILS4EU data. Weighted results. Total observations: see Table 10.1. Complete models available upon request. Significance level: *** $p<0.01$; ** $p<0.05$; * $p<0.1$. As no variation in the dependent variable is detected for Caribbeans, Europeans and Other students in England, these students are excluded from Table 10.3.

linguistic competency acquisition. In other words, our analyses suggest that the ethnic penalty in achievements, highlighted by several previous studies, does not seem to depress continuation into post-mandatory education. This is true for most of the addressed ethnicities, with the important exception of Turks in Sweden. For the latter, the difficulties in mastering the destination country's language seem to be so substantial, that they impede the total effect of ethnicity to be driven by its positive direct effect.

The type of post-mandatory education

A generalized positive total effect of ethnicity on the probability to regularly continue full-time education at age 15–16, however, cannot be taken as proof of equal educational opportunities for children of immigrants in Europe. Avoiding the risk of early school leaving is fundamental, but not all transitions mean the same in terms of successful labour market outcomes. Our models in Table 10.5 estimate the influence of ethnicity on the probability to attend the most prestigious and remunerative track available, i.e. the academic track. Our results are presented following the same strategy as in Table 10.3. However, here the dependent variable changes and only students that made the transition are considered.

In line with previously discussed findings, the estimation of the bivariate effect of ethnicity shows mixed results. While some ethnic groups report an advantage over natives (as of Caribbean students in England and Surinamese students in the Netherlands), others show a penalty. A descriptive gap is particularly strong for Turks and Southern Europeans in Germany, but also for young Pakistani and Bangladeshi in England (model 1b). It is interesting to notice that, when we control for the migration experience from model 2, little to nothing changes. Differently, when we add in our models' parental cultural and economic capital (model 3), several previous negative coefficients stop to be statistically significance. As we also found when analysing vertical choices, the impression of a penalty for children of immigrants in the simple comparison to children of natives largely depends on the overrepresentation of immigrant parents within the less advantaged social strata. When offspring of families with a similar level of socio-economic resources are compared, no difference remains for Pakistani and Bangladeshi in enrolling into courses in preparation of A levels, and Turks now show a significantly greater propensity to enrol in the prestigious *Högskoleförberedande* programme in Sweden.

Finally, our last model adds previous achievement, sex and age in order to estimate the direct effect of ethnicity on track choice. In model 4, ethnic advantages are now visible for even more ethnicities, however not without interesting dissimilarities across national educational systems, which are going to be discussed further in the next session. What is important to stress here is that no ethnic minority reports a statistically significant negative effect. Instead, 43 per cent of all country-specific ethnic groups report a positive effect. The latter is particularly noticeable for some ethnicities. Indians in England, for example, not only report a 5 percentage points higher propensity to remain in full-time post-mandatory education, but also a 22 percentage points higher probability to enrol in courses in preparation for college. Other ethnicities, such as Dutch-Surinames and Swedish-Former Yugoslavian students, do not report any advantage upon transition, but when they continue schooling, they feature a substantially higher propensity to enrol in academic tracks (respectively +37 and +20 percentage points). It

Table 10.5 Estimated effect of ethnicity on the probability to be enrolled in academic full-time education at age 15–16 across countries. Average marginal effects from logistic regression models with standard errors clustered at school level (in brackets)

Ethnicity	*Model 1b*		*Model 2*		*Model 3*		*Model 4*	
England								
India	0.206***	(0.049)	0.219***	(0.049)	0.228***	(0.044)	0.221***	(0.049)
Pakistan & Bangl.	−0.179***	(0.062)	−0.156**	(0.069)	−0.063	(0.056)	0.001	(0.045)
East Africa	−0.114	(0.082)	−0.073	(0.091)	−0.068	(0.086)	−0.062	(0.082)
Africa (other)	−0.037	(0.120)	0.010	(0.098)	−0.050	(0.105)	0.008	(0.080)
Carib. & Lat. America	0.211***	(0.061)	0.225***	(0.062)	0.217***	(0.063)	0.197***	(0.058)
Asia (other)	0.096	(0.081)	0.136**	(0.064)	0.133**	(0.058)	0.140**	(0.065)
Europa	−0.096	(0.096)	−0.041	(0.114)	0.001	(0.107)	0.020	(0.116)
Others	0.258***	(0.060)	0.273***	(0.058)	0.236***	(0.087)	0.152	(0.134)
Sweden								
Nordic country	0.067	(0.129)	0.130	(0.112)	0.091	(0.126)	0.039	(0.135)
Turkey	0.081	(0.058)	0.095	(0.059)	0.160***	(0.044)	0.213***	(0.038)
Iran	−0.0004	(0.104)	0.041	(0.100)	0.058	(0.103)	0.158*	(0.081)
Former Yugoslavia	0.040	(0.053)	0.060	(0.050)	0.147***	(0.040)	0.195***	(0.036)
America	−0.019	(0.116)	0.045	(0.105)	0.072	(0.095)	0.136	(0.097)
Africa	0.019	(0.068)	0.059	(0.066)	0.131**	(0.052)	0.202***	(0.045)
Asia (other)	0.079**	(0.034)	0.123***	(0.038)	0.186***	(0.032)	0.231***	(0.029)
Europe (other)	0.080	(0.053)	0.140**	(0.056)	0.168***	(0.049)	0.198***	(0.050)
Netherlands								
Suriname	0.380***	(0.114)	0.416***	(0.109)	0.413***	(0.104)	0.365***	(0.105)
Antilles	0.018	(0.260)	0.086	(0.238)	0.010	(0.210)	0.034	(0.154)
Morocco	0.071	(0.173)	0.101	(0.174)	0.193	(0.157)	0.271*	(0.142)
Turkey	−0.031	(0.225)	−0.015	(0.233)	0.123	(0.188)	0.235	(0.147)
Africa *(other)*	0.004	(0.110)	0.176	(0.130)	0.229**	(0.117)	0.218**	(0.094)
America *(other)*	0.382***	(0.142)	0.473***	(0.102)	0.482***	(0.095)	0.443***	(0.091)
Asia *(other)*	0.379***	(0.101)	0.450***	(0.091)	0.454***	(0.089)	0.444***	(0.079)
Europe	0.236*	(0.138)	0.367***	(0.119)	0.311***	(0.123)	0.241**	(0.115)
Germany								
Turkey	−0.206***	(0.070)	−0.201***	(0.071)	−0.085	(0.062)	0.084	(0.051)
Former USSR	−0.071	(0.080)	−0.030	(0.092)	0.044	(0.076)	0.094	(0.060)
Former Yugoslavia	−0.125	(0.111)	−0.107	(0.111)	−0.036	(0.197)	0.099	(0.080)
Poland	−0.091	(0.109)	−0.072	(0.117)	0.035	(0.096)	0.044	(0.073)
Southern Europe	−0.333***	(0.115)	−0.290**	(0.117)	−0.173*	(0.096)	−0.109	(0.097)
Asia *(other)*	−0.051	(0.086)	−0.028	(0.086)	0.017	(0.077)	0.116*	(0.059)
Africa	−0.158	(0.133)	−0.134	(0.128)	−0.035	(0.109)	0.102	(0.090)
Others	−0.055	(0.135)	0.020	(0.132)	0.010	(0.113)	0.017	(0.085)

Source: CILS4EU data. Weighted results. Total observations: see Table 10.1. Complete models available upon request. Significance level: *** $p<0.01$; ** $p<0.05$; * $p<0.1$. Contrary to Tables 10.2 and 10.3, the groups of Caribbeans, Europeans and Other students in England do show heterogeneity in their choices of the field of study and are thus considered in the models of Table 10.5.

has to be stressed, however, that no ethnic premia are reported in Germany at a confidence level of 95 per cent. In the country featuring the most selective and stratified educational system in Europe, only Asian students seem to show a marginally significant higher propensity to be enrolled at the *Gymnasium*.

Conclusions

This chapter aimed at providing a more comprehensive view of the sources of disparity for children of immigrants attending school in Western European countries. Not only are immigrants compared to natives, but also different ethnicities are contrasted. Moreover, the assessment of secondary school track choice adds to that of enrolment in post-compulsory education. Our analyses on Germany, the Netherlands, Sweden and England highlight the centrality of the role played by students' ethnic background in shaping educational choices, compared to the non statistically significant influence of migration experience. Only the former exerts a significant net effect on the probability of regularly enrolling in full-time school-based education at age 15–16 as well as chooosing the academic track. In line with a rational action theory framework, we interpret this result as a sign of how ethnicity leads to upward changes of students' evaluations of, both, probability of success (due to migration optimisms devaluating potential sub-optimal grades) and benefits of prestigious educational alternatives (due to anticipated labour market discrimination). Two important aspects emerge as particularly relevant in this regard. Firstly, the direct positive effect of ethnicity on choices is so conspicuous that it substantially shapes the total effect of the variable. As our decomposition analysis shows, its positive direct effect surmounts the indirect negative effect exerted through achievements. In other words, even if ethnicity negatively influences competency acquisition, children of immigrants will, nonetheless, overtake children of ethnic majority parents in educational choice, everything else kept equal. Secondly, as a consequence of what has just been mentioned, children of immigrants will succeed in meeting the most prestigious choices in a (relatively) "natural" way, if i) the negative effect stemming from the over-representation of their parents in less remunerated jobs on the external sector of the labour market will be mitigated; ii) the educational system of the destination country will allow an easy translation of their higher aspirations into choices. Our analyses show that the ethnic premium in choices expresses itself differently across countries. In England 100 per cent of the identified ethnic groups outperform British students in avoiding early school leaving, while circa 40 per cent of them also report a statistically significant higher propensity of enrolling in academic education. In Sweden only circa 40 per cent of ethnicities show a premium in regular full-time education, but conditional on the latter, 75 per cent of ethnicities take more prestigious track choices. The Dutch sample, which has, however, to be interpreted with caution due to an above average panel attrition in the ethnic subsample (CILS4EU 2016), provides results very similar to the Swedish case. Finally, in Germany the two quantities are, respectively, 40 per cent and 13 per cent. Our results, thus, suggest that, in the highly stratified and selective German education system, students' choices are much more bonded by institutional constraints than in any of the other considered country.

One limitation of the present study is the impossibility of identifying further single ethnicities within macro groups such as Asian or African, in order to understand if all minorities grouped in these broader categories report the same premium or if the final coefficient is the result of a composition of over- and underperforming ethnicities. Comparing bigger datasets generated by national surveys could represent a solution in this regard, however, to the cost of a lower direct comparability of estimates. As the number of observations affects *p* values too, some of the separately identified groups might have generated statistically non-significant estimates because of a relatively low number of cases. As these coefficients were usually positive, our considerations on how widespread the ethnic premium in educational choices has to be is considered as a rather conservative estimation. Another limitation is the restricted number of countries considered, which impedes running pooled regressions in order to identify the effect of specific aspects of educational systems (such as the independent effect of age at first selection, of occurrence of mandatory exams, of the incidence of professional education etc.) net of other macro-level variables (such as GDP, unemployment rate, type of welfare regime etc.). Further studies are needed in order to better understand the role of specific contextual features in the educational integration of ethnic minorities. The study presented constitutes just a first step in this direction. It is also worth considering here that the present study does not aim at identifying causal effects, but rather at describing the mechanisms underlying the influence exerted by the migration background (disentangled in its two components of migration experience and ethnicity) on educational choices. Finally, future studies should explore the possibility of mapping the whole educational career of children of immigrants, from an early age to entrance into the labour market. This would allow for a better understanding of the independent effects of migration and ethnicity on educational choices at age 15–16 conditional on previously made choices (something especially important to understand the role of exam-based educational system on ethnic minorities' integration chances).

Despite limitations, our analyses highlight relevant novel findings regarding the sources of ethnic premia in educational choices in comparative perspective, stressing the role of ethnicity, socio-economic resources and institutional features in shaping educational trajectories. Based on our findings and in line with the previous public policy literature on minimizing educational inequalities of less advantaged students (Baker et al. 2014), we identify as a relevant area for public intervention in favour of children of immigrants the stage at which educational aspirations translate into choices.

In this regard, policies should focus on the stratification character of destination countries' systems of education. However, a general reform of education in countries featuring highly selective systems would be very complex to implement. On the contrary, smaller scale interventions targeting ethnic minorities during their school careers might be equally effective in supporting their integration, yet less costly. The Dutch case seems to provide a best practice in this regard. Although tracking in this country starts at an early age, dedicated information campaigns and programmes to increase the "permeability" of tracks at specific turning points (track changing), provide "second chances" for ambitious students to match the progression of their studies to their personal aims. Interventions aimed at disseminating information on which further steps are needed to reach prestigious degrees might grant positive outcomes even when targeted students already own a (less prestigious) diploma. Such programmes could be organized, with limited expenses, by non-academic schools, where students with lower availability of resources and, thus, also children of immigrants, tend to cluster. If activities are targeted at the entire population attending these curricula, without distinction on the basis of ethnicity, positive outcomes in terms of equality of opportunities can be achieved for ambitious children of less advantaged native parents as well.

Acknowledgements

Considerations and analyses discussed in this chapter have been developed within the author's PhD thesis (Vlach 2017). I would like to thank Asher Colombo, Martina Cvajner, Markus Gangl, Jara Kampmann, Debora Mantovani, Antonio Schizzerotto, Giuseppe Sciortino, and Loris Vergolini for their useful suggestions and comments on a previous version of the chapter.

Notes

1 Where not differently stated, numbers come from Eurostat data for 2018, online data code: migr_pop1ctz.
2 Where not differently stated, information come from Eurydice data available at: https://eacea.ec.europa.eu/national-policies/eurydice/national-description_en (20.06.20).
3 The CILS4EU project took place thanks to the funds of the programme *NORFACE ERA NET Plus Migration in Europe*.
4 Third wave's response rates conditional on participation in the first wave are: 51.6% for England, 51.8% for Sweden, 58.3%% for the Netherlands, and 67.1% for Germany.
5 It should be noted, however, that the Netherlands reports a slight reduction in the incidence of children of immigrants from the first to the third wave (from 34% to 28%), thus results from the Dutch need to be interpreted with caution (CILS4EU 2016).
6 In addition to a better intelligibility of results, AME allows estimates from nested models (Wooldridge 2002) and from different national contexts (Allison 1999; Mood 2010) to be compared.

7 As stressed by models numbering, evidences in the last three columns of Table 10.3 originate from the same regression models presented in the last three columns of Table 10.2. Thus, only the focus of our attention changes, from the effect of the migration experience to that of ethnicity.

References

Allison P.D. (1999). Comparing Logit and Probit Coefficients across Groups. *Social Methods & Research*. 28(2): 186–208.

Azzolini D. (2012). *Immigrant-native Educational Gaps: A systematic Inquiry into the Schooling of Children of Immigrants throughout the Italian Educational System*. Tesi di Dottorato: Università degli Studi di Trento.

Baker W., Sammons P., Siraj-Blatchford I., Sylva K., Melhuish E.C. and Taggart B. (2014). Aspirations, Education and Inequality in England: Insights from the Effective Provision of Pre-school, Primary and Secondary Education Project. *Oxford Review of Education*. 40(5): 525–542.

Ballarino G. and Checchi D. (2006). Sistema scolastico e disuguaglianza sociale: scelte individuali e vincoli strutturali. Bologna: Mulino.

Ballarino G. and Panichella N. (2013). The Occupational Integration of Male Migrants in Western European Countries: Assimilation or Persistent Disadvantage? *International Migration*. 53(2): 338–352.

Bandura A. (1993). Perceived Self-Efficacy in Cognitive Development and Functioning. *Educational Psychologist*. 28(2), 117–148.

Bandura A. (1995). *Self-Efficacy in Changing Societies*. New York: Cambridge University Press.

Barone C., Assirelli G., Abbiati G., Argentin G. and De Luca D. (2018). Social Origins, Relative Risk Aversion and Track Choice: A Field Experiment on the Role of Information Biases. *Acta Sociologica*. 61(4): 441–459.

Becker B. (2013). *The Educational Aspiration of Turkish-Origin Parents of Three-Year-Old Children in Germany: A Comparison by Generational Status*. Trento: Paper presented at the ISA-RC28 Spring Meeting.

Becker B. and Gresch C. (2016). Bildungsaspirationen in Familien mit Migrationshintergrund. In Diehl C., Hunkler C. and Kristen C. (eds.). *Ethnische Ungleichheiten im Bildungsverlauf*. Wiesbaden: Springer VS. Seiten, 73–88.

Bennett P.R. and Xie Y. (2003). Revisiting Racial Differences in College Attendance: The Role of Historically Black Colleges and Universities. *American Sociological Review*. 68(4): 567–580.

Boudon R. (1974). *Education, Opportunity, and Social Inequality*. New York: Wiley.

Breen R., Karlson K.B. and Holm A. (2011). Total, Direct, and Indirect Effects in Logit and Probit Models. *Sociological Methods & Research*. 42(2): 164–191.

Bukodi E. and Goldthorpe J.H. (2012). Decomposing Social Origins: The Effect of Parents' Class, Status and Education on the Educational Attainment of their Children. *European Sociological Review*. 29(5): 1024–1039.

CILS4EU (2014). *Children of Immigrants Longitudinal Survey in Four European Countries. Technical Report. Wave 1 – 2010/2011, v1.1.0*. Mannheim: Mannheim University.

CILS4EU (2016). *Children of Immigrants Longitudinal Survey in Four European Countries. Technical Report. Wave 3 – 2012/2013, v3.1.0*. Mannheim: Mannheim University.

Covington M. (1984). The Motive for Self-Worth. In Ames R. and Ames C. (eds.). *Research on Motivation in Education, vol. 1, Student Motivation.* New York: New York University Press.

Crul M. and Schneider J. (2009). Children of Turkish Immigrants in Germany and the Netherlands: the Impact of Differences in Vocational and Academic Tracking systems. *Teachers College Record.* 111(6): 1508–1527.

Dalla Zuanna G., Farina P. and Strozza S. (2009). *Nuovi Italiani. I giovani immigrati cambieranno il nostro paese?*. Bologna: Il Mulino.

Erikson R. and Jonsson J.O. (eds.). (1996). *Can Education Be Equalized? The Swedish Case in Comparative Perspective.* Boulder: Westview Press.

Erikson R., Goldthorpe J.H., Jackson M., Yaish M. and Cox D.R. (2005). On Class Differentials in Educational Attainment. *PNAS.* 102(27): 9730–9733.

Eurostat (2019). *Key Figures on Europe.* Luxembourg: Publications Office of the European Union.

Fekjaer S. (2007). New Differences, Old Explanations: Can Educational Differences between Ethnic Groups in Norway Be Explained by Social Background? *Ethnicities.* 7(3): 367–389.

Feliciano C. (2005a). Does Selective Migration Matter? Explaining Ethnic Disparities in Educational Attainment among Immigrants' Children. *International Migration Review.* 39(4): 841–871.

Feliciano C. (2005b). Educational Selectivity in U.S. Immigration: How Do Immigrants Compared To Thos Left Behind? *Demography.* 42(1): 131–152.

Foster P., Gomm R. and Hammersley M. (1996). *Constructing Educational Inequality: An Assessment of Research on School Processes.* London: Falmer.

Ganzeboom H., De Graaf P. and Treiman D. (1992). A Standard International Socio-Economic Index of Occupational Status. *Social Science Research.* 21(1): 1–56.

Heath A. and Cheung S.-Y. (eds.). (2007). *Unequal Chances: Ethnic Minorities in Western Labour Markets.* Oxford: Oxford University Press.

Heath A., Rothon C. and Kilpi E. (2008). The Second Generation in Western Europe: Education, Unemployment, and Occupational Attainment. *Annual Review of Sociology*, 34: 211–235.

Heath A. and Brinbaum Y. (2014). *Unequal Attainments. Ethnic Educational Inequalities in Ten Western Countries.* Oxford: Proceedings of the British Academy.

Herzog-Punzenberger B. and Schnell P. (2014). Race and Ethnic Inequalities in Education in Austria. In Stevens P.A. and Dworkin G.A. (eds.). *The Palgrave Handbook of Race and Ethnic Inequalities in Education.* Basingstoke: Palgrave Macmillan, 70–106.

Hoenig K., Leopold L. and Shavit Y. (2013). *Cultural Capital and Achievement Differences between Immigrants and Natives in Germany.* Trento: Paper presented at the ISA-RC28 Spring Meeting.

Ichou M. (2014). Who They Were There: Immigrants' Educational Selectivity and Their Children's Educational Attainment. *European Sociological Review.* 30(6): 750–765.

Ichou M. (2015). Origine migratoire et Inégalités scolaires: Etude longitudinale des résultats scolaires des descendants d'immigrés en France et en Angleterre. *Revue Française de Pédagogie.* 2(191): 29–46.

Jackson M. (2012). Bold Choices: How Ethnic Inequalities in Educational Attainment Are Suppressed. *Oxford Review of Education.* 38(2): 189–208.

Jackson M. (2013). *Determined to Succeed? Performance Versus Choice in Educational Attainment*. Stanford: Stanford University Press.

Jackson M., Jonsson J.O. and Rudolphi F. (2012). Ethnic Inequality and Choice-Driven Educational Systems: A Longitudinal Study of Performance and Choice in England And Sweden. *Sociology of Education*. 85(2): 158–178.

Jonsson J.O., Kilpi-Jakonen E. and Rudolphi F. (2014). Ethnic Differences in Early School-Leaving. In Heath A.F. and Brinbaum E.Y. (eds.). *Unequal Attainments: Ethnic Educational Inequalities in Ten Western Countries*. Oxford: Oxford University Press, 95–118.

Kalter F., Heath A.F., Hewstone M., Jonsson J.O., Kalmijn M., Kogan I. and van Tubergen F. (2014). Children of Immigrants Longitudinal Survey in Four European Countries (CILS4EU): Reduced version. Cologne: GESIS Data Archive.

Kao G. (1999). Psychological Well-Being and Educational Achievement among Immigrant Youth. In Hernandez D.J. (ed.). *Children of Immigrants: Health, Adjustment and Public Assistance*. Washington: National Academic Press, 410–478.

Kao G. and Thompson J.S. (2003). Racial and Ethnic Stratification in Educational Achievement. *Annual Review of Sociology*. 29: 417–442.

Kao G. and Tienda M. (1995). Optimism and Achievement: The Educational Performance of Immigrant Youth. *Social Science Quarterly*. 76(1): 1–19.

Karlson K.B. and Holm A. (2011). Decomposing Primary and Secondary Effects: A New Decomposition Method Research. *Social Stratification and Mobility*. 29(2): 221–237.

Kilpi-Jakonen E. (2011). Continuation to Upper Secondary Education in Finland: Children of Immigrants and the Majority Compared. *Acta Sociologica*. 54(1): 67–94.

Kogan I. (2006). Labor Markets and Economic Incorporation among Recent Immigrants in Europe. *Social Forces*. 85(2): 697–721.

Kogan I. (2007). *Working through Barriers. Host Country Institutions and Immigrant Labour Market Performance in Europe*. Dordrecht: Springer VS.

Kogan I. (2011). The Price of Being an Outsider: Labour Market Flexibility and Immigrants' Employment Paths in Germany. *International Journal of Comparative Sociology*. 52(4): 264–283.

Kristen C. (2005). *School Choice and Ethnic School Segregation: Primary School Selection in Germany*. Münster: Waxmann Verlag.

Lessard-Phillips L., Brinbaum Y. and Heath A. (2014). Academic and Vocational Tracking in Upper Secondary Education. In Heath A.F. and Brinbaum Y. (eds.). *Unequal Attainments: Ethnic Educational Inequalities in Ten Western Countries*. Oxford: Oxford University Press, 119–148.

Lucas S.R. (2001). Effectively Maintained Inequality: Education Transition, Track Mobility, and Social Background Effects. *American Journal of Sociology*. 106(6): 1642–1690.

Lutz A. (2007). Barriers to High-School Competition among Immigrant and Later-Generation Latinos in the USA: Language, Ethnicity and Socio-Economic Status. *Ethnicities*. 7(3): 323–342.

Maki P. and McHugh M. (2014). *Immigrant Parents and Early Childhood Programs: Addressing Barriers of Literacy, Culture, and System Knowledge*. Washington: National Center of Immigrant Integration Policy.

Marks G.N. (2005). Accounting for Immigrant/Non-Immigrant Differences in Reading and Mathematics in Twenty Countries. *Ethnic and Racial Studies*. 28(5): 925–946.

Mantovani D. and Gasperoni G. (2018). Native and Immigrant Parents' Involvement in School-Related Activities in France and Italy. *Italian Journal of Sociology of Education*. 10(3): 110–139.

Mood C. (2010). Logistic Regression: Why We Cannot Do What We Think We Can Do, And What We Can Do about It. *European Sociological Review*. 26(1): 67–82.

Müller W. (2005). Education and Youth Integration into European Labour Markets. *International Journal of Comparative Sociology*. 45(5-6): 461–485.

Müller W. and Pollak R. (2010). Weshalb gibt es so wenige Arbeiterkinder in Deutschlands Universitäten? In Rolf Becker R. and Lauterbach W. (eds.). Bildung als Privileg. Wiesbaden: Springer VS Verlag, 305–317.

Murray À. and Sundin S. (2008). Student Flows and Employment Opportunities before and after Implementation of a Third Year in Vocational Programmes at Upper Secondary School. *European Journal of Vocational Training*. 44(2): 110–131.

OECD (2005). *From Education to Work: A Difficult Transition for Young Adults with Low Level of Education*. Paris: OECD.

OECD (2017). *Catching Up? Intergenerational Mobility and Children of Immigrants*. Paris: OECD.

OECD (2019). *International Migration Outlook 2019*. Paris: OECD.

Padilla A.M. and Durán R. (1995). The Psychological Dimension in Understanding Immigrant Students. In Rumbaut R.G. and Cornelius W.A. (eds.). *California's Immigrant Children: Theory, Research, and Implications for Educational Policy*. La Jolla San Diego: University of California, 131–160.

Phalet K., Deboosere P. and Bastiaenssen V. (2007). Old and New Inequalities in Educational Attainment: Ethnic Minorities in the Belgian Census 1991-2001. *Ethnicities*. 7(3): 390–415.

Portes A. and Rumbaut R.G. (1996). *Immigrant America: A Portrait*. Berkeley: University of California Press.

Portes A. and Rumbaut R.G. (2001). *Legacies: The Story of the Immigrant Second Generation*. Berkeley: University of California Press.

Relikowski I., Schneider T. and Blossfeld H.P. (2009). Primary and Secondary Effects of Social Origin in Migrant and Native Families at the Transition to the Tracked German School System. In Cherkaoui M. and Hamilton P. (eds.). *Raymond Boudon: A Life in Sociology. Vol. 3*. Oxford: Bardwell Press, 149–170.

Reimer D., Noelke C. and Kucel A. (2008). Labor Market Effects of Field of Study in Comparative Perspective. *International Journal of Comparative Sociology*. 49(4–5): 233–256.

Riach P.A. and Rich J. (2002). Field Experiments of Discrimination in the Market Place. *The Economic Journal*. 112(483): F480-F518.

Riphahn R.T. (2003). Cohort Effects in the Educational Attainment of Second Generation Immigrants in Germany: An Analysis of Census Data. *Journal of Population Economics*. 16(4): 711–737.

Rist R.C. (1970). Student Social Class and Teachers' Expectations: The Self-Fulfilling Prophecy in Ghetto Education. *Harvard Educational Review*. 40(3): 411–450.

Rothon C. (2007). Can Achievement Differentials Be Explained by Social Class Alone? An Examination of Minority Ethnic Educational Performance in England and Wales at the End of Compulsory Schooling. *Ethnicities*. 7(3): 306–322.

Rumberger R.W. and Lamb S.P. (2003). The Early Employment and Further Education Experiences of High School Dropouts: A Comparative Study of the United States and Australia. *Economics of Education Review*. 22(4), 353–366.

Shavit Y. and Blossfeld H.P. (eds.). (1993). *Persistent Inequality: A Comparative Study of Educational Attainment in Thirteen Countries*. Boulder: Westview Press.

Schnepf S.V. (2004). *How Different Are Immigrants? A Cross-Country and Cross-Survey*. IZA Discussion Paper (1398).

Schneider B. and Coleman J.S. (1993). *Parents, their Children, and Schools*. Boulder: Westview Press.

Stevens P.A. and Dworkin A.G. (2014). *The Palgrave Handbook of Race and Ethnic Inequalities in Education*. New York: Palgrave Macmillan.

Storen L.A. and Helland H. (2010). Ethnicity Differences in the Completion Rates of Upper Secondary Education: How Do the Effects of Gender and Social Background Variables Interplay? *European Sociological Review*. 26(3): 339–351.

Triventi M. (2013). Stratification in Higher Education and its Relationship with Social Inequality: Evidence from a Recent Cohort of European Graduates. *European Sociological Review*. 29(3): 489–502.

Triventi M., Vlach E. and Pini E. (2020). Understanding the Sources of Children of Immigrants' Penalty in Academic Performance: Evidence from Italian Compulsory Education. *Journal of Ethnic and Migration Studies*. Forthcoming.

Vallet L.A. (1996). L'assimilation scolaire des enfants issus de l'immigration et son interprétation: un examen sur données francaises. Revue francaise de pédagogie. 117(1): 7–27.

Vlach E. (2017). *Diseguali su quale base? Lo svantaggio scolastico dei figli di immigrati in Europa*. PhD Thesis. Trento: Unitn-eprints.PhD (http://eprints-phd.biblio.unitn.it/2059/).

Vlach E. (2019). Nazionalità, migrazione e apprendimenti in Italia: una comparazione tra livelli scolastici. In Falzetti P. (eds.). *Uno sguardo sulla scuola. II Seminario "I dati Invalsi: uno strumento per la ricerca"*. Milano: Franco Angeli, 73–94.

Weiss H., Caspe M. and Lopez E.M. (2006). *Family Involvement in Early Childhood Education*. Cambridge: Harvard Family Research Project.

Wooldridge J. (2002). *Econometric Analysis of Cross Section and Panel Data*. Cambridge: MIT Press.

Xie Y. and Hsin A. (2013). *Growing Gains, Growing Pains: What Explain Asian-American Youth's Academic Advantage Over Whites?* Trento: Paper Presented at the ISA-RC28 Spring Meeting.

Index

Note: Page numbers in **bold** refer to tables and in *italics* to figures.

Taylor & Francis eBooks

www.taylorfrancis.com

A single destination for eBooks from Taylor & Francis with increased functionality and an improved user experience to meet the needs of our customers.

90,000+ eBooks of award-winning academic content in Humanities, Social Science, Science, Technology, Engineering, and Medical written by a global network of editors and authors.

TAYLOR & FRANCIS EBOOKS OFFERS:

A streamlined experience for our library customers

A single point of discovery for all of our eBook content

Improved search and discovery of content at both book and chapter level

REQUEST A FREE TRIAL

support@taylorfrancis.com